HISTORIC PRESERVATION HANDBOOK

HISTORIC PRESERVATION HANDBOOK

J. KIRK IRWIN

McGRAW-HILL

New York Chicago San Francisco Lisbon London
Madrid Mexico City Milan New Delhi San Juan
Seoul Singapore Sydney Toronto

The McGraw·Hill Companies

Copyright © 2003 by The McGraw-Hill Companies, Inc. All rights reserved. Printed in the United States of America. Except as permitted under the United States Copyright Act of 1976, no part of this publication may be reproduced or distributed in any form or by any means, or stored in a data base or retrieval system, without the prior written permission of the publisher.

1 2 3 4 5 6 7 8 9 0 DOC/DOC 0 9 8 7 6 5 4 3 2

ISBN 0-07-136411-0

The sponsoring editor for this book was Cary Sullivan and the production supervisor was Sherri Souffrance. It was set in Versailles by Lone Wolf Enterprises, Ltd.

Printed and bound by RR Donnelley.

This book is printed on recycled, acid-free paper containing a minimum of 50% recycled, de-inked fiber.

McGraw-Hill books are available at special quantity discounts to use as premiums and sales promotions, or for use in corporate training programs. For more information, please write to the Director of Special Sales, McGraw-Hill Professional, Two Penn Plaza, New York, NY 10121-2298. Or contact your local bookstore.

Dedicated to my grandmother
Florence A. Irwin

CONTENTS

Acknowledgments xi
About the Author xiii
Introduction xv

PART ONE: BUILDING FORM   1

The Formal Archetypes 3

Size, Mass, Proportion, and Scale 46

Fenestration 50

Base, Middle, and Top 56

Legend and Ornament 61

Spaces Between Buildings 62

Districts 63

Compatibility 71

References 74

PART TWO: CRAFT   75

Building Components and Materials 78

  Vinyl 78

  Brick Masonry 83

  Terra Cotta 86

ADA 95

Building Elements **96**

   Columns 96

   Corners 98

   Windows 103

   Window Casing 108

   Skylights 108

   Stained Glass 114

   Dormers 116

   Doors and Casing 119

   Entablatures 119

   Gutters, Downspouts, and Vents 120

   Fireplaces 123

   Flashings 124

Mechanical Equipment **126**

   HVAC 128

   Lighting 132

   Light Pollution 133

   Elevators 134

Foundation Systems **135**

Wall Systems **139**

   Curtain Walls 141

   Plaster 141

Floor Systems **141**

Roof Systems **144**

Posts **145**

Additions **145**

   Garages 153

   Fences 156

Public Space **164**

References **170**

PART THREE:
MEANING AND POLICY   171

Interpretation 173
Policy 180
    Scope of Authority: Binding versus Advisory Review 190
    Contributing and Non-Contributing Structures 192
References 203

APPENDICES

Appendix A: The Athens Charter 205

Appendix B: International Charter for the Conservation and Restoration
of Monuments and Sites...211

Appendix C: Appleton Charter for the Protection and Enchancement of the
Built Environment..215

Appendix D: Charter for the Preservation of Quebec's Heritage.................221

Appendix E: Congress on the European Architectural Heritage,
21-24 October, 1975 233

Appendix F: European Charter of the Architectural Heritage 241

Appendix G: Historic Gardens..247

Appendix H: Conservation of Historic Towns 253

Appendix I: Charter for New Urbanism 257

Appendix J: Charleston Zoning Ordinance Part 6...........................261

Appendix K: Protection of Historic Properties, 36 cfr part 800 273

Appendix L: Worksheets 313

Index 343

ACKNOWLEDGMENTS

There are several individuals and organizations that I would like to acknowledge and thank for their support and encouragement in the preparation of this book. First are the members of the Evanston Preservation Commission who served during the year 2000. These include Mark Sarkisian, Vice-Chair, George Halik, Secretary, Jessica Deis, Barbara Gardner, Micheal Girard, Lynne Heidt, Michael Imlay, Heidi Pawlowski-Carey, and Susan Regan. Additionally, I would like to acknowledge the members of the Board of Directors of the Northeast Evanston Historic District Association: Mark Burnette, Judy Fiske, Jeanne Kamps Lindwall, James McGuire, and Mary McWilliams.

Furthermore, I am grateful to the City Council and Mayor of the City of Evanston, the Honorable Lorraine Morton, who provided me with the opportunity to serve as Chair of the Evanston Preservation Commission. Also, I would like to acknowledge and thank Carlos Ruiz, Senior Planner and Preservation Coordinator for the City of Evanston, for his continued hard work and support and for teaching me how to work with local city government.

Further acknowledgment is in order for The International Council on Monuments and Sites (ICOMOS) International Secretariat in Paris, along with the UNESCO ICOMOS Documentation Centre, who were instrumental in making possible the inclusion of several international documents and charters.

All illustrations and photographs are by the author.

ABOUT THE AUTHOR

J. Kirk Irwin is a licensed architect with extensive experience in historic preservation. He has renovated dozens of buildings in Chicago and vicinity and has been active in grass roots historic preservation initiatives. He is the former Chair of the Evanston Preservation Commission and co-author of several reports and documents pertaining to the establishment of landmark status and district designation for numerous properties in the City of Evanston, Illinois.

Irwin holds a Master's Degree in Architectural History from the University of Virginia where he studied European influences on the development of the American suburb.

INTRODUCTION

The manner in which architects, urban planners, private developers, politicians, and private citizens come together to establish the physical and social fabric of urban, suburban, and rural settings will have a long-lasting impact on the quality of life for a great number of people. Historic preservation has a role in this process as a discipline concerned with the character of public space through the making, re-making, and conservation of meritorious buildings and sites. In this regard, the current condition of American architecture is of particular interest. What may be said about character in an American context is twofold: first, that the character of the physical environment often exists in a decayed and isolated condition, and second that the definition of character is usually developed within a debate regarding the extent of the rights of individual property owners as measured against the needs of the larger community. An historical analysis of why American cities, towns, and villages have come to look the way they do lies outside the scope of this book. This book addresses how preservation contributes to the making of attractive physical settings that also address vital social needs by providing people with humane places for working, living, and amusement.

To preserve historic buildings and sites is to preserve the character of public spaces. Most public spaces are comprised by, and often bounded by privately owned properties. Historic preservation as policy has to do with the exteriors of buildings viewed from a public perspective and publicly accessible sites. Historic preservation appropriately includes the restoration of interior spaces in addition to the exteriors of buildings and surrounding sites. As a profession, historic preservation must define its mission in a way that protects individual property rights while protecting cultural and architectural resources, and the character of public space. Regulatory policies must be clear as to the reach of historic preservation.

The debate balancing the rights of the individual with the rights of the community gives rise to several arguments. First is that anyone can do what ever they want with their own property. This argument assumes that property rights are absolute. It does not consider that all property is subject to zoning and other restrictions enacted for the welfare of the public that would tend to limit what one could do with privately owned property. Another popular argument against preservation is that the government cannot legislate taste because of the concept that beauty is in the eye of the beholder. This argument assumes that preservation ordinances are based on taste rather than the thoughtful analysis based on criteria for review. The argument does not recognize that preservation ordinances include criteria that refer not to taste, but to principles of architectural design as applicable to historic contexts. An additional argument is that regulating Individual landmarks is appropriate, but regulating districts constitutes "forced" preservation. This argument fails to recognize the significance of groups of buildings. The implication is that left alone and considered in isolation, each building will automatically contribute to a larger whole by virtue of its individual significance. The problem with this argument is that it provides no way to look at groups of buildings, streets or urban form. The idea that a district must have one style or one architect in order to have significance is argued in support of those opposed to historic preservation. There are many styles of architecture and there are many ways in which multiple architects can make buildings compatible with one another in a district, while maintaining the individual quality of each property. Historic preservation is attacked as an attempt to preserve architecture in amber. This is incorrect, because within preservation there is considerable flexibility to allow for innovative work and to allow a community to grow while recognizing the historical essence of the community. Additionally, the premise of preservation does not often reflect museum quality preservation, although there are certainly instances where buildings should be preserved as museums. All of the arguments above misrepresent the purpose of preservation, which is to identify and conserve what it is that makes places meaningful to those who live in live in them, and to re-establish a sense and spirit of place.

When the character of public spaces is preserved, the physical and social fabric of cities, towns, and the countryside is also preserved, thereby providing a viable platform for maintaining meaningful architectural surroundings.

This handbook serves as a practical guide to understanding historic architecture and its preservation. Presented within is a method for observing and evaluating historic buildings and sites for the purpose of renovating existing buildings, for constructing new buildings in historic contexts, and for the implementation of public policy supportive of historic buildings and sites. The book's scope is limited to an analysis of the influence of historic preservation on public space and the public face of architecture. Building renovation will be considered with respect to building exteriors exclusively, while recognizing that there are many opportunities for historic preservation with regard to historic interior spaces.

Character is the physical setting of a building or site understood with regard to architectural form, craft, and meaning. Public spaces, for the purposes of this discussion, are areas within direct view from the public way of anyone, regardless of ownership or accessibility. For example, the exterior of privately owned buildings would contribute to public space. A person's front yard could be considered public space as would a parking lot in front of a large commercial establishment.

This is an introduction to the historic preservation process, and is intended to supplement the work of federal, state, and local preservation officials, and neighborhood organizations who are qualified to assist individuals and groups who intend to develop local preservation programs or renovate historic properties. The text and supporting diagrams focus primarily on the architecture of buildings and sites and is written from the point of view of an architect, while recognizing that historic preservation includes a wide range of other disciplines. Because local conditions vary considerably, legal and architectural professionals should be consulted during any preservation project. This book is not a substitute for specific professional advice.

The form of buildings and sites, the craft of how buildings and sites are put together, the shared meanings of historic places, and the fair and correct establishment of policies that protect cultural resources are each essential components of historic preservation.

BUILDING FORM

A focus on building form, rather than style, is essential for a more complete understanding of historic preservation to be implemented. Building form (for the purposes of this analysis, the exterior form), may be viewed with regard to fundamentals of architectural composition. Architectural composition entails an understanding of the underlying geometry, structure, and ornament of historic buildings and sites. The geometry of buildings and sites includes use of scale, proportion, massing, and spatial configuration in architectural design. Many historic preservation debates have to do with the addition onto an existing structure or the addition of a new building into an existing historic context. Reviewing the compatibility of new construction with an existing context, whether the existing context is a single building or a group of buildings, involves looking at the composition of the new construction in relation to the composition of existing construction. The illustrations that supplement the text are intended to graphically show the fundamentals of architectural composition.

THE CRAFT OF BUILDING

The craft of architecture is the way in which the elements of architecture are physically put together. How a column is attached to a base, how an arch connects to the wall in which it creates an opening, and how a dormer window is detailed, will determine how well a building fits to its surroundings. How a building relates to the surrounding landscape and how a building relates to adjacent sidewalks, streets, or roads will determine the quality of the urban, suburban, or rural setting. The craft of assembling materials and the craft of making public spaces is to a great extent a lost art especially in residential construction and new development in areas outside urban centers. Learning to recognize the quality of existing materials and crafts-manship, and learning to perceive quality in the public environment is a step toward restoring a fundamental part of the physical environment.

MEANING

This section will review the need for interpretation of historical attitudes and sensi-bilities in historic preservation. To accomplish this, there are several interpretative positions that should be challenged. First is that of age based merit. This position states that anything over a certain age has historic merit. A second interpretive posi-tion is that of appearance based merit. This position states that popular styles from the past should be kept. A third position is value based. This position states that everything old is good and everything new is bad. Each of these will be discussed within the context of making or remaking meaningful architectural settings.

Relating history to historic preservation is a matter of telling the social and archi-tectural story of buildings and places. How the story is told, by whom, and from what point of view becomes critical, especially in a multicultural environment. How sensibilities change over time and from place to place is another concept essential to conveying and interpreting the architecture of buildings and sites. Current sen-sibilities with respect to a building's color, spatial configuration, and ornamentation are not the same as the sensibilities of prior generations. Furthermore, current social structures and relationships are not the same as those of the past. Interpre-tive programs should show an understanding of this in order to bring historic preservation to the widest audience possible. How primary and secondary struc-tures are interpreted is clearly important in this context. For example, preservation needs to look at a secondary structure, such as a coach house, and tell the story of the coach house from the perspective of the driver of the coach as well as from the perspective of the owner of the primary structure, which is the house to which the coach house is associated.

POLICY

Determining historical merit and the character of public space in an inclusive multi-cultural setting depends upon the establishment of agreed upon and commonly under-stood preservation standards and criteria, and their fair and equitable implementation. In this regard historic preservation is a public policy tool for use in deciding the char-acter of public space. While building conservation and restoration address the entire building fabric from outside to inside, historic preservation, as policy, has purview over the external characteristics of buildings and spaces that are in public view. Limiting historic preservation policy in this way guarantees individual citizens their right to privacy while maintaining the community's right to decide matters relating to public character. Zoning ordinances, as distinguished from preservation ordinances, are tools for deciding building use, building size, and the placement of buildings on a parcel of property. Historic preservation does not mandate building use. In fact, historic preservation encourages changes in use for existing buildings when the change in use promotes the saving of an existing structure. Building use is not the same as building type. An historic house may be used as an office; a warehouse may be used as a commercial retail establishment, and a commercial office building may be used as a hotel.

CURRENT HISTORIC PRESERVATION PRACTICES

Historic preservation has moved to a new phase due in part to the phenomenon of aging Modernism and the desirability of increased densification in urban and suburban areas as expressed in the new urbanism movement. Previously, historic preservation could employ a stylistic analysis to aptly evaluate the value and merit of buildings and groups of buildings. Now that many Modernist buildings have crossed the 50 year threshold for consideration as historic structures, preservationists must seek out new approaches. Additionally, recognition of the economic and environmental advantages of planning techniques of new urbanism has led to the construction of new buildings and towns based on traditional pre-modernists methods. Buildings that look old are new and buildings that look new are old.

Another influence on current preservation practice is the breakdown of the language people use to describe the physical environment. One task of this book is to re-establish a working language to allow for an improved discourse having to do American cities, towns, and rural areas. The description of places and the buildings that comprise them, is often left to the marketing programs of the real estate or housing industries. What results is a discordant relationship between what is built and what is talked about or described. Parks are not parks but rather parking. Town centers are not towns nor are they centers. These are often privately owned commercial enterprises that may be very well planned as such, but are disastrous to the making of meaningful communities.

Style is often debased in an effort to portray an imagined environment resulting in the destruction of historic time and place. Often the very names of places have little or nothing to do with the places themselves, physically or socially. Recognizing existing historic fabric is what allows the reconstitution of meaningful environments. Historic preservation is about places, buildings, communities, and the stories of the people who live in them.

Seen within the context of place making, and the physical and social re-establishment of communities in American urban, suburban, and rural settings, Historic preservation serves several purposes:

1. Historic preservation ensures that enduring works last more than one generation

2. Historic preservation provides a means for people to participate in the making of the physical environment

3. Historic preservation is a means by which communities may define the character of public space

4. Historic preservation provides architects with an expanded architectural vocabulary

5. Historic preservation ensures the continuation of the historic urban infrastructure of streets, alleys, and public spaces

6. Historic preservation provides a basis upon which meaningful environments may be reconstituted.

Significant efforts to address these purposes are now an imperative, and gaining a working method aimed at fulfilling these purposes seems a greater priority, particularly now that the very fabric of American cities has been shaken by violent attacks within the borders of the continental United States. The act of re-building and re-making is now being undertaken in a new context that one can not fully comprehend from such a close historical position. Historic preservation is itself historically significant, with its ability to include within its purview discussions relating to cultural identity or identities, architectural symbolism, public spaces, and the quality of life of the people who live in and around historic buildings, objects, and sites. The following chapters will help to clarify a role for Historic preservation and to clearly delineate its working methods.

PART
ONE

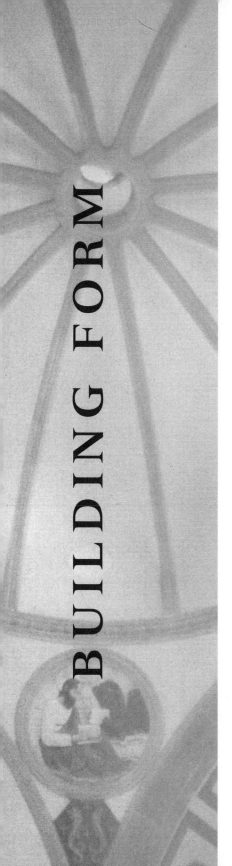

BUILDING FORM

The purpose of this chapter is to outline a method for describing the appearance of buildings and groups of buildings. Stylistic categories are frequently employed when writing descriptions of buildings and places. Categorization provides a common language and understanding that is easily learned and easily put to use. There are many handbooks describing the difference between Gothic, Romanesque, Classical, Federal, Georgian, Queen Anne, and Prairie Style buildings. However, for preservation to take part more fully in establishing the character of public space descriptions of buildings, the concept needs to expand to include articulate knowledge of architectural form. Architectural form consists of geometry expressed through structure and ornament. Geometry in architecture is pervasive, and is evident in six formal archetypes: cylinders, thickened planes, pyramids, spheres, cubes, and pediments (Figure 1.2).

THE FORMAL ARCHETYPES

Each formal archetype has its unique primary structural expression. The structure of each archetype may be employed in such a way that the archetype is expressed either as a void or a solid. The six archetypes define centers and edges, tops, bottoms and middles, and may be combined in a variety of ways and applied to any building, in any time or place. Figures 1.3 and 1.4 present diagrams of how the primary archetypes may be combined into familiar architectural forms.

The primary structural expression of a cylinder is a column. A thickened plane is expressed as a wall, floor or ceiling, a sphere as a dome, a pediment as a gable front, a pyramid as a rooftop, and a cube as a room or town square. By looking at each archetype individually, the variations and multiple expressions of each become clear.

A cylinder, or column, can exist alone or in groups. Columns exist as solids. When a column stands alone the column defines a center (Figure 1.5). When columns are grouped, the group of columns defines a center as the void

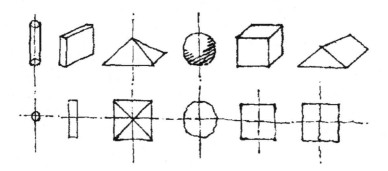

FIGURE 1.1   From left to right: cylinder, plane, pyramid.

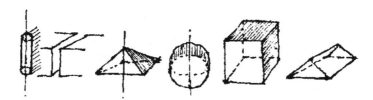

FIGURE 1.2   Diagram showing archetypal geometry. From left to right: sphere, cube, and pediment.

between the columns, and defines an edge by means of repetition at a perimeter (Figure 1.6). Seen in elevation, columns define a middle between a base and roof structure.

A built example of this compositional use of columns is B. Henry Latrobe's Water Works in Philadelphia (Figure 1.7). The buildings that comprise the Water Works employ a classical set of architectural elements to create a unified stage set made up of several buildings each with an individual identity within the whole. The consistent use of columns to define the middle portions of the buildings is one way in which Latrobe accomplishes this. Figure 1.8 further describes the compositional function between bases and tops of columns on the fronts of buildings with the examples of the Erechtheum and the Temple of Athena Nike. Figure 1.9 shows a built example of a double row of columns that defines a two-story exterior portico front. While this building, Belle Mont Plantation in Muscle Shoals, Alabama, is an Early American example, the use of double columns on exterior front elevations may be traced to Italian Renaissance sources in the work of Andrea Palladio [1]. Palladio's architecture

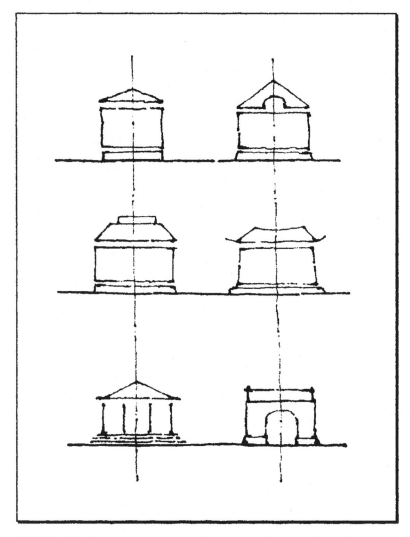

FIGURE 1.3 Diagram showing varieties of architectural form. Geometric archetypes expressed as buildings.

provides a basis for American architecture that is Classically derived. Many of his buildings serve as models for buildings built centuries later and his books on Architecture articulate a clear approach to building in the Classical language. Figure 1.10 shows Palladio's Villa Rotonda near Vicenza, Italy. This building dramatically represents a columnar portico repeated on all four sides of a centrally placed dome.

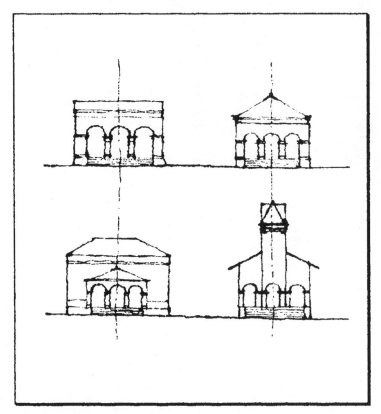

FIGURE 1.4 Diagram showing varieties of architectural form. Geometric archetypes expressed as buildings.

FIGURE 1.5 Diagram showing a center defined by a cylinder or column.

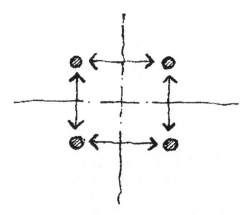

FIGURE 1.6 Diagram showing a perimeter defined by cylinders or columns

FIGURE 1.7 Water Works. B. Henry Latrobe, Philadelphia, Pennsylvania.

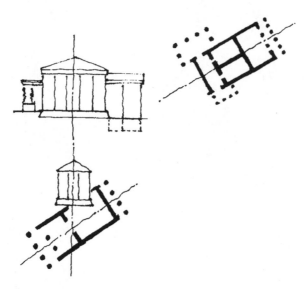

FIGURE 1.8 Diagram showing column placement at the Erectheum and Temple of Athena Nike in Athens, Greece.

FIGURE 1.9   Belle Mont, Muscle Shoals, Alabama.

FIGURE 1.10 Villa Capra, Andrea Palladio, Vicenza, Italy.

Figure 1.11 shows an example of the same use of columns, this time for the face of St. Paul's Covent Garden in London. This building, dating from the early 1600s and designed by a follower of Palladio, Inigo Jones, is a bold and simple expression of the classical language that is repeated in numerous buildings throughout the world. With origins in Greek and Roman architecture of the ancient world, such as the Pantheon in Rome (Figure 1.12), a variety of architectural expressions and building uses is possible within the classical language. These expressions range from Elvis Presley's Graceland (Figure 1.13), which has taken on obvious and additional significance beyond its existence as a competent piece of residential architecture, to Union Terminal (Figure 1.14) in Cincinnati, Ohio, which is a fine example of art deco design.

The Classical language is a codified set of details based on Greek and Roman architecture called *the Orders* [2]. The Orders of architecture, Tuscan (Figure 1.15), Doric (Figure 1.16), Ionic (Figure 1.17), Corinthian (Figure 1.18), and Composite (Figure 1.19) have their own architectural vocabulary, or expression. Traditionally, the placement or disposition of the Orders on or in a building is stratified based upon the building's use and siting. For example, a rural building will employ the Tuscan Order.

FIGURE 1.11   St. Paul's Covent Garden, Inigo Jones, London.

FIGURE 1.12   The Pantheon, Rome.

FIGURE 1.13 Graceland, Memphis, Tennessee.

FIGURE 1.14 Union Terminal, Cincinnati, Ohio.

A building of great significance and standing will employ either a Corinthian or Composite Order. The hierarchy of Orders can occur within one building as well as from building to building. When the Classical Orders are stratified in one building the lowest order is at the bottom of the building and successively higher Orders are placed in ascending order toward the top of the building. A primary example of stratification occurs in the exterior wall surface of the Flavian Amphitheater in Rome. The supporting arch structure is flanked by applied columns, or pilasters, representing the Orders.

Figures 1.20 and 1.21 show American examples of the Tuscan Order and the Roman Doric Order. The Tuscan Order at the University of Virginia exists within a classically designed and inspired ensemble of buildings following Thomas Jefferson's plans.

An example of a Greek Doric Order is seen in the Church of Christian Science in Evanston, Illinois, designed by Solon Beman (Figure 1.22). The difference between a Roman Doric and Greek Doric is easiest to see in the entablature just above the column capital. In a Greek Doric, the vertical surface above the capital is divided roughly in half, while in the Roman Doric the relationship is about 1:3. Additionally, in the Greek Orders, the shaft of the column may extend directly to the plinth of the building without a base.

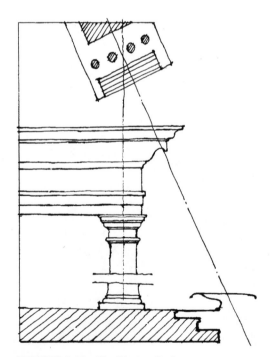

FIGURE 1.15 The Tuscan Order.

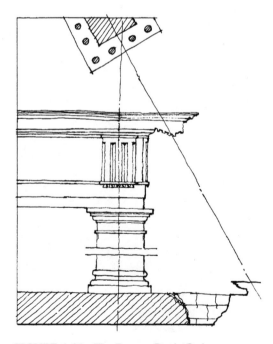

FIGURE 1.16 The Roman Doric Order.

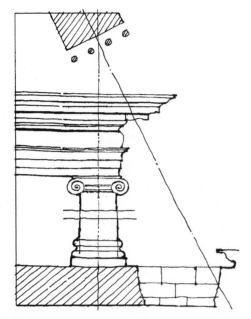

FIGURE 1.17 The Ionic Order.

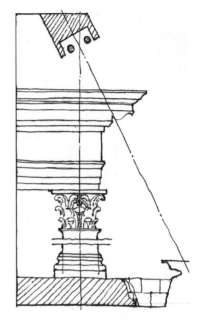

FIGURE 1.18 The Corinthian Order.

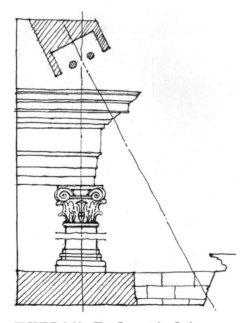

FIGURE 1.19 The Composite Order.

FIGURE 1.20 The Tuscan Order, University of Virginia, Charlottesville.

The Roman Ionic is used at Pavilion II at the University of Virginia (Figures 1.23 and 1.24) and Waverly Plantation in Mississippi (Figures 1.25 and 1.26). The Ionic Order is differentiated from other Orders by means of volutes which are the roughly circular elements that occur at the top of the column capital. The Ionic Order is also more slender than the Tuscan and Doric Orders and its detailing is more elaborate.

FIGURE 1.21 The Roman Doric Order, Water Works, B. Henry Latrobe, Philadelphia, Pennsylvania.

Figure 1.27 shows an example of a column that represents a break from classical ornamental tradition. This column at the Rookery building in Chicago is cylindrical and has at its base a series of rings rather than an alternating torus (a convex curve) and scotia (a concave curve).

FIGURE 1.22 Church of Christian Science, Solon Beman, Evanston, Illinois.

Another example of columns that are the exception to the rule rather than the rule themselves are the central columns at the Strauss Building by Graham Anderson Probst and White (Figure 1.28), also located in Chicago. The columns in this case are on a central axis and relate to the pyramid top that is a representation of the Mausoleum at Halicarnassus. The mausoleum motif, when following the Greek example, has an odd number of columns in each elevation. This is in reference to the original building at Halicarnassus, which is thought to have had 36 columns with columniation of nine on two sides and 11 on the remaining two.

FIGURE 1.23   Pavilion II, University of Virginia, Charlottesville.

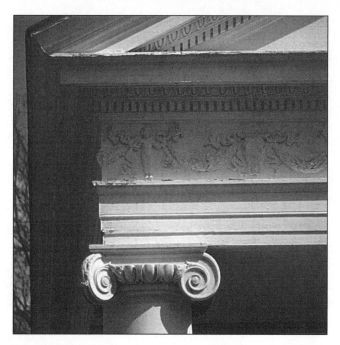

FIGURE 1.24   Pavilion II, University of Virginia, Charlottesville.

FIGURE 1.25   Waverly Plantation, Mississippi.

FIGURE 1.26 Waverly Plantation, Mississippi.

FIGURE 1.27 Column Detail, Rookery Building, Burnham and Root, Chicago, Illinois.

Cylinders may be built either as rings or as stacks of solid material as represented in Figure 1.29. They can also be used to mark significant points in an urban or rural setting. Thus far, cylinders have been described in their relationship to other building components. However, a cylinder may be added to or modified to become a freestanding monument as seen in Nelson's Column at Trafalgar Square (Figure 1.30). Another example of a freestanding column is shown in Figure 1.31, which shows a detail from Cranbrook, in Bloomfield Hills, Michigan, where the freestanding column is placed adjacent to a wall that repeats the vertical qualities of the column in its window design and placement.

Figure 1.32 shows how cylinders relate to points in space which designate centers and points of significance. Figure 1.33 shows Spider Rock, located in the Navajo Nation in Arizona, which is a natural expression of the idea of a vertical marker defining space. Other more conventional examples include the Eiffel Tower (Figure 1.34) and the Washington Monument (Figure 1.35).

FIGURE 1.28 Strauss Building, Graham Anderson Probst and White, Chicago, Illinois.

FIGURE 1.29 Diagram showing column types. (Left) fluted, no base. (Right) non-fluted with base.

FIGURE 1.30 Nelson's Column, London.

FIGURE 1.31   Cranbrook, Eliel Saarinen, Bloomfield Hills, Michigan.

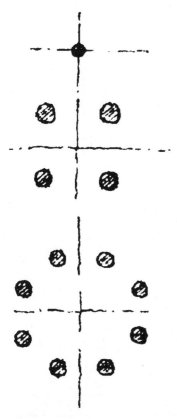

FIGURE 1.32 Diagram showing column placement.

FIGURE 1.33 Spider Rock, Canyon de Chelly, Navajo Nation, Arizona.

The structural expression of the thickened plane can be either a vertical or horizontal surface such as a wall, floor, or ceiling. Openings in walls can be made of post and beam construction, arches, or load bearing construction (Figure 1.36). A thickened plane as a ceiling structure, can be made of joists or slab construction. A thickened plane as a floor surface can also be made from joists or slab construction (Figures 1.37 and 1.38). Vertical planes can be grouped to define a center as a void (Figure 1.39).

As with columns, vertical planes define edges when grouped at a perimeter (Figure 1.40). Greek temple architecture combines columns and planes by defining interior space with a *cella*, and providing rows of columns at the perimeter called a *peristyle*. Figure 1.41 illustrates the varieties of column placement found in Greek architecture.

FIGURE 1.34   The Eiffel Tower, Paris.

FIGURE 1.35 The Washington Monument, Washington, D.C.

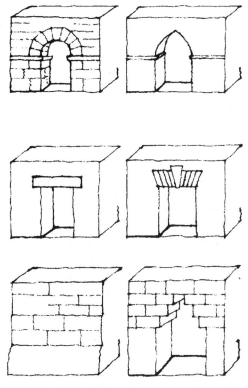

FIGURE 1.36 Diagram showing thickened planes as walls with several varieties of wall openings.

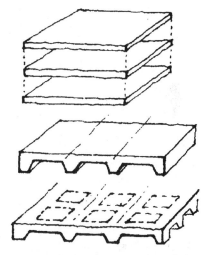

FIGURE 1.37 Diagram showing construction of horizontal planes as slab, joist, and waffle.

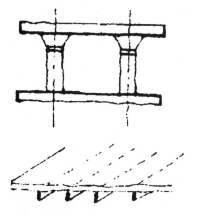

FIGURE 1.38 Diagram showing supports for horizontal planes.

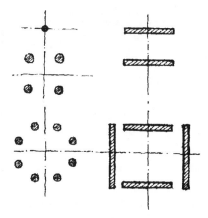

FIGURE 1.39 Diagram showing vertical planes and columns defining centers and edges.

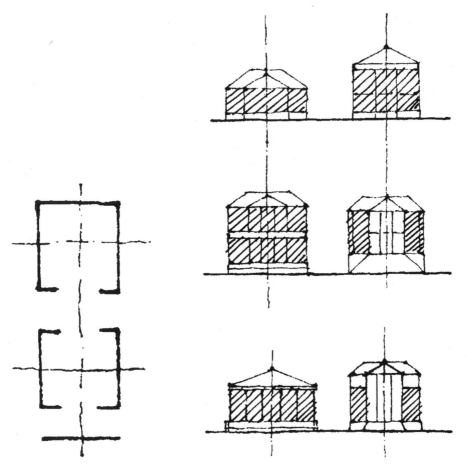

FIGURE 1.40 Diagram showing vertical planes defining edges.

FIGURE 1.41 Arrangement of columns in Greek temples. (Top left) columns in Antis. (Top right) prostyle. (Middle left) pseudodipteral. (Middle left) amphiprostyle. (Bottom left) peripteral. (Bottom right) dipteral.

Buildings meet the ground by means of a floor plane. Figure 1.42 shows variations of how a floor plane may be varied to link a building to the ground, literally and figuratively. Buildings can link themselves to a depressed plane that corresponds to the adjacent terrain, or a building can sit above the terrain on a plinth. A building can also integrate itself completely with the terrain through a series of gradually recessing surfaces. Examples of buildings that recess into the ground include the Theater at Epidaurus in Greece (Figure 1.43), and Frank Lloyd Wright's Taliesin West in Scottsdale, Arizona (Figure 1.44).

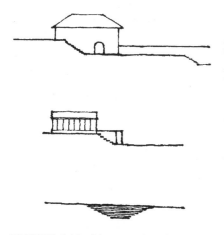

FIGURE 1.42 Diagram showing floor planes.

FIGURE 1.43 The Theater at Epidaurus, Greece.

FIGURE 1.44 Taliesin West, Frank Lloyd Wright, Scottsdale, Arizona.

Urban piazzas may be seen as horizontal planes. An example of this is Sienna's Piazza Publico (Figure 1.45). An example of a plane that is expressed as a floor surface, also designed by Wright is the Gale house in Oak Park, Illinois which has a projecting horizontal balcony facing the adjacent street (Figure 1.46). Another American example of horizontal planes being expressed as ceilings and floor surfaces is the Black Mountain College Building in North Carolina designed by Lawrence Kocher (Figure 1.47). Planes expressed vertically are seen at Saarinen's Cranbrook, where a set of four thickened walls create an entry as if designed like solid buttresses to the main mass of the building (Figure 1.48).

Thickened planes are ornamented with applied columns or by means of rustication. Applied columns may be stratified in accordance with the classical language and may either be literally load bearing, or may represent or depict load bearing construction. Rustication is another method of differentiating a wall surface. A rusticated wall is one that is stratified with surface treatments that increase in smoothness from the bottom to the top of a building. Examples of rusticated surfaces include the Palazzo Riccardi in Florence (Figure 1.49), and The Rookery Building (Figure 1.50), and Adler and Sullivan's Auditorium Building, both in Chicago (Figure 1.51).

FIGURE 1.45 Piazza Publico, Sienna, Italy.

FIGURE 1.46 Gale House, Frank Lloyd Wright, Oak Park, Illinois.

FIGURE 1.47 Black Mountain College, North Carolina.

FIGURE 1.48   Cranbrook, Eliel Saarinen, Bloomfield Hills, Michigan.

FIGURE 1.49 Palazzo Riccardi, Michelozzo di Bartolommeo, Florence.

FIGURE 1.50 The Rookery Building, Burnham and Root, Chicago.

FIGURE 1.51   The Auditorium Building, Adler and Sullivan, Chicago.

Spheres are expressed structurally as domes with variations expressed as vaults. A dome is an arch rotated about a center axis. A dome is a half sphere when the arch is a semi circular arch (Figure 1.52). Spheres as archetypes exist as voids in the form of domes and vaults. An arch extended in along a straight line is a barrel vault. Intersecting domes are groin vaults. All of these exist as voids, with regard to their archetypal form—the sphere. Domes create centers as voids, and they also create tops. A dome or vault can create an edge through the emphasis of the edge supports of the dome or vault. Domes and vaults often represent the sky, and are literally ornamented with clouds, stars, or other representations of the heavens.

Figure 1.53 shows the multiple domes above the Church of San Marco in Venice. Figure 1.54 shows an example of a domed structure from the American southwest called a hogan. Both examples define centralized spaces, although they are extreme in how remote they are from one another. The Arc de Triomphe in Paris (Figure 1.55), is a part of a public space, but rather than defining an edge, the structure defines a center along a line. American examples include the brick vault at Cranbrook (Figure 1.56), and the arches forming the colonnade at Pullman, Illinois (Figure 1.57).

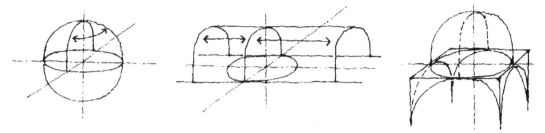

FIGURE 1.52 Diagram showing the dome archetype. From left to right: arch as dome, arch as vault, arch as dome on pendentives.

FIGURE 1.53 The Church of San Marco, Venice.

FIGURE 1.54 Navajo Hogan, Canyon de Chelly, Navajo Nation, Arizona.

FIGURE 1.55 The Arc de Triomphe, Paris.

FIGURE 1.56 Cranbrook, Eliel Saarinen, Bloomfield Hills, Michigan.

FIGURE 1.57   Pullman neighborhood, Solon Beman, Chicago.

Examples of arches include Frank Lloyd Wright's Winslow House in River Forest, Illinois, where an arch is used to create a porte cochere (Figure 1.58), and the structure at Arcosanti in Arizona, designed by Paolo Soleri, which shows an arch that forms a part of a vault (Figure 1.59). And finally, the stone that forms the arch over the ruins at Canyon de Chelly dating from the 900s AD is an example from nature that illustrates most vividly the effectiveness of vaulted construction (Figure 1.60).

Pyramids exist as solids or voids and, as with the sphere archetype, create the top of buildings. Structural expression is achieved through corbelling of masonry or by means of truss construction (Figure 1.61). In Egyptian funerary architecture, pyramids are expressed as solids, while in American residential architecture, pyramids are formed by roof structures. Wright's Robie and Winslow Houses both have pyramid tops (Figures 1.62 and 1.63). Figure 1.64 shows a simple example of a small building in Charleston, South Carolina, that has a pyramid top for a roof structure.

An example of the pediment archetype include the Scott Mansion by Ernest Mayo located in Evanston, Illinois (Figure 1.65). This building has a distinct triangular top floor which not only points dramatically to the sky, but cantilevers out from the lower level to emphasize the triangular shape of the top level.

FIGURE 1.58   Winslow House, Frank Lloyd Wright, River Forest, Illinois.

FIGURE 1.59   Arcosanti, Paolo Soleri, Arizona.

FIGURE 1.60 Canyon de Chelly, Navajo Nation, Arizona.

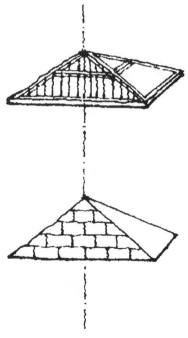

FIGURE 1.61 Diagram of pyramid shaped archetype. (Top) expressed in wood. (Bottom) expressed in stone.

FIGURE 1.62 Robie House, Frank Lloyd Wright, Chicago, Illinois.

FIGURE 1.63 Winslow House, Frank Lloyd Wright, River Forest, Illinois.

FIGURE 1.64 Example of a pyramid top, Charleston, South Carolina.

FIGURE 1.65 Scott Mansion, Ernest Mayo, Evanston, Illinois.

Frank Lloyd Wright's home and studio in Oak Park includes a truss articulation of the pyramid forming a large triangular pediment with a Palladian window centered within (Figure 1.66). The entrance to Drayton Hall in South Carolina includes a pediment articulation centered above a doorway to the central hallway and is another example of the variety found within this archetype (Figure 1.67). Figures 1.68 and 1.69 show two ways to frame a pediment, and two stylistic variations.

The expression of the cube archetype is accomplished through post and beam, vaulting and bearing wall construction. A cube can exist either as a solid as in the example of a house or palazzo, or as a void as in the example of a piazza or town

FIGURE 1.66 Frank Lloyd Wright home and studio, Oak Park, Illinois.

FIGURE 1.67   Drayton Hall, Charleston, South Carolina.

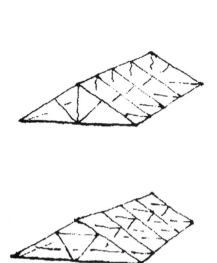

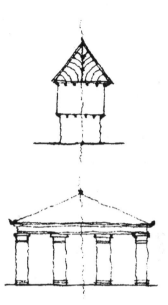

FIGURE 1.68 Diagram showing pediment archetype expressed in two truss types.

FIGURE 1.69 Diagram of two pediments. (Top) Tudor expression. (Bottom) Classical expression.

square (Figures 1.70, 1.71, and 1.72). Cubes can form the middles of buildings and sometimes form the bases of buildings. Groups of cubes form cities when heights are consistently maintained. An example of the cube geometry expressed as an urban center may be seen in Figure 1.73. Figure 1.74 shows a corner of a town square in Sidney, Ohio. This particular town square has one of its corners defined by a building designed by Louis Sullivan, the People's Savings and Loan Association Bank building. The bank itself is a box defined as a solid. It forms the corner of a square that is expressed as a void. Sullivan's bank building concentrates its ornament within the perimeter of the cube that forms the main mass of the building.

Another building that is cube-like is the Monadnock Building at 53 West Jackson in Chicago. Commonly known for being the tallest masonry bearing wall structure in Chicago, the Monadnock is also known for the interior street that is carved out of its middle. The building, which along with its later addition, extends from Jackson to Van Buren, includes an interior passage that runs in a north to south direction parallel to Dearborn Street. Shops on the first floor of the building face both the interior and exterior streets without compromising the integrity of either the interior or exterior spaces. Other buildings emphasize corners with ornamentation. Examples of buildings with corner ornamentation include quoining at the corners of the entrance to the Monadnock (Figure 1.75), and similarly detailed quoining at the corners of Gunston Hall in Springfield, Virginia (Figure 1.76).

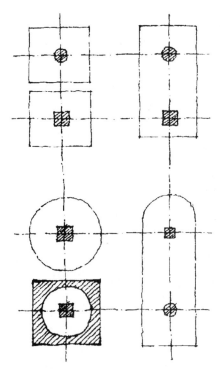

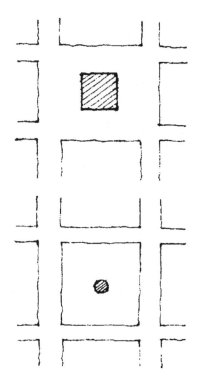

FIGURE 1.70 Diagram showing circles and cubes. (Top left) two squares as perimeters, one with a circle as a center, the other with a square as a center. (Top right) two squares combined as a perimeter with two centers, one as a square, the other as a circle. (Bottom left) combinations of edges as circles with solid squares as centers. (Bottom right) combination of squares and circles into one space with two centers, one as a square, the other as a circle.

FIGURE 1.71 Diagram showing cube geometry in an idealized urban plan.

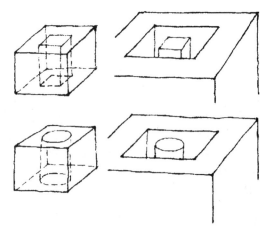

FIGURE 1.72 Diagram showing cube geometry. (Top left) center as a square void. (Top right) center as a square solid. (Bottom left) center as a circular void. (Bottom right) center as a solid circle.

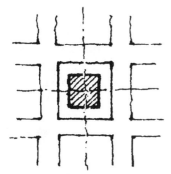

FIGURE 1.73 Diagram showing cube geometry expressed as an urban center.

FIGURE 1.74 Peoples Savings and Loan, Louis Sullivan, Sidney, Ohio.

FIGURE 1.75 Monadnock Building, William Holabird, Chicago.

FIGURE 1.76 Gunston Hall, Springfield, Virginia.

SIZE, MASS, PROPORTION, AND SCALE

The manipulation of the relative size, mass, proportion, and scale of the underlying geometry in architecture is a fundamental part of what makes a building or place humane, livable, and enjoyable. Geometry underlies window placement, trim details, and the massing or blocking out of the building or place as a whole. For example, roofs of buildings are usually formed by either the sphere or pyramid archetype. The connection between the pediment and the wall below is called an *entablature,* and is made of a successive addition of trim work and moldings. If the triangle formed by the roof is too high in relation to the wall below the entablature, then the massing will appear too heavy and the building will appear oppressive. Conversely, if the top of the building lacks enough emphasis then the building will appear unfinished or unsubstantial (Figures 1.77, 1.78, 1.79, and 1.80).

Mass, scale, proportion, and size are the means by which the elements of architecture are made coherent. A building's mass results from the relationship of solid to void. The size of a building is the building described in terms of a unit of measure. The scale of a building is the building's size expressed in relation to the human figure. The proportion of a building refers to the relative size of the parts of the building.

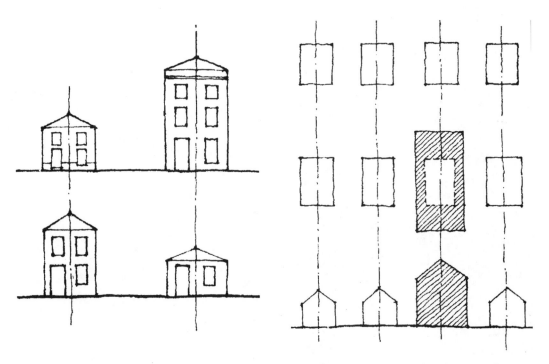

FIGURE 1.77 Diagram showing variations of size with similar shapes and elements.

FIGURE 1.78 Diagram showing mass. Increase in mass shown within an existing context.

Figure 1.81 helps explain this further. Represented in this photograph are three columns located in the Jeffersonian portion of the University of Virginia. All three are of the same Order, two are the same size, and one is considerably larger. The mass of the larger one is heavy compared to the mass of the smaller two because the large amount of solid compared to the small amount of void. The larger column is a larger scale than the smaller two because it is larger in relation to the human figure. The proportion of the three columns are identical since the relationship of base to shaft of the small columns is the same ratio as the relationship between the base and shaft of the large column.

Another way to illustrate these principles is to look at the ATT Building by Phillip Johnson located in New York (Figure 1.82). The building is well known for what some term its Chippendale top. The top is large in scale and size, but like the columns in the previous example, would be roughly the same proportion as a piece of Chippendale furniture. The furniture would be a small-scale version of the building and the building would be a large-scale version of the furniture.

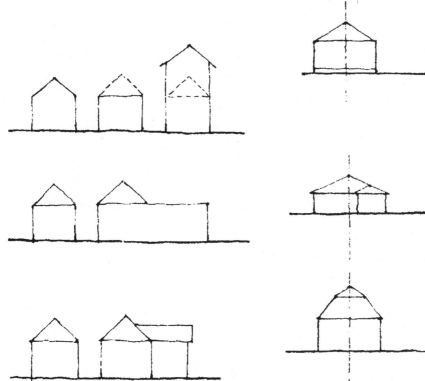

FIGURE 1.79 Diagram showing proportion. New additions shown out of proportion with existing context.

FIGURE 1.80 Diagram showing scale. Secondary buildings represented as small scale versions of primary buildings.

FIGURE 1.81 University of Virginia, Charlottesville, Virginia.

A third example is the relationship of the tower to the column shown in Figure 1.83. The tower at Cranbrook is seen in the background with a column in the foreground. The tower is heavy in terms of mass because of the relationship of solid to void. There is very little void in the tower compared to solid. It is a large size and scale in relation to the human figure. The column is small in size and light in terms of its mass, because of the relationship of mass to void around it. The proportion of the column is different than that of the proportion of the tower, because of the relationship of width to height and the relationship between the column capital to the column shaft, compared to the relationship of the observatory top to the shaft of the tower.

FIGURE 1.82 ATT Building, New York.

FIGURE 1.83   Cranbrook, Bloomfield Hills, Michigan.

FENESTRATION

Fenestration is the placement of openings, usually windows, in a wall of a building. Whether the windows are large or small, placed axially or non-axially, will have bearing on the character of the building or adjacent space. Typically, in axially symmetrical buildings, openings are placed such that the center axis of a building creates a void.

This implies that if columns are to be placed on the exterior, there will be an even number of columns to place a void at the center axis. In an axially symmetrical building, a void is usually in the center.

Geometry is used in placing windows and doors either axially symmetrical or axially asymmetrical. Figure 1.84 illustrates the difference between the two kinds of composition. Axial symmetry is when one side of a building is a mirror image of the other. Axial asymmetry is when a building appears balanced with respect to a vertical axis but does not have two equal halves on either side of a vertical axis. An example of an axially symmetrical building is any Greek or Roman temple. A specific example of an axially asymmetrical building is Mount Vernon (Figures 1.85 and 1.86). The beauty of this kind of composition is that the building is balanced about an axis yet not equal on each side. Additionally, the eye struggles to make the front elevation axially symmetrical but is not able to because of the asymmetrical placement of the elements of the elevation. To illustrate this further using buildings from another era Figure 1.87 shows axial asymmetry as seen in Modernist buildings such as the Farnsworth House, the Glass House and the Villa Savoy. Figure 1.88 shows axial symmetry in other Modernist structures such as the Chicago Loop Post Office, Crown Hall, and the Seagram's Building located in New York.

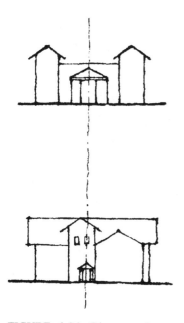

FIGURE 1.84 Diagram showing kinds of composition.

FIGURE 1.85 Mount Vernon, Virginia.

FIGURE 1.86   Mount Vernon, Virginia.

Historical architecture provides a rich set of fenestration patterns (Figures 1.89 and 1.90). Figure 1.91 shows a special case where the fenestration pattern is broken by the placement of a chimney on axis with a ridge line. In one case, the chimney becomes transparent below the eave, and in the other, the chimney is exposed on the outside of the structure. Figure 1.92 shows a variety of institutional fenestration patterns, where windows are placed either in the center or to the sides depending upon the overall composition of the building.

Usually with urban row houses, the front door is placed off axis regardless of whether the windows create a void in the center axis or if the center axis is solid (Figure 1.92). Axially asymmetrical buildings with mass on the center axis rather than void can vary considerably in size and shape. They may have pediment or pyramid tops or have a flat articulation formed by a cornice line. They may be multi storied or simple one story structures.

While there are many ways to place windows within an exterior wall, there are clear examples of what not to do when adding or subtracting windows from a building. Figure 1.93 represents a several fenestrations patterns that should not be implemented. The variation evident in window openings themselves is infinite. Figures 1.94 and 1.95 show some possibilities that exist in historic architecture, including triple and double hung windows, pointed arch openings, double arched openings, and eyelet window.

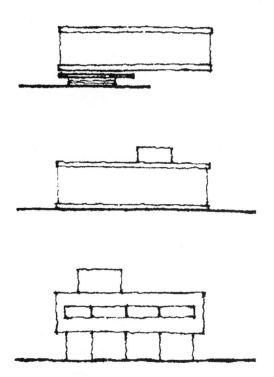

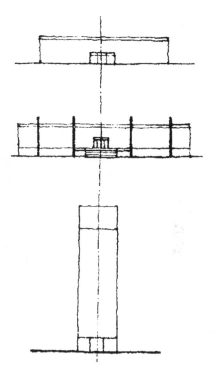

FIGURE 1.87 Diagram showing Modernist composition. (From top to bottom) the Farnsworth House, the Glass House, the Villa Savoy.

FIGURE 1.88 Diagram showing Modernist compositions. (From top to bottom) Loop Post Office, Crown Hall, Seagram's Building.

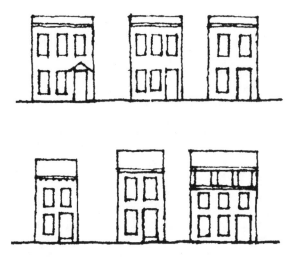

FIGURE 1.89 Diagram showing fenestration patterns.

FIGURE 1.90   Diagram showing residential fenestration patterns.

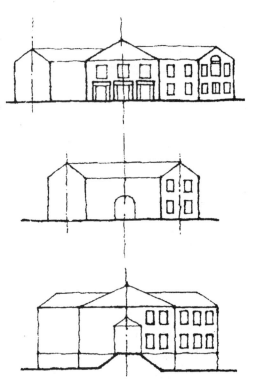

FIGURE 1.91   Diagram showing institutional fenestration patterns.

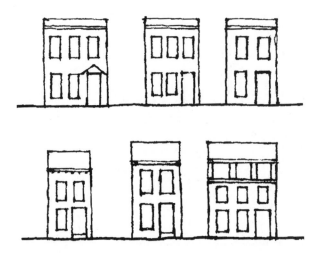

FIGURE 1.92   Diagram showing row house fenestration.

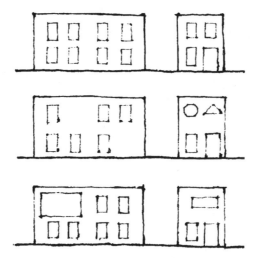

FIGURE 1.93 Diagram showing incompatible fenestration patterns.

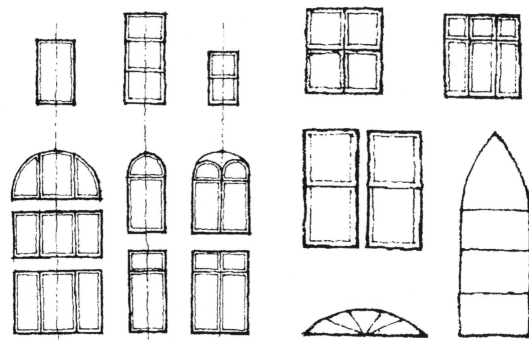

FIGURE 1.94 Diagram showing window variations. (Top left to top right) casement, triple sash, double-hung. (Bottom left to bottom right) basilican, single transom arch, double transom arch.

FIGURE 1.95 Diagram showing window variations.

BASE, MIDDLE, AND TOP

The division of the elevation of a building into base, middle, and top is called tripartite composition, or three-part composition. What divides a building into three parts is usually a differentiation of materials between the three parts. For example, the base of a building divided into three parts may be rusticated to look like large rough-hewn stones. The articulation of the middle portion would include slightly smaller looking stone pieces and the top would have refined articulation and ornament. Another expression of tripartite composition is to have the base of the building several stories tall, the middle several dozen stories tall, and the top one or two stories tall.

Tripartite composition can be applied to any building use and any size structure (Figures 1.96, 1.97, and 1.98). The Villa Capra, for example, is composed in a tripar-

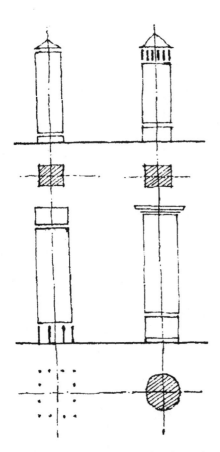

FIGURE 1.96 Diagram showing tripartite composition in tall buildings.

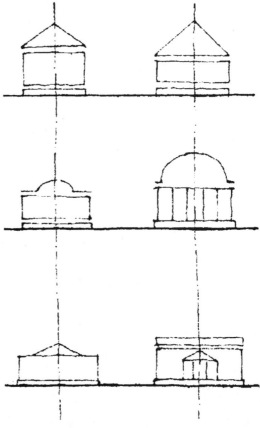

FIGURE 1.97 Diagram showing tripartite composition in moderately scaled buildings.

tite format (Figure 1.99). Rome's Flavian Amphitheater, more commonly known as the Coliseum, is also a tripartite composition in that the columns divide the elevation into three parts and vary from Doric at the base to Ionic in the center to Corinthian at the top (Figure 1.100). This is similar to the compositional division of the wall in the Court of the Urbino Palace (Figure 1.101), where the arches form the base. In this case, a middle is formed by rectangular window openings, and a top is defined by square window openings.

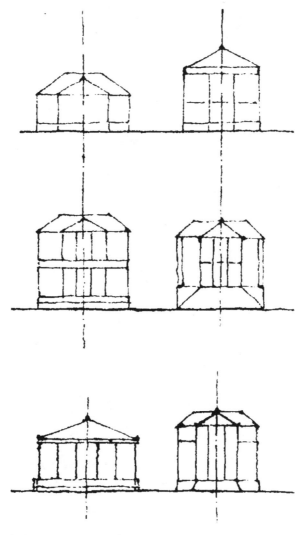

FIGURE 1.98 Diagram showing varieties of tripartite composition using columns.

FIGURE 1.99 The Villa Capra, Vicenza, Italy.

FIGURE 1.100 The Flavian Amphitheater, also known as the Coliseum, Rome.

FIGURE 1.101   Urbino, Italy.

LEGEND AND ORNAMENT

Architectural ornament, either though its use or its elimination is one way in which architectural character is expressed in buildings. Ornament depicts structure, imitates nature, or tells a story. In Classical architecture the vocabulary of ornament represents in stone, the expression of wood structure. Triglyphs depict the ends of wood joists. Fluting, the vertical indentations in columns represents the story of how reeds were once bound together in bundles, then placed vertically as building supports.

The rustication of stone from bottom to top depicts the structural capacity of stone with larger stones at the base, and successively smaller ones placed on top of one another toward the top of the wall. In Modernist architecture, the architectural expression results from a spare ornamental expression. The representation of nature in Modernism results from a literal introduction of natural materials such as marble or wood. Veining of wood and stone is used ornamentally, by repeating patterns resulting from the splitting of stone or wood.

The myths and legends associated with architecture and expressed through its ornamentation are significant because they provide examples of how architecture can become a part of the tradition of a place or a group of people. The primitive hut, the Corinthian girl, and the caryatids, are three legends or myths which provide a metaphoric understanding of architecture.

The primitive hut, the Corinthian girl, the caryatids, are three legends or myths which provide a metaphoric understanding of architecture. The Primitive Hut legend is described by the Roman Architect and author Vitruvius in *The Origins of the Dwelling House* [3]. He says, *"Among the Colchians in Pontus, where there are forests in plenty, they lay down entire trees flat on the ground to the right and the left, leaving between them a space to suit the length of the trees, and then place above these another pair of trees, resting on the ends of the former and at right angles with them. These four trees enclose the space for the dwelling."*

A second legend from Vitruvius describes the representation of human figures as columns as a means to humiliate a conquered people [4]. Vitruvius says,*"...the Persian armies, infinite in number, with a small force at the battle of Plataea, celebrated a glorious triumph with the spoils and booty, and with the money obtained from the sale thereof built the Persian Perch, to be a monument to the renown and valour of the people and a trophy of victory for posterity. And there they set effigies of the prisoners arrayed in barbarian costume and holding up the roof, their pride punished by this deserved affront, that enemies might temple for fear of the effects of their courage..."*

A third legend from Vitruvius describes the origin of the Corinthian Order [5]. Vitruvius says, *"A freeborn maiden of Corinth, just of marriageable age, was attacked by an illness and passed away. After her burial, her nurse, collecting a few little things which used to give the girl pleasure while she was alive, put them in a basket, carried it to the tomb, and laid it on top thereof, covering it with a roof-tile so that the things might last longer in the open air. This basket happened to be placed just above the root of an acanthus. The acanthus root, pressed down meanwhile through it was by the weight, when springtime came around put forth leaves and stalks in the middle, and the stalks, growing up along the sides of the basket, and pressed out by the corners of the tile through the compulsion of its weight, were forced to bend into volutes at the outer edges."*

Extensive literature exists describing in metaphoric terms how elements of architecture represent nature or natural processes. A column is a tree, groups of columns are a forest. A column is a human figure, a group of columns is a society of human beings. The acanthus leaf symbolizes the natural process of life and death by describing the death and rebirth of a young maiden. Triglyphs represent thighbones, and relate to animal sacrifice rituals which took place within ancient temples.

Architectural elements imitate nature, both literally and figuratively. Paradoxically, the material of buildings crafted into columns, walls, roofs, and arches become the means by which architecture relates to its natural surroundings. For example, architecture connects to the sky by means of roof profiles seen against the horizon (Figures 1.102 and 1.103). Examples of profiles against the sky include church steeples, castle towers, or the exterior profile of domed buildings and the pointed roof shapes so frequently used in residential architecture. Cities also have profiles, and the preservation of an entire skyline could easily become the focus of preservation if threatened with inappropriate development.

SPACES BETWEEN BUILDINGS

Porches, verandas, loggias, and terraces provide spaces that are both inside and outside. Spaces such as these are all too familiar, yet plans for communities and for new buildings often exclude elements such as these in favor of maximized parking spaces or maximized interior retable square footage. While most often associated with suburban environments, each of these—porches, verandas, loggias, and terraces—is vital to successful urban suburban and rural settings.

Porches, for example, provide a space within view of the public way, yet are protected from public access. Porches placed at the fronts of buildings provide a space for social interaction on the street side of a building. Compared to the option of placing lawn chairs in front of an open double garage door, or to the brutality of an environment with no place whatsoever designated for outdoor enjoyment, the inclusion of porches in a residential setting is far from a nostalgic whim. For the preservationist, the challenge is to identify and conserve elements of the physical environment that permit this kind of interaction. Often homeowners will want to close-in a porch or tear down a porch that has decayed without proposing a replacement for

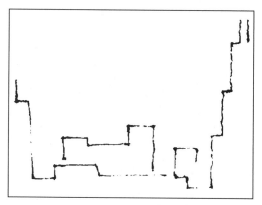

FIGURE 1.102 Diagram showing large building profiles.

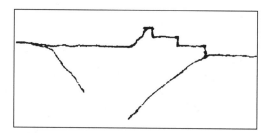

FIGURE 1.103 Diagram showing small building profiles.

the inside/outside space that is to be lost. This should be prevented as much as possible so that an essential part of the physical environment allowing an essential set of social patterns to develop may be preserved.

Porches on the street side of a building are typical of true suburban settings, and are one element in a suburban setting that creates a well defined intermediate zone between building and street. In urban environments, this intermediate zone is closer to the street and is comprised most often by stairs to a first floor, and porch and stairs down below grade to a small recessed area that permits access to a lower apartment. In an urban setting the stairs are often fenced in or gated for a feeling of security or privacy. In rural settings, however, elements such as porches and terraces are ways in which a building can connect to the natural landscape.

As with the suburban and urban examples, the porch element creates a place that is both inside and outside, and creates a link to whatever is at the exterior of the building. Furthermore, the social function allowed by the inclusion of an inside/outside area is no less important in a rural setting as it is in a suburban or urban setting (Figures 1.104 through 1.109).

DISTRICTS

The idea of a district is at the center of many intensely debated preservation dialogues. Architecturally, the challenge of identifying a district is to recognize the common elements of a district and the limits of these elements. The common elements of

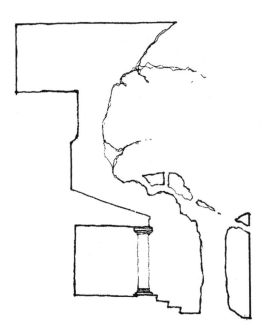

FIGURE 1.104 Diagram showing spaces between buildings. Space between a porch and a tree.

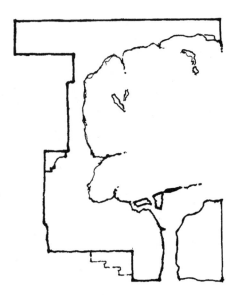

FIGURE 1.105 Diagram showing spaces between buildings. Space between a terrace, a projected Tudor gable, and a tree.

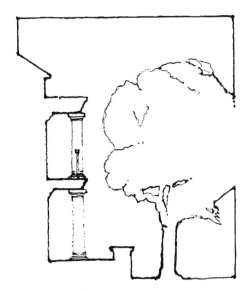

FIGURE 1.106 Diagram showing spaces between buildings. Space between a double exterior portico and a tree.

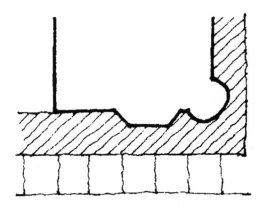

FIGURE 1.107 Diagram showing spaces between buildings. Diagonal shading indicates area between building and sidewalk.

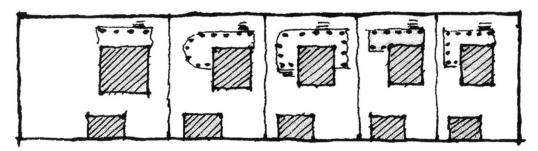

FIGURE 1.108 Diagram showing spaces between buildings. Diagonal shading indicates areas between building and sidewalk.

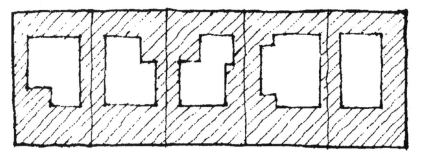

FIGURE 1.109 Diagram showing spaces between buildings. Diagonal shading indicates area between building and sidewalk.

a district may include common massing of buildings, common material construction of buildings, common scale, proportion and size, or common quality construction. The limits of the district could include a natural boundary such as a river or stream, a change in topography, a change is mass, scale, proportion or size of the buildings in the district, or a radical change in building use.

Once the common elements are identified and the limits of the district are established, the uniqueness of the elements seen as a whole should be articulated. This second step is important; if overlooked, one might argue that since the district has so much in common, there is nothing unique about the district and the district should not be designated as having significance and merit. The emotion surrounding the establishment of districts has some relationship to the way in which the form of a district is defined. If a district is defined in a way which equalizes all of the buildings, but the people in the buildings do not feel equal to one another, then there will be disparity between the architectural definition of the district and the politics surrounding its designation. If a district is defined with strong boundaries, then those outside the boundaries may resist the establishment of a district because of their exclusion from an area defined as significant. No one likes to be told that they live on the other side of the tracks, but how then can a group of buildings be designated as a singular district?

The idea of style should be separated from the idea of quality. Preservation limits its role by assigning moral and qualitative attributes to visual analysis. This happens when one style is described as being more popular or more advanced than another style. Stating that an architect "just hadn't gotten rid of the old style yet," or "these old buildings were popular styles back then" is not defensible. First, architects do not design one style at a time. Architects of today, as well as those who lived during the 19th and early 20th centuries, often design many styles at once and mix architectural languages and expressions in singular buildings. Second, who knows what was or was not popular at any given time, and even if one were able to determine a standard of popularity, this would not matter since our concern is the making of socially and architecturally viable communities in the present.

Furthermore, the idea of style should be separated from the idea of social station. There is a long-standing American tradition that links a building's style to class. This is not a useful paradigm for preservation, since a style of building can exist at any economic level. Architectural expression is not limited to class—building styles can be designed for any economic level.

With this in mind, a clear analysis of architectural form is possible that defines in precise terms the merits of groups of buildings, the spaces in between the buildings, and the street and alley infrastructure that defines how the buildings relate to one another. This relationship differs in rural, suburban, and urban settings. In rural areas, buildings are placed far from the main street or road. Many are accessed by means of secondary single lane roads that lead to a house with several outbuildings nearby. Where main roads cross a center is usually defined by a set of buildings at each of the four corners of the road crossing. The main road often passes through small villages or towns that have been laid out in a grid pattern. This environment is threatened when the definition of the corner crossing is destroyed or the primacy of the main road is diminished. This can happen when a large area is paved for the purpose of parking automobiles or when the main road is no longer permitted to pass through a small village and is replaced by a multiple lane thoroughfare. Additionally, this pattern of development is destroyed when the single lane roads leading to single houses become over burdened and are expanded to accommodate more houses (Figures 1.110 through 1.115).

The suburban setting is more complicated. For the purposes of this discussion suburban setting will be defined as true suburban and suburban sprawl. A true suburb is a city that is adjacent to a major metropolitan center and has its architectural roots in 19th century planning. True suburbs have a hierarchy of boulevards, streets, and alleys that are usually planned in a grid pattern. There is a clear relationship

FIGURE 1.110   Diagram showing varieties of urban intersections and centers.

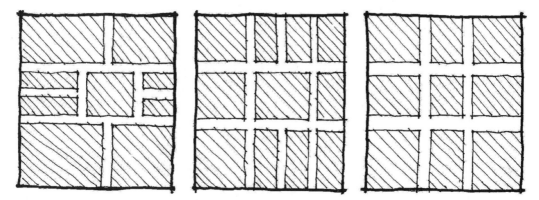

FIGURE 1.111   Diagram showing varieties of urban intersections.

between street sidewalk and building and there is a well-defined intermediate zone comprised of landscaping and terraces, porches, and verandas. Public space is provided and people are able to walk from place to place instead of using motorized transportation.

True suburbs include a pattern of primary and secondary structures in residential areas. The secondary structures—outbuildings currently used for automobile storage—are often small scale versions of the larger scale primary buildings which are usually single family residences (Figure 1.116). True suburbs include institutional and commercial buildings that are scaled to the size of adjacent residences. All of the elements of true suburbs should be preserved and enhanced. Suburban sprawl has none of this. Sprawl provides no public space, there is no intermediate zone, no sidewalks are provided, and the planning is based on the economics of the automobile.

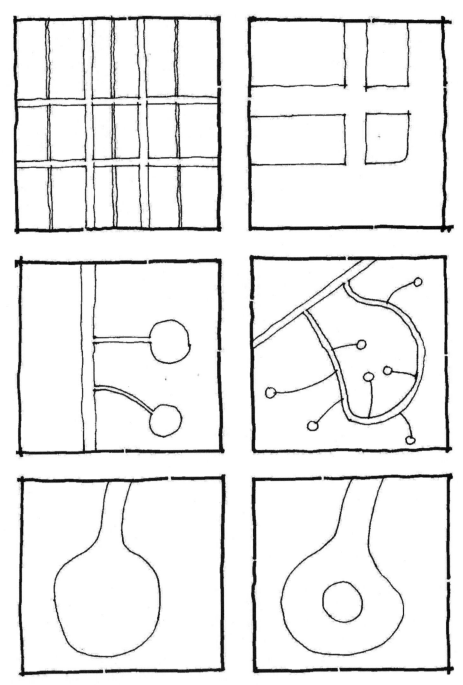

FIGURE 1.112 Diagram showing varieties of suburban intersections.

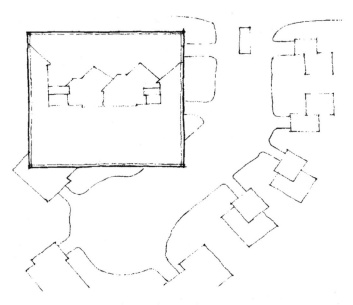

FIGURE 1.113 Diagram showing contemporary suburban land use where vistas are blocked.

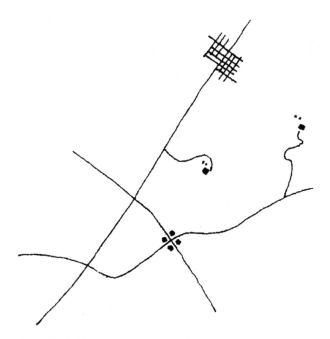

FIGURE 1.114 Diagram showing rural land use. Cross roads, individual buildings, and village grid are integrated into natural surroundings.

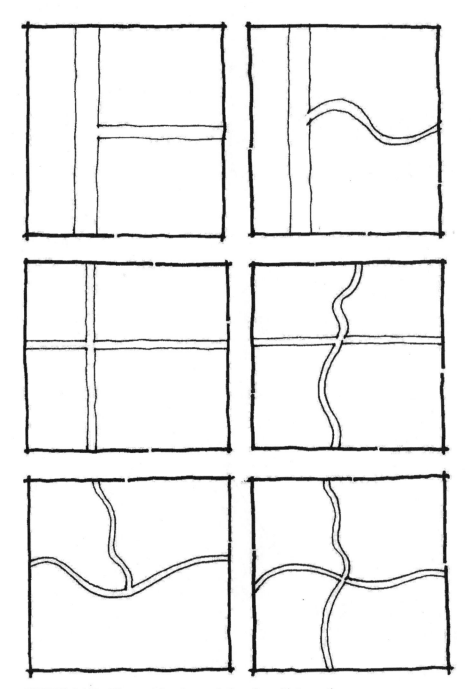

FIGURE 1.115 Diagram showing varieties of rural intersections.

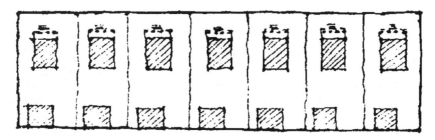

FIGURE 1.116 Diagram showing primary and secondary structures in a consistent pattern.

Buildings do not link to nature, do not provide appropriate spaces for groups of people to gather, nor do they do not provide a sense of privacy. Sprawl fails socially, architecturally, and economically, and can occur in urban, suburban, and rural areas.

Urban settings are similar in some ways to the true suburban setting, in that there is a clear distinction between types of streets, and the definition of public and private space is clearly delineated in the architecture. Links to nature are provided by tree-lined boulevards and recreational parks. Buildings in urban settings often are placed with no space between them. Urban residences also include outbuildings at the rear alleys. Institutional and commercial buildings, when adjacent to residences, are scaled to the size of the adjacent residences. In urban areas residential buildings are sometimes scaled to the size of institutional and commercial buildings, as seen in large multi-story residential structures.

COMPATIBILITY

Compatibility is the way in which a new building or addition fits its context, or the way in which a group of buildings settles into a landscape. There are several ways to describe compatibility using the language described above. First is with regard to the way in which the five archetypes define centers, edges, tops, middles, and bases. If a group of buildings creates an edge, then an addition to this group of buildings should maintain the edge. If a group of buildings creates a center, then an addition to the group of buildings should maintain the definition of the center. In the case of an individual building, if a building has a tripartite elevation, then an addition to the building should maintain the tripartite composition. If a building has a fenestration pattern that places an opening on a central axis, then modifications to that building should maintain the opening on the central axis.

A second way to look at compatibility is to view it with regard to mass, scale, proportion, and size. If a building has a heavy massing, or very few openings, then adding a great number of new openings may not be compatible. If a building were scaled to the human figure so that it feels small, then an addition that changes the scale to feel large would not be compatible. If changes to a building alter the proportions of a horizontally proportioned building such that the proportions are vertical instead of horizontal, then the alterations are not compatible (Figures 1.117 through 1.120).

A third way to view compatibility is to consider whether or not existing urban infrastructure is maintained. For example, if a new building were planned which blocks an existing grid pattern of streets, then the building would not be compatible with its surroundings. If a parking lot is planned for an area that is currently a part of a system of parks and green space, then the new parking lot is not compatible with

FIGURE 1.117 Diagram showing central building inconsistent with pattern of adjacent pattern of primary and secondary structures.

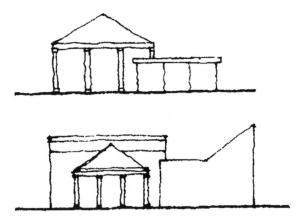

FIGURE 1.118 Diagram showing incompatible additions.

the surrounding landscape. In a rural setting, if buildings are planned that block natural views or vistas, then the buildings are not compatible with the rural landscape.

Structure and ornament in buildings include commonly understood elements of the built environment such as columns, arches, walls, roofs and floors among others. In towns structure and ornament include streets, boulevards, parks, plazas and alleys. Observing and describing the placement and disposition of archetypal structures and the relation of these to one another and to a surrounding context results is the first part of making, re-making and conserving livable, humane and meaningful places. What follows is the craft of how this is accomplished.

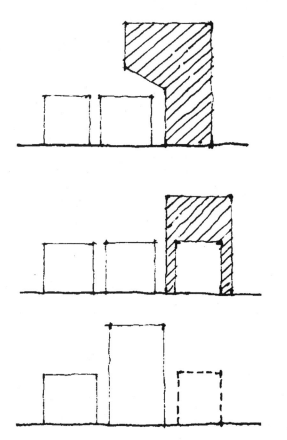

FIGURE 1.119 Diagram showing incompatible additions and subtractions.

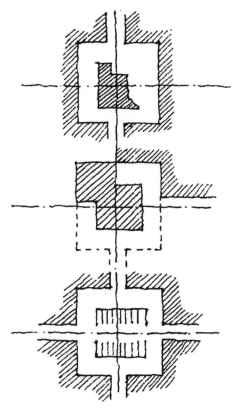

FIGURE 1.120 Diagram showing incompatible additions and subtractions in an urban setting. (From top to bottom) subtraction from a center, addition to a center and subtraction from a perimeter, and subtraction from a center to create a parking lot.

REFERENCES

1. Palladio, Andrea. 1997. *The Four Books on Architecture*. Trans. Robert Tavernor and Richard Schofield. MIT Press, Cambridge, Massachusetts. (Originally published as *I Quattro Libri dell' Architettura*, Book I, 1570.)

2. Palladio, Book XVI.

3. Vitruvivius, *The Ten Books on Architecture*. Ed. Morris Hicky Morgan. 1960. Dover, New York. 38.

4. Vitruvius, 7, 8.

5. Vitruvius, 104.

PART
TWO

CRAFT

The craft of architecture concerns the making of buildings and sites through the artful assembly of materials and space. Preservation has much to say about the craft of architecture. First there is the matter of replacing materials, then second the modification of elements and structures, and third the reconstitution of public space.

Historic preservation employs techniques that range from meticulous museum conservation to what amounts to emergency room triage where a building is threatened by structural decay and requires immediate stabilization. Most preservation work happens somewhere in the middle of this range where decisions are made to save some pieces of a building, replace others, and dispose of others.

Preservation practice encourages the replacement of materials in kind if possible. What this means is that, for example, if a wood balustrade is deteriorated and needs to be replaced, then the balustrade should be replaced with a wood balustrade that looks like the original. If a masonry wall needs to be replaced, then the wall should be re-built with a new masonry wall that looks like the original. Matters become complicated when the wood balustrade mentioned above needs to be replaced but new building codes require a higher railing height than the original. In the case of the masonry wall, if the wall needed to be replaced because it was not built well to begin with, then to build a new one just like the original would only create a problem for future owners of the masonry wall. In the example of the wood balustrade, the owner of the balustrade and the owner's architect have a responsibility to follow current building codes that protect public health safety and welfare. At the same time, the owner and the owner's architect have a responsibility to the historic integrity of the structure that they are proposing to modify.

One possibility to resolve this would be to keep all of the post spacing identical to the original, keep the wood profiles identical to the original, keep all of the intermediate vertical slats the same as the original, and construct a balustrade that is higher than the original but includes the same elements as the original (Figure 2.01). There are many varieties of balusters present in residential architecture made from either wood or stone (Figure 2.02).

Generally stone balusters are found in larger buildings or buildings that are in urban areas. The connections between pieces of stone and the base upon which the stone is placed sometimes deteriorate. This most often occurs due to moisture penetration and the effects of salt used to prevent the build up of ice during the winter months.

In the case of the masonry wall, the owner of the wall and the owner's architect also have a responsibility to the public health safety and welfare, and must build the new wall in compliance with current building codes. If the wall could be reinforced properly and a proper footing could be designed without affecting the external appearance of the wall, then current code requirements could be met while maintaining the historic integrity of the wall.

This being said, historic preservation should recognize that architectural history is, among other things, a history of replacement materials. Columns and Classical detailing may not only be expressed in wood or stone, but the very appearance of the Classical language is based upon the imitation of wood construction in stone. The vertical grooves seen in columns represent bundled reeds. Varieties of fluting include the flutes that extend to the ground in a column without a base, flutes that stop short of the ground with no base, and flutes that stop short of a column or pilaster base. Pilasters differ from columns in that they are engaged to walls and most often do not have entasis or a curvature of the shaft between the base and capital (Figure 2.04). Another Classical detail seen in Figure 2.05 represents a bundle of reeds placed horizontally at the base of a building. This detail is more literal than fluting as the straps that hold the representative reeds together form a cross pattern at the base.

BUILDING COMPONENTS AND MATERIALS

Vinyl

An important issue relating to materials is that of replacing wood with vinyl. This occurs in three areas; first with siding, second with fences, and third with windows. Vinyl siding is generally considered detrimental to the material that the siding covers up—usually wood siding. The reason for this is that vinyl does not let air flow properly underneath the siding, and does not let moisture properly move through the wall. Vinyl siding only replicates the look of wood clapboard siding but does not have the properties of wood clapboard siding. The overlapping effect of clapboard siding provides an air space within the wall. This air space helps the wall breath and naturally regulates condensation. Another problem with vinyl siding is that the detailing of corners and eaves is often clumsy and inarticulate compared to what is possible with wood installed by a good carpenter. Ironically, vinyl siding is often so poorly crafted that the sloppiness of the installation mitigates the effects of the vinyl with regard to moisture build-up in the wall.

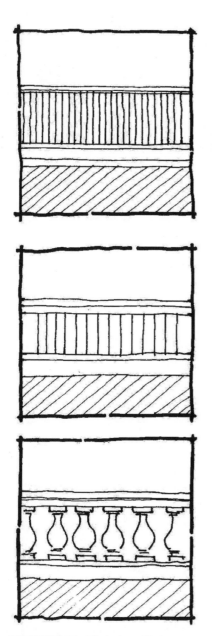

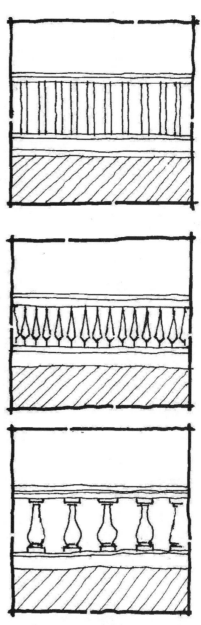

FIGURE 2.01 Varieties of balusters. Top: wood balusters at 1:1 spacing. Middle: wood balusters at 1:1 spacing but made from wider posts. Bottom: stone or wood balusters.

FIGURE 2.02 Varieties of balusters. Top: wood balusters at 1:2 spacing. Middle: wood balusters with open areas cut to make a pattern. Bottom: stone or wood balusters widely spaced.

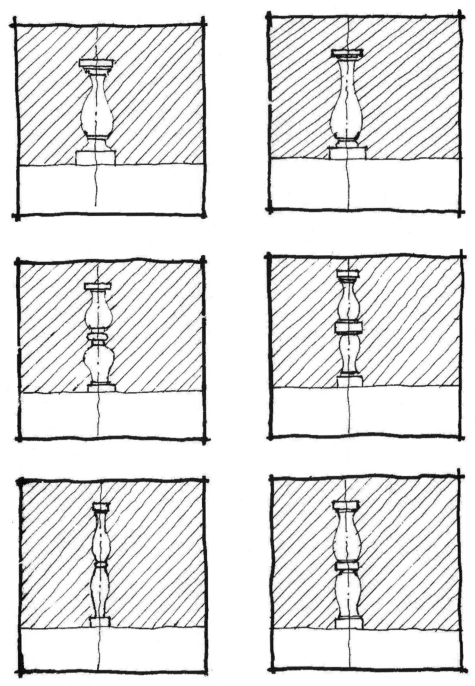

FIGURE 2.03a Varieties of Classical balusters [1].

FIGURE 2.03b *(continued)* Varieties of Classical balusters [1].

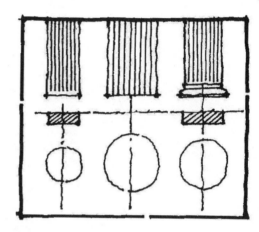

FIGURE 2.04a Top: fluting of a pilaster based on Asher Benjamin's method outlined in *The American Builder's Companion*. Pilaster is divided into 29 equal parts. Each flute is 3 parts, each rib is 1 part.

FIGURE 2.04b Varieties of fluted pilasters and columns.

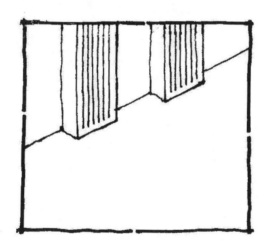

FIGURE 2.04c Pilasters with flutes stopping short of the ground [2].

Wood fences are sometimes replaced with vinyl fences. There are vinyl fences that look almost identical to wood fences that have been painted with acrylic paint. Both have a glossy finish. The advantage of vinyl over wood for fences is that the owner will not need to paint the vinyl fence. The disadvantage is that there is a possibility that the vinyl will discolor over time if it is of a poor quality.

FIGURE 2.05 Base detail, Marquette Building, Holabird and Roche, 1895, Chicago.

Vinyl windows often replace wood frame windows. The advantage, as with vinyl fences, is that the vinyl windows will not need to be painted while wood windows will need to be painted. The disadvantage from a preservationist's point of view is that there are limits to how narrow the frame profile can be manufactured. This is a problem when narrow wood frames are to be replaced. Good practice states that the frame width should be maintained in the replacement windows, as should the mullion widths. In historic properties with windows that have wide frames and mullions, and historic buildings that are not of a museum quality, vinyl windows are quite possibly a suitable alternative to reconstructing wood windows.

Brick Masonry

When replacing brick masonry, when adding onto an existing brick building, or when tuckpointing existing masonry, the new bricks and mortar should match the existing bricks in color, texture, coursing, mix, and size. Each of these is possible, although the contractor may not be pleased with the work required to accomplish a good match.

Tuckpointing is the process of replacing the mortar between bricks. The mortar should match the color of the original mortar and the type of mortar joint should be replicated. Ideally, a brick building will be cleaned prior to brick replacement or tuck-pointing. Then a color match can be determined. The color of a brick wall is determined by the mix of bricks. Usually there are several colors of bricks in a mix of bricks. If some of the colors are placed too closely or too far apart then the color match will not be adequate and the work should be rejected and replaced at no cost to the owner. The texture of the brick may also vary depending on how it is cut. The size of the brick can vary also. Brick sizes have changed over time and occasionally an existing building will have a brick size that is a true eight inch width. If cost prohibits the use of the exact match, the mason should be instructed to compensate for the variation in width by slightly adjusting the vertical mortar joints so that none of the bricks will need to be cut.

The mortar joints between the bricks should be replaced with the same kind of mortar color and the same kind of joint as the original construction would indicate. Occasionally, as in some Prairie School buildings, the vertical joint is struck flush with the brick and the horizontal joint is recessed. This produces a horizontal effect. This effect would need to be preserved. There are several kinds of mortar joints including flush, struck, convex, concave, grooved, and beaded. Each should be replicated in accordance with what was used in the original construction. During tuck-pointing it is important to avoid cutting into the brick when removing old mortar. Mortar may be removed by chiseling or *tooling* the old mortar out from in between the bricks, or the mortar may be removed by using small hand-held saws. New mortar should be specified such that the mortar is softer than the brick. If the mortar is harder than the brick then the bricks will spall, which means that the outer surface of the brick will flake off. There are specialty mortars called lime based mortars that are used in conditions where archaic bricks or stones are to be restored. (Figures 2.6, 2.7, 2.8, and 2.9) [3].

Brick masonry repair also involves the investigation of brick tie-backs. When brick masonry units are laid properly, metal tabs are placed in the mortar and attached to either a masonry backing, or to another means of support. Additionally, a masonry clad wall may contain steel angles, called relieving angles because they act as reinforcing to distribute or relieve the load of the masonry units. Figure 2.10 shows spot checks that are underway at the Carbide and Carbon building in Chicago.

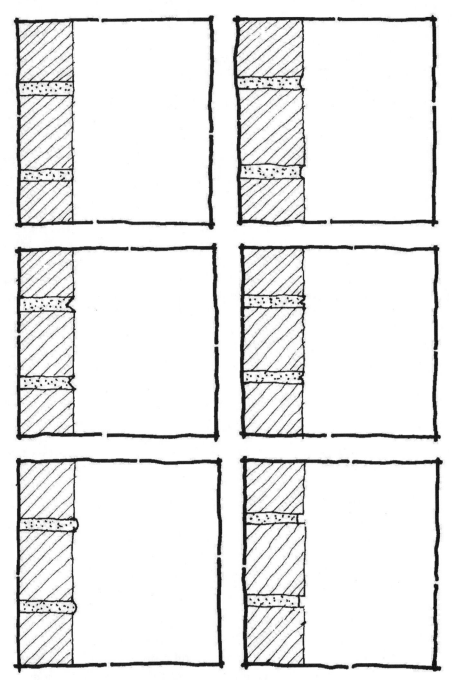

FIGURE 2.06   Diagram showing mortar joint profiles. Top left to bottom right: flush, concave, v groove, groove, convex v, and struck.

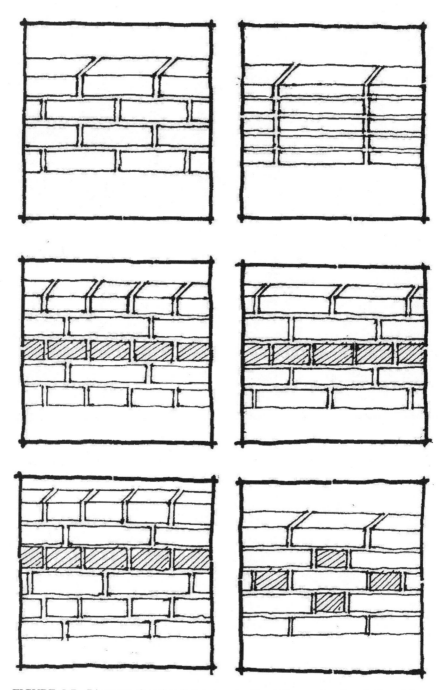

FIGURE 2.7 Diagram showing brick bonds. Top left: running bond. Top right: Roman stacked bond. Middle left: English bond. Middle right: American bond. Bottom left: English cross bond. Bottom right: Flemish bond.

FIGURE 2.8 Thinly set mortar and convex or beaded mortar at the Monadnock Building (North Building), Burnham and Root, 1891, Chicago.

Brick has been removed at intervals so that the condition of the inner wall may be evaluated. Figure 2.11 shows the brick face removed from the south elevation of the same building exposing the structural steel frame. Another example of similar repairs to brick masonry is seen in Figure 2.12 where a corner has been removed to expose an internal steel column.

Terra Cotta

Terra cotta is a clay material that is usually used as ornamental trim in buildings dating from the 1920s and earlier. Terra cotta is attached to a building by means of steel clips. Terra cotta pieces are very heavy and do not often exceed two or three feet in length. Cracks in the material are usually caused by the shifting of individual pieces as a result of corrosion of the steel support clips, rather than a failure of the clay material itself.

FIGURE 2.9 Beaded or convex mortar joint.

FIGURE 2.10　Carbide and Carbon Building north wall.

FIGURE 2.11 Carbide and Carbon Building south wall.

FIGURE 2.12   Garland Building, Chicago.

Corrosion is often caused by moisture that has penetrated the interior of the wall cavity. If the terra cotta is replaced along with the support clips but the moisture penetration is not stopped, then the newly replaced terra cotta will crack as a result of the moisture penetration.

Terra cotta clay color and glaze color should be reviewed during the construction process prior to fabrication. As with masonry work, terra cotta should be cleaned prior to and after construction to assure a good color match. If replacement is out of the question, then a suitable replacement material is precast concrete or fiberglass reinforced concrete that matches the profile of the existing terra cotta and that comes as close as possible to a color match as is reasonable. An additional possibility is the repair of the existing terra cotta by gluing the pieces back together. Again, unless the potential moisture problem is solved, the terra cotta will subsequently crack. Therefore, if either approach is taken, repair or replacement, then the support mechanisms should be checked as should all flashings and caulking in the area of the terra cotta where moisture could penetrate the wall (Figures 2.13 through 2.18).

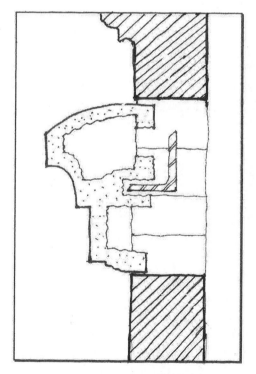

FIGURE 2.13 Diagram showing terra cotta detail. Terra cotta trim attached to masonry with steel lintel.

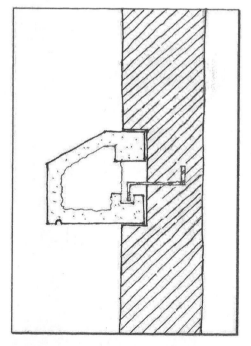

FIGURE 2.14 Diagram showing terra cotta detail. Terra cotta trim attached to masonry with steel ties.

FIGURE 2.15 Terra cotta restoration at the 111 West Washington Building, Chicago.

FIGURE 2.16 Terra cotta restoration at the 111 West Washington Building, Chicago.

FIGURE 2.17 Terra cotta repairs, Montgomery Ward Building, Burnham and Root, Chicago.

FIGURE 2.18 Terra cotta repairs, Montgomery Ward Building, Burnham and Root, Chicago.

ADA

Many old and historic buildings require modification to provide full access under the Americans with Disabilities Act or ADA. The ADA is a federal law in the United States mandating that public buildings be accessible to anyone with a disability, usually interpreted to mean anyone in a wheelchair, or who is unable to see, or unable to hear. Most ADA modifications involve the addition of ramps and elevators to provide access to all levels of a building to people in wheelchairs and the modification of restroom facilities to provide proper clearances and access. Also, included in ADA modifications are changes to door hardware, the addition of signs indicating room numbers and names in Braille, and the addition of strobe lights to alarms.

Adding a ramp to the front of a building is possible while respecting the original design intent of a building. In historic structures, there are several principles that when applied properly will allow accessibility while maintaining the existing historic fabric of a building intact (Figure 2.19). First is that the primary entrance to the building should remain unaltered. Second is that windows should not be blocked by the ramp, and third, the ramp should be configured to fit within the existing configuration of the building to which it is being added. Further concerns include the detailing of materials to match existing materials and compliance with applicable codes regulating the slope or pitch of the ramp as well as its width and length.

Another requirement mandated by the ADA is the reconfiguration of restroom facilities to accommodate use by individuals in

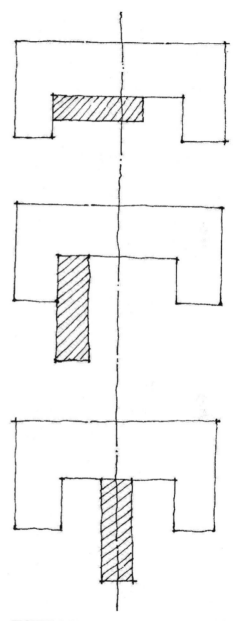

FIGURE 2.19 Top: diagram showing ramp placement within the existing outline of a building. Middle: diagram showing the placement of a ramp extending too far in front of an existing building. Bottom: diagram showing the placement of a ramp too far in front of an existing building and obstructing a primary axis.

wheel chairs. In most cases, reconfiguration is achieved by simply reorganizing the locations of restroom fixtures within an existing restroom space. There are obvious advantages to taking this approach, not the least of which is the minimization of plumbing reconfiguration and the costs associated with relocation of piping. When there is simply not enough space within an existing restroom for new ADA compliant fixtures, then a suitable unobstructed location within the building should be sought.

BUILDING ELEMENTS

Columns

The Classical language has been described with regard to architectural form. With regard to craft, there are specific techniques that are important to the proper construction and implementation of Classical elements. Often, wood columns rot and decay as do railings and balustrades. Wood columns are typically hollow tubes usually made from redwood that are attached to a wood or steel framework hidden within the column. The columns need to be vented to prevent moisture from building up within the column. This is possible by installing the column on a plinth base that contains a vent and by detailing the entablature in a way that provides a vent at the top. This detail will permit convection from the bottom of the column to the top, and will prevent decay due to moisture building up within the column (Figures 2.20 and 2.21).

Figures 2.22 and 2.23 both show double columns that would appear too narrow had the columns not been placed side by side. Both are very well-detailed and both examples indicate a properly detailed relationship between the column and the trim above the column. The abacus is the square piece of wood that provides a transition from the column to whatever exists above it. The correct way to detail this piece is to have it project outboard of the column and frieze trim above. Very often the abacus is either not present or is recessed too far in from the front of the outermost trim to be noticeable.

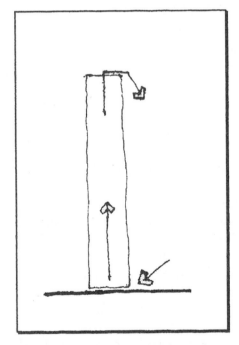

FIGURE 2.20 Diagram showing column venting. Convection from bottom to top to prevent moisture built-up.

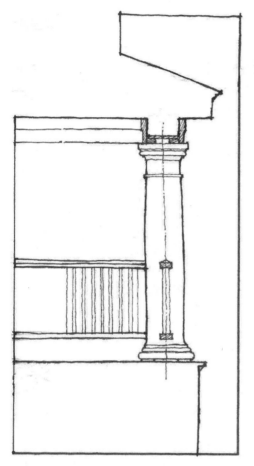

FIGURE 2.21 Diagram showing column detail at a porch. Porch detail with gaps shown for convection.

FIGURE 2.22 An example of double columns at a front porch.

Another matter relating to the craft of Classicism is the use of entasis and the diameter of the column in relation to its height. Entasis is the proper curvature or flare of a column shaft. If a column is to be replaced and the existing column has an entasis, then the new column should also have an entasis. In Classical design, column shafts are rarely straight shafts. Entasis is achieved through establishing points along a shaft that describe a curve. The proportion of the column shaft to its diameter is based on units based on the measure of the diameter. The Orders, which have been described earlier in relation to architectural form, each have different requirements for the length to diameter proportion. For the Tuscan Order, the relationship is one column width to seven for the height. For the Doric, Ionic, and Corinthian

FIGURE 2.23   An example of double columns in a front and side porch.

Orders, the proportion is one to nine. For the Composite Order the proportion is one to ten. Regarding column placement, the proportions are also set by ratios relating to column shaft width. A common Classical column placement is to place the outer two columns with seven and one half widths between them, with six column widths between the center columns (Figures 2.24 through 2.27) [4].

A third item relating to proportion is how to establish the vertical dimension of a building. The method for determining height is based on the length and width of a space in plan. This is done by adding the width of the room BC to the length CD then dividing the overall length DE by two to calculate the overall height of the space (Figure 2.28a). Another method is to add the width of the room BD to the length CD. Then divide CE in two and strike a semicircle from the mid-point. Extend BD to the circle to create point F which determines the height of the space (Figure 2.28b). A third method for determining height is to take the same room ABCD and extend the width with line DE, as in the previous example. Then strike line EB until it intersects the extension of line AC to determine the height of the room (Figure 2.28c) [5].

Corners

The way in which corners of buildings are detailed is critical to the success of compatible design. There are many ways to detail a corner, but all too often, corners are poorly executed with a *pork-chop* eave condition that is easy to build, but results in

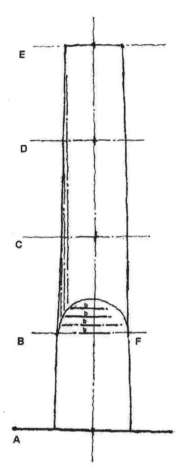

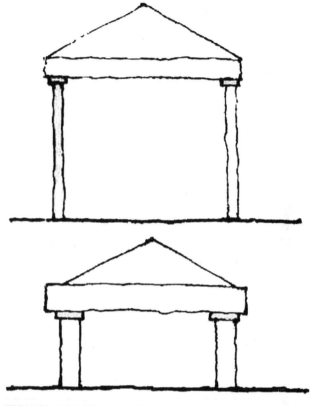

FIGURE 2.25 Diagram showing incompatible column proportions relative to column height and spacing.

FIGURE 2.24 Diagram showing entasis. Divide A to E by 4. Divide B to F by 8. Project lines to circle and perpendicular to c, d, and e to create entasis [5].

an inarticulate connection between the components of a building. The best way to make a corner in a building is to wrap the trim from the main elevation around to the secondary elevation. Once that is achieved, then place under the trim a series of quoins or a pilaster with a column capital. Quoins are meant to represent blocks of masonry at corners of buildings. They can be made by projecting brick masonry out from the face of the building, by inserting stone veneer at the corners, or by using stucco to represent stone. The advantage of using a pilaster is that the pilaster provides an edge for horizontal wood siding to end into (Figures 2.29 through 2.32).

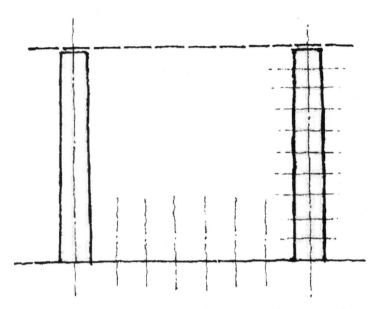

FIGURE 2.26 Diagram showing column proportions, ten column widths high by seven column widths wide [6].

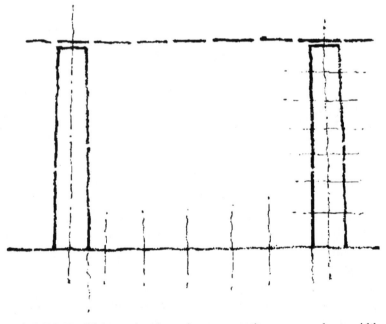

FIGURE 2.27 Diagram showing column proportions, seven column widths high by 5½ column widths wide [7].

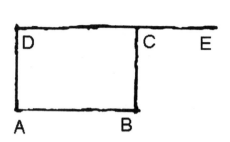

FIGURE 2.28a Diagram showing determination of height.

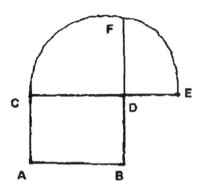

FIGURE 2.28b *(continued)* Diagram showing determination of height.

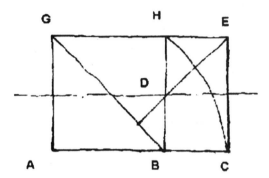

FIGURE 2.28c *(continued)* Diagram showing determination of height.

FIGURE 2.29a Clapboard siding and pilaster corner.

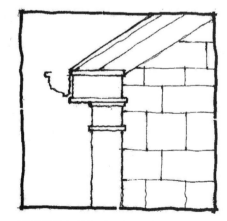

FIGURE 2.29b Stone cladding and pilaster corner.

FIGURE 2.30a Narrow clapboard siding with pilaster corner.

FIGURE 2.30b Brick veneer with no pilaster at the corner.

FIGURE 2.31a Alternating quoins.

FIGURE 2.31b Vertical quoins.

Another way to detail a corner is by creating a reverse corner detail. A reverse corner shows detail where the corner is articulated by two pilasters placed at right angles to one another instead of one column at the corner. The space between the pilasters is thereby set back from the face of the building. This detail is seen in Classical and Modernist architectures. An example of a Classical expression is in Figure 2.33 which

FIGURE 2.32a Pilaster corner.

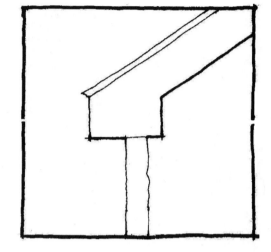

FIGURE 2.32b Pork-chopped detailing.

shows the corner of the Rothschild Building on State Street between Jackson and Van Buren Streets in Chicago, originally designed by Holabird and Roche in 1912 and recently renovated for DePaul University. The negative space between the corner pilasters is articulated with a volute, a round element set back from the outer face of the building. This same kind of corner is seen at the Kluczynski Federal Building designed by Mies van der Rohe which serves as a classic example of Modernist detailing and planning (Figure 2.34). Rather than a Classically inspired volute filling the void at the corner, Mies details a vertical element that extends the entire height of the building from the top of the upper level, as seen in the illustration, to the column at the base.

How all this relates to historic preservation is seen in Figure 2.35. This building at 11 South Quincy Place in Chicago is clad in terra cotta. The detailing of the corner is similar to the detailing seen at the Rothschild Building in that the detail is a classicized reverse corner. The difference is that at some point an additional floor was added above the cornice. The reverse type detail was not carried through to the top of the new structure. Compatible design practice would provide a detail that would extend the existing detail into the addition.

Windows

The restoration of windows and trim is essential to good preservation practice. The division of the window into smaller panes of glass with mullions and muntins can affect the compatibility of an addition to an existing building, or affect the appearance of an existing building with windows that need to be replaced.

FIGURE 2.33 Corner detail from the Rothschild and Co. Building, Holabird and Roche, 1912, Chicago.

FIGURE 2.34 Corner detail from the Kluczynski Federal Building, Mies van der Rohe, begun 1964, Chicago.

FIGURE 2.35   Corner Detail, 11 South Quincy Place, Chicago.

If at all possible, it is best to maintain the look of the original window mullion and muntin pattern. Additionally, the thickness of the new mullions and muntins should be as close as possible to the original mullion and muntins as possible. Generally, windows that exist in historic buildings have mullions and muntins that are narrower than those found in newly manufactured windows. Mullions and muntins in historic buildings usually create a separation between smaller pieces of glass that comprise the overall window. These are called *true divided lites*, and are available through modern window manufacturers or may also be replicated by craftsmen trained in making historic windows (Figure 2.36).

Modern window manufacturers also provide applied mullions which are mullions and muntins which are glued or applied to the glass portion of the window. Another option provided by manufacturers is mullions that are sandwiched between the two panes of glass that make insulated glass. Each of these options has a cost associated with it, and each has implications for preservation (Figure 2.37a and 2.37b).

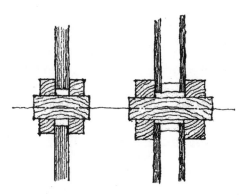

FIGURE 2.36 Diagram showing true divided lites.

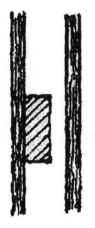

FIGURE 2.37a
Mullion within two panes of glass.

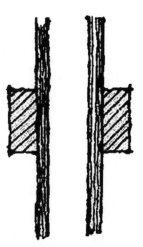

FIGURE 2.37b Mullions applied to outside face of glass.

Another element relating to windows is the mechanism within the wall adjacent to the window. A pulley and weight system is usually contained within the wall on either side of old windows. Very often, the ropes that hold the pulley break over time with use and the weights fall to the bottom of the wall cavity. When windows are completely removed from an existing building and manufactured windows are to be installed, the wall areas immediately beside the windows will need to be refurbished because of the removal of the pulley and weight system.

Window Casing

Window casing is the trim surrounding the window. Casing can be either interior or exterior or both. It is possible to replace windows without replacing trim, depending upon the detailing of the existing window and trim. Ideally, historic windows should be renovated to match the existing windows and all trim should be saved or replaced to match the existing. However, if costs prohibit the renovation of existing windows and manufactured windows are specified, then the original trim should be saved or replicated.

There are many varieties of window mullion patterns possible. Figure 2.38 shows how mullions may be configured differently within a double-hung frame mechanism. When researching or renovating a building, matching the number of panes of glass formed by the mullions is essential to the renovation program for the building being renovated. Figure 2.39 describes windows and doors configured within a basilican window frame. These configurations usually occur in institutional buildings of a larger mass and scale than the windows shown in the previous example.

A third kind of window configuration is a Palladian window, usually comprised of two rectangular windows flanking a center rectangular window with a semi-circular window above. Key to the success of the restoration of a Palladian window is the alignment of the mullions from the centers to the side, and the detailing of the trim at the intersections of the round window with the rectangular window. It is virtually impossible to find a manufactured Palladian window that is properly detailed, although there are *circle-top* windows on the market that are sometimes passed off as Palladian windows. Figure 2.40 is a sketch of a Palladian window indicating aligned mullions and muntins. Figure 2.41 and 2.42 are additional examples of Palladian windows in houses dating from early in the 20th century.

Skylights

One does not always think of skylights as historically compatible elements in building design, but skylights were very often used as they are today, to admit natural light into the center of a building (Figure 2.43). Examples of this include numerous

FIGURE 2.38 Varieties of mullion patterns in double hung windows.

FIGURE 2.39   Varieties of window shapes possible within a basilican window and door configuration.

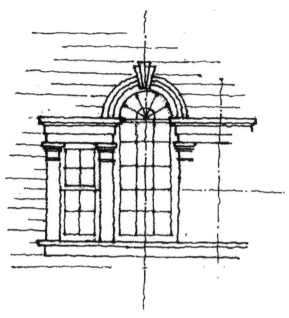

FIGURE 2.40 Palladian window with aligned mullions and trim.

FIGURE 2.41 An example of a well-detailed Palladian window used as an attic window.

FIGURE 2.42   An example of a Palladian window above an Ionic front porch.

commercial buildings such as the Santa Fe Building or the Rookery Building that contain centralized public spaces with rental space along the perimeter. This allows natural light to enter from at least two sides of the rental space, which accomplishes two effects. First is that the amount of natural light is nearly double the amount if light were admitted from the exterior only and second, the light distribution throughout the day tends to be more even throughout the rental space as the sunlight moves from one side of the building to another.

In residential architecture, skylights are normally thought of as modern additions to the roof line of a building. In historic residential buildings, skylights are sometimes found at the top of stairwells. When evaluating an existing building, it is sometimes wise to verify if a skylight had been located above the stairs and either removed or simply covered over with roofing material. Skylights become problematic for historic preservation when they obstruct a roof line in an existing building. Modern skylights, sometimes referred to as roof windows, are just that—they are windows placed within a roof. Very often homeowners install skylights to admit natural light into an attic apartment or into a bathroom addition without consideration of the effects on the exterior appearance of their building. The problem with skylights is that they look like windows, not skylights, from the exterior and are usually inconsistent with the original fenestration patterns that exist within a house, nor are they compatible in detailing, proportion, and materials with the original materials found within the building. Therefore, if the addition of a skylight is required, the best solution would be to install it in a location where it is not visible from the exterior. This is easier than one might think. The sight lines to the proposed skylight should be figured either though a measured diagram or through photography in order to place the skylight in the least obtrusive location.

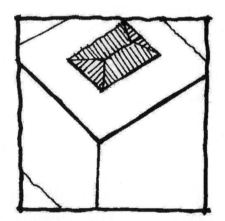 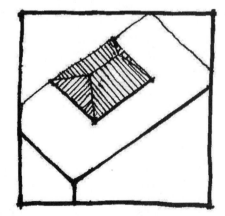

FIGURE 2.43 Left: skylight in the center of a donut-shaped building. Right: skylight within the center of a u-shaped building.

Stained Glass

Stained glass, although normally and most readily associated with ecclesiastic architecture, may exist in historical residential and commercial buildings. Stained glass is made from colored pieces of glass set within a lead frame. Between the glass and frame is a material called caming that creates a buffer between the metal material and the glass. The entire lead and glass system is then installed within a larger frame usually made of wood.

As stained glass ages, the lead frames in which the glass pieces are placed very often sag and buckle. Also, the caming between the glass and lead will deteriorate over time and will need to be removed and replaced. The restoration of stained glass is a craft rather than a trade and should be undertaken by craftsmen rather than window installers. The stained glass restoration craftsmen will remove the entire panel of lead and glass and place the panel on a horizontal surface in order to remove any sags or buckles and to reinstall caming.

For a period of time in the 1970s, accepted practice was to place an outer layer of plastic at the exterior surface of the stained glass assembly. Two problems occurred with this method. The plastic sheets used as an outer protective covering discolored after about 15 or 20 years. Plastic sheets are evident by their grayish yellowish hue and by stress lines within the plastic that are visible in direct sunlight. A second problem with plastic sheets is that they often were not installed in a manner that allowed for the dissipation of heat and condensation that built up between the plastic and the original stained glass. When a sandwich of plastic on the outside air, space in the middle, and stained glass on the inside is made without being properly ventilated moisture and heat damage the frame of the entire assemble along with the original glasswork. The moisture built up between the plastic and glass settles into the exterior frame and accelerates the deterioration of the frame. The heat that is built up between the panels accelerates the sagging of the leaded components of the assembly. This is because the heated air expands and then exerts pressure on the plastic and stained glass. Since the leaded components are the softest parts of the assembly, these pieces yield by bending inward (Figure 2.44). The lead framework or beads that hold the individual pieces of glass sometimes have a profile designed into them. This should be matched as closely as practicable, as should the original color of the lead beading. The intersections between the lead beads should be smooth and should not detract from the glass patterns that the beads are framing. The thickness of the lead components should match the existing also.

In some cases it is possible to place a new window assembly at the outer portion of a stained glass assembly. This is advantageous for several reasons. First, is that the external window may have installed double paned glass with a coating to prevent damage from ultra violet rays. Also, if the new window is sealed properly, it will prevent air infiltration and moisture penetration into the cavity of the existing wall and window assembly. However, it is essential to properly vent the space between the

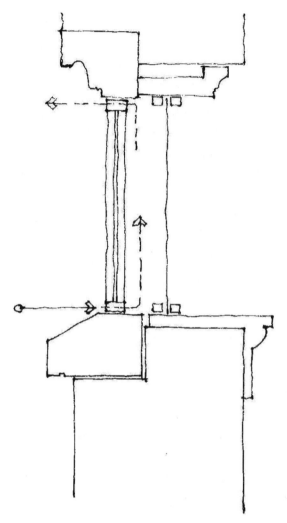

FIGURE 2.44 Diagram showing new insulated glass assembly at the exterior with existing stained glass on the interior, with ventilated area between the two.

new window and the existing stained glass to prevent moisture build-up and increased air temperature in the space between the new window and existing.

Local conditions will affect how particular window assemblies should be vented. Typical practice is to create several small slots in the sill and head of the window frame to allow air to flow from the bottom to the top of the window, thus venting moisture and heated air.

Dormers

Dormers are windows that are built above the eave line of a building. They are rarely built properly in new construction and frequently downgraded when repaired. Dormers should be detailed as small temples. This means that the areas to the left and right of the window should be detailed like a column with a shaft base and capital. The horizontal area above the window should be detailed to look like an entablature. Substituting crown mold trim for a column capital is not proper nor is pork-chopping the corners (Figures 2.45 through 2.48).

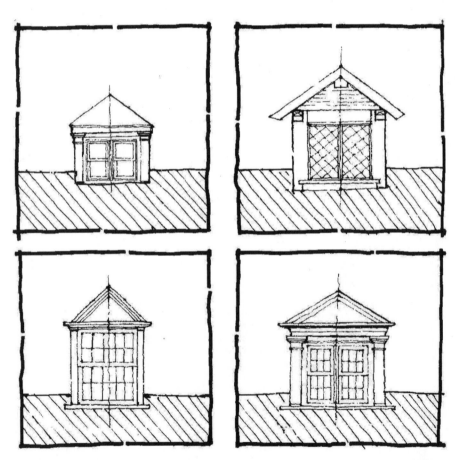

FIGURE 2.45a Varieties of dormers.

FIGURE 2.45b Dormers showing pork-chopped detailing.

FIGURE 2.46 Two dormers with hip roofs.

FIGURE 2.47 Dormer combining Prairie School roof pitch with Classical elements.

FIGURE 2.48 Dormer with sea shell arch motif above windows.

Doors and Casing

If doors in historic buildings require replacement, then they should be replaced to replicate the existing doors. The size of the panels that comprise the doors should be kept in mind, as should the profiles of the wood panels. Door hardware could be saved from an existing door and reinstalled in a new door if the original door hardware has not decayed. Weatherstripping may be installed onto existing doors without affecting the appearance of the door. Locks can also be installed sensitively without destroying a door's original appearance (Figures 2.49, 2.50, and 2.51). Most doors are held in place with three hinges, sometimes four. Hinges are set into the surface of the door to create a flush surface on the face of the door and the end. Piano hinges are applied to the surface of the door and are not an acceptable substitute for recessed butt hinges.

Entablatures

An entablature is the assembly of molding that is above a column capital in Classical architecture. Entablatures are made of specific shapes of wood or stone. If an entablature needs to be replaced, it should be replaced to match the existing identically. When replacing an entablature or replicating one either from a built example or from a drawing, the curved pieces should remain curved and the linear pieces should remain linear. The relationship between curved elements and linear ones is critical to the success of Classical detailing. An example is the way in which a column attaches

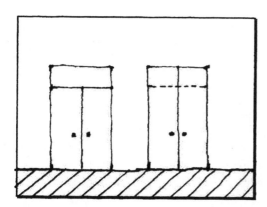

FIGURE 2.49 Diagram showing door detail. Left: door with transom. Right: new door with transom removed.

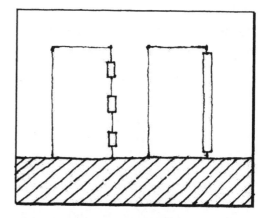

FIGURE 2.50 Diagram showing door detail. Left: triple butt hinges. Right: triple hinges removed and replaced with continuous surface mounted and incompatible piano hinges.

FIGURE 2.51 Diagram showing door detail.
Left: panel door. Right: flush door.

to the entablature above it. Normally, the column capital attaches by means of an element called an abacus. The abacus is square and the column is round. The abacus
creates the transition between the round column and the linear wall above. Elimi-
nating it is not consistent with the Classical language of architecture.

Figures 2.52 and 2.53 illustrate two examples of Italianate entablatures. Most
entablatures of this kind include ornate brackets that project out from the front of a
building at least one foot or so. The entablature often includes a gutter assembly. The
entablature also includes ornament that extends down the face of the building and
sometimes includes attic vents.

Gutters, Downspouts, and Vents

Gutters and downspouts are sometimes designed as a part of an entablature. When
gutters and downspouts must be replaced, as with other building elements, these
should be remade to match the existing pieces of the building. At times, gutters and
downspouts are ornamental features of a building, especially in Victorian buildings.
Ornamental elements such as these should be kept in tact and repaired as much as is
reasonably possible.

Vents have the purpose of allowing moisture to be discharged from a building
through natural air convection through a space or cavity. If an attic or air space is
not properly vented, moisture will force its way through to the interior portion of a
wall or ceiling. This will cause blistering of paint and plaster. Vents can exist as crawl

FIGURE 2.52   An example of an Italianate entablature.

FIGURE 2.53   An example of an Italianate entablature.

space vents, soffit vents, or attic vents. Attic vents can be designed into the upper-most parts of a gable end, appearing like small triangles just below the uppermost ridge. These are usually louvers that are located on opposite ends of an attic space. Soffit vents allow air to flow from the lower part of a roof structure to the ridge of a roof. Soffit vents should be designed in conjunction with ridge or roof vents, allowing airflow upward through a roof assembly. Ridge vents run in a line along the high point of a roof. They are unobtrusive and preferable over the alternative of placing metal mushroom vents at successive places along a roof (Figures 2.54 and 2.55).

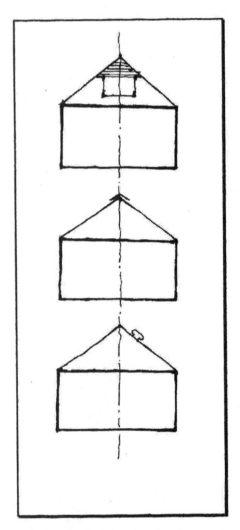

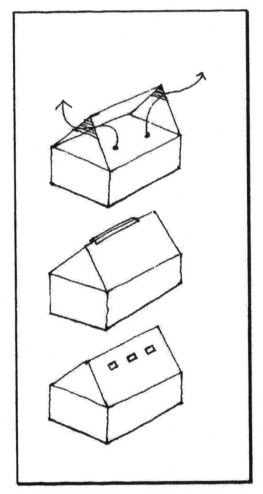

FIGURE 2.54 Diagram showing vents. Top: eave vent. Middle: ridge vent. Bottom: mushroom vent.

FIGURE 2.55 Diagram showing vents. Top: eave vent. Middle: ridge vent. Bottom: mushroom vent.

Fireplaces

Fireplaces are comprised of several parts. The parts visible from the inside are the fireplace surround, mantle, and hearth. The parts visible from the exterior are the chimney stack and chimney cap. Within the chimney are several other components including the flue, damper, ash disposal, and birdscreen. The main points that need to be heeded in the restoration of a chimney are first, the proportion of opening as it relates to flue size, second, the existing condition of the flue, and third, the condition of the exterior construction. Other items to bear in mind are the condition of the chimney cap and the condition of the visible interior.

If a new fireplace is to be built attached to an existing fireplace then the proportion of opening to flue size must be verified by an architect, mason or chimney sweep. The proportion of opening to flue size affects the upward draft within and through the chimney and is therefore critical to the proper functioning of the fireplace. If a building is to be renovated in a manner that requires the extension of a chimney, the proportion of opening to flue size must also be verified.

The existing condition of the flue must be verified as a fire precaution. The flue is the hollow area extending from the hearth to the top of the chimney. Soot may accumulate over time and ignite within the flue. Therefore it is wise to hire a chimney sweep to examine the interior of the flue and to remove any existing soot. Additionally, the chimney sweep will be able to verify the condition of the existing flue lining to see if any cracks exist that could cause water damage or damage resulting from fire. Chimney flues are often made of clay tiles within a chimney enclosure. Repairing a flue liner can require access to the inside of the flue, as in the case of a very large smokestack, or with smaller structures, a new flue lining may be installed by means of inserting a balloon form within the chimney. A slurry mixture is then poured between the balloon lining and the existing chimney construction to create a new lining.

Chimney caps are sometimes ornamented pieces of terra cotta and should be saved or repaired as a part of a building's restoration program. Also, to prevent birds or other animals from entering the structure from the exterior it is advisable to place a bird screen at the top of the chimney. Lightning rods are also recommended for the tops of chimneys.

The hearth of the fireplace is where the fire is contained. Hearths are usually made of a hard clay brick masonry. This differs from other kinds of bricks that may be used in the construction or reconstruction of the exterior portions of chimneys. The fireplace surround includes the vertical surface that extends from the opening of the fireplace to the ornamental wood or stone work that comprises the mantle. The vertical surfaces are often made of tile.

In some buildings, flues are contained within an existing wall cavity. This is evident where a chimney projects from the eave of a building but there is no stack projecting out from the wall. Sometimes with internal flues, the path the flue takes through the wall is not directly vertical. There may be many reasons for this, including making a window pattern symmetrical or to avoid other components of the building such as structural or mechanical elements.

Chimney stacks project outboard of the main wall of a building. At the intersection of a chimney and an existing roof, flashing will be required to prevent water damage. Flashings should match existing flashings, and roofing materials should match existing roofing materials (Figures 2.56a, b, and c).

Flashings

Flashing is the material used to prevent water infiltration. Flashings may either be made of roofing materials such as bituminous asphalt sheets or metals such as copper or aluminum. In restoration work, the existing flashing material should be matched if it is reasonable to do so. With metal flashing, the gauge of the existing metal flashing should be verified so that the new flashing is of the same quality as the existing. If a lighter gauge metal is used that only looks the same as the existing, the new material may decay at a more rapid rate that the adjacent existing material. Also, if the new metal flashing is not the same kind of metal as the adjacent material, then both the new and the existing will decay due to the electrolytic action that occurs between dissimilar metals.

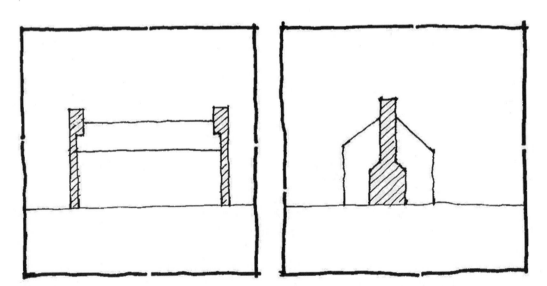

FIGURE 2.56a Varieties of chimney locations. End placement with stack external to the face of the building.

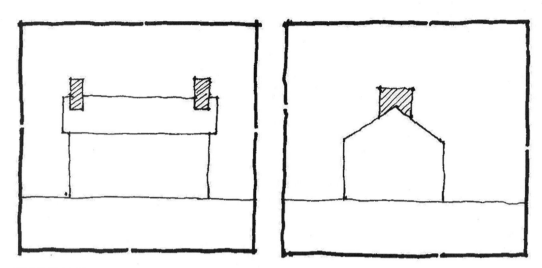

FIGURE 2.56b End placement with internal stack.

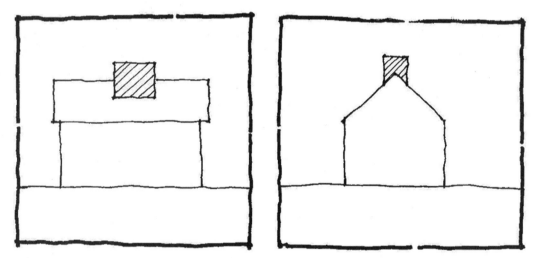

FIGURE 2.56c Mid-point placement with stack entering the interior of the structure.

A cricket or saddle is required where a chimney intersects a pitched roof. The cricket or saddle allows rainwater and melting snow to divert from the back side of the chimney. If this element is missing then moisture damage is likely if not inevitable. Crickets or saddles may be made of roof framing material or be made entirely of metal flashing.

Some flashings have an ornamental quality to them. Photographic documentation of the ornamental metals would be wise, if replacement becomes necessary due to damage during construction. Although metal work is a trade distinct from the roofing trade, some roofers will also be able to do the metal work associated with the metal flashings required on a restoration [9].

MECHANICAL EQUIPMENT

The proper installation of new mechanical systems in existing buildings is critical to the ability of a building owner to use the building to its fullest potential. There are several factors to be considered in the removal and upgrading of mechanical systems. First is how to remove the old system, and second is how to fit the new system into the existing building fabric without destroying the appearance of the existing building (Figure 2.57a and 2.57b).

Often, especially with institutional buildings such as large school buildings or commercial structures, heat is provided to the building by means of aging boilers. Boilers have a life span of about 75 years. When they need to be removed, they are simply dismantled by being cut into small pieces and thrown away. This requires torches and open flame, so the process needs to be carefully coordinated. The condition of existing ductwork, if there is any, will need to be verified at this point to

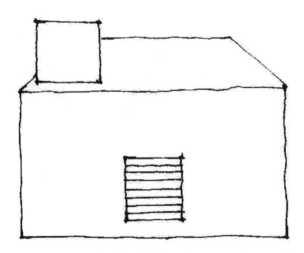

FIGURE 2.57a Diagram showing a roof top unit breaking the line of an existing roof and a large louver vent inserted in a primary façade.

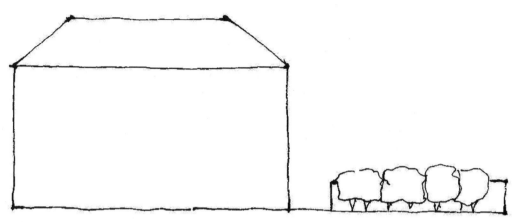

FIGURE 2.57b An existing building left intact with mechanical equipment placed at grade and screened by landscaping.

assure that there are no holes caused by corroding metal. In addition, the existing controls to the boiler system will most likely be removed so that a computerized set of controls may be installed. Another component requiring attention is the system of pipes that supply the existing radiators with heated water. Pipes on the supply side of the radiators are under more pressure than those on the return side because the water temperature in near boiling for a hot-water system, and of course above boiling for a steam-based system. The pressure increases the potential for supply pipes to decay. Condensate pipes also tend to decay but for different reasons. These pipes corrode due to slow moving moisture rather than moisture under pressure. Other machinery that may or may not need to be replaced or repaired includes pumps, fans, and tanks. The seals between components should be checked, as should the motors in any of the mechanical components.

Installing the new systems into an existing building should be done in a manner that avoids the removal of or destruction of the historical fabric of the building. For example, if a building such as a post office or a school has murals painted on the wall dating from the 1930s and executed by the U.S. Federal WPA program, these should remain intact and not cut into with vents and grilles. In another example from the exterior of a building, if additional louvers are required for air intake or exhaust, then the placement of the louvers should be such that the louvers are not visible from the main parts of the building. If new louvers are required, then ideally they should be placed in an existing wall opening by replacing a window not visible from the street. If a new opening must be cut, then the opening should be in the least visible spot in the building but that makes the new system feasible. When new openings are cut, the structural integrity of the existing wall and footing must be maintained. For example, if openings are cut near the base of a large masonry wall and the footing below the wall is a continuous footing, then care must be taken to verify that when the openings are made, the remaining wall will not puncture the existing footing. The existing loads must still be transferred to the footing and to the soil beneath the footing. Also, a steel lintel will need to be engineered to carry the masonry above the newly cut opening. The contractor will need to have access to both sides of the wall to properly cut the wall. Openings in masonry need to be specified as *saw-cut* to assure that the opening will not be created with a jack-hammer (as absurd as that seems) or hammered out with a sledge hammer.

HVAC

Heating, ventilation and air conditioning systems (HVAC) include components that are inside as well as those that require placement outside. As for the components that are within a building, these need to be located in places that allow the system to work efficiently, that allow access for maintenance, and in an area where sound transmission is not an issue. Pumps and fans are typically placed on vibration isolators that are effectively shock absorbers for sound. When the mechanical engineer specifies the pumps and fans, he or she should also specify an associated set of sound controls achieved by means of reducing vibrations emanating from the moving parts within pieces of equipment.

For exterior equipment, often municipal codes will require a specific sound level be achieved at the lot line of a property. This is accomplished by placing exterior vibration isolators and/or surrounding the equipment with sound absorbing panels. The vibration isolators also prevent damage to the existing building from the transmission of vibration through the building's structure. Additionally, new equipment should be located such that it is hidden from primary views. Figure 2.58 shows how mechanical equipment has been placed on the roof of the Art Institute of Chicago building in full view of Michigan Avenue. Figure 2.59 shows how a mechanical system has been hidden by metal panels after being placed on a rooftop above the Civic Opera Building in Chicago. Although an attempt was made to hide the equipment, the panels degrade the existing building fabric. A third example of a poorly placed piece of mechanical equipment in Figure 2.60 shows how the ductwork placed high atop a high rise in Chicago's Loop has discolored the stone below it.

Another factor in adding systems into existing buildings is how to hide piping. Pipes are required to deliver heating and cooling to the perimeter of buildings. This means that sets of pipes will run along the outside walls of a building and extend vertically usually from the basement boiler room. In pre-modernist buildings there are often voids in between walls in which to run pipes vertically. In modernist buildings usually there is little room for additional piping, more than what was installed initially.

FIGURE 2.58 Mechanical equipment placed too close to primary view.

FIGURE 2.59 Mechanical equipment placed above the Civic Opera House, Chicago.

FIGURE 2.60 Mechanical equipment discoloring adjacent materials.

For the horizontal runs of pipes at the perimeter of a building, a chase is often required to conceal the pipes. By constructing the chase in the first floor ceiling, a set of pipes may be used to access both the first and second floors. The drawback of this approach is that in buildings with very tall windows the pipes block the windows. A solution to this problem is to pull the chase back from the windows approximately nine inches in order to let the window appear unobstructed from the exterior. The nine inch dimension is adequate for the workmen to access with a paint brush.

This solution is only appropriate for spaces that have no historical value or that have been completely altered from their original appearance. A solution for a building of historic value is to run the pipes in a concealed location below the floor and place grilles in concealed locations near the floor. Replacing the exterior window opening size or the window configuration for the purpose of installing pipes or ductwork is not advisable.

Exterior equipment is required for the air conditioning component of an HVAC system. If a building already has a heating system and a full HVAC system is proposed, then a suitable location for the exterior machinery will need to be determined. There are several factors that will affect the outcome of this determination; first is the structural load of the equipment, second is the size of the equipment, and third, the visibility of the equipment. The weight of a compressor unit can easily exceed several tons in weight. The weight of the unit and its physical size are different than the size of the unit. The amount of air conditioning required for any given interior space is measured in tons. Tons of air conditioning refers to the amount of Btu's (a measure of heat) required to melt one ton of ice. With regard to air conditioning it is the amount of heat extracted from the air that provides the unit of measure.

Piping will need to be placed on vibration absorbing hangers that include an apparatus called a roller that allows the pipe to expand and contract along its length. Also, where pipes intersect fire rated walls a fire rated assembly comprised of fireproofing sometimes installed with metal rings or sleeves will be required by code. Fireproofing around pipes is a type of caulking that expands in the event of a fire. A proper substrate or backup for the fireproofing is required so that if the material expands, it will provide a proper seal between the pipes and the adjacent surfaces. This is a critical component to any larger construction project and, if overlooked, could create a safety hazard or could place in jeopardy buildings that are of historic merit. It is not unheard of to require a contractor to provide proof of purchase for fireproofing to validate that fireproofing was installed rather than a red color caulk that looks like the fireproofing material.

Lighting

Lighting design is critical to successful restorations. There are two elements to lighting design; the first is the fixture, the second is the light source itself. In a space that has existing wall sconces, for example, an auditorium with art deco lights, the existing light source may be changed and the fixture may be re-wired for a more energy efficient and effective lighting scheme. Local codes should be consulted with regard to electrical requirements. Electrical codes will often require new fixtures to be UL listed which means that the fixture bears a label certifying that it was tested by Underwriters Laboratories. If a fixture is re-wired and re-lamped, meaning that it is to receive new bulbs, then the UL listing needs to appear on the new parts of the fixture and possibly, depending upon local codes, the entire fixture would require UL testing to verify code compliance.

If existing lighting does not exist within an historic space, the lighting scheme needs to be thought of in terms of the restoration program for the building. There are many ways in which this may be approached.

Most old buildings contain electrical wiring that is not compliant with current codes. Most municipalities require that wiring be placed within a small metal tube rated for use as a conduit for wiring. But many old buildings still contain wires that are not encased within conduit, such as old cloth covered wiring and flexible conduit. The purpose of placing the wires within conduit is to prevent electrical shock if a nail is driven through a wall and accidentally hits a wire.

In some old buildings, new conduit may be threaded through existing but unused pipes that were previously used for gas lighting. The advantage of using the old pathways for the new conduit is that less disturbance to the building would result because the cavity in the wall is already made. Conduit may also be placed in unused chase spaces or through other voids in the wall cavity. Placing the conduit within the wall rather than on the external face of the wall is good historic preservation practice.

The electrical loads required for any building should be verified by an engineer or electrician. If a significant amount of new equipment is required, then the electrical capacity of the existing electrical service may need to be upgraded. This, of course, will happen on a case by case basis. If new electrical service is required, space must be found for new electrical panels, and transformers. Local codes should be consulted with regard to panel and transformer installation, but with regard to historic preservation the transformer should be placed in an unobtrusive location. Some transformers may be located in a building's interior while others are for placement out of doors.

Light Pollution

Another item to bear in mind concerning lighting is what is becoming known as light pollution. For historic preservation, light pollution could be an issue with regard to the exterior appearance of individual landmarks and districts. Lighting from parking lots or from large buildings often is not contained within the parking lot or within the large building. Also, since light has color as well as intensity, the color of the light may adversely affect historic properties or districts. One way to mitigate the negative affects of light pollution or eliminate it completely would be to reduce light levels in commercial and retail establishments that are adjacent to or within historic districts. Another method would be to hide the light source to eliminate glare whether through proper design of the light source or by designing the overall footprint of the building to shield historic properties from excessive light levels.

Elevators

Elevators present two issues for historic preservation. The first is the historic elevator and door assembly, and second is the installation of a new elevator into an existing historical building. Most elevators have had their mechanical components replaced years ago and are powered by new equipment. Elevators are inspected on a regular basis by code officials and due to safety concerns must be mechanically up to date. Occasionally, a non-public elevator dating from early in the 20th century may still be in use, but since these are used mainly as service elevators, they have little or no historical significance beyond their age.

Very often elevator doors and the frames in the walls that surround the elevator door opening are made with ornate metalwork that relates to a program of ornamentation in a building.

Installing an entirely new elevator into an existing building presents an additional set of issues. The first is the placement of the elevator in a location that is workable on all levels of the building. The second is that the elevator needs to be accessible to corridors and public areas of the building. Third is that the space above the elevator needs to be adequate for elevator override. Fourth is the design of the elevator pit area, and last is the design of the cab and elevator door assembly.

The new elevator shaft should be in a location that minimizes the reconfiguration of adjacent spaces. Additionally, since a large area of floor and ceiling structure will be removed to create the new elevator shaft, structural components should analyzed by a structural engineer. Because the purpose of the elevator is normally to transport people from a lower corridor to a higher corridor, the location will need to be near public spaces on all levels of the building. The elevator override is the amount of space required for the elevator cab and machinery above to top floor when the elevator is lifted to its maximum height. Ideally, the elevator override will not require modifications to the existing roof structure and may fit into an existing attic space, but often this is not the case. For example, if an elevator requires a 12 foot override and there is only four feet of space above the top floor of a building, then the elevator override will project beyond the roof of the building by about eight feet. This could have an adverse affect on the appearance of the building from the outside (Figures 2.61 and 2.62a, b, and c).

FOUNDATION SYSTEMS

The foundation of a building is the means by which the weight of the building is transferred into the ground upon which the building sits. A foundation system is comprised of a footing and a foundation wall. In some old buildings, footings simply do not exist. The foundation walls in buildings like this simply extend into the ground and no provision is made to spread the load of the wall horizontally at the base of the wall. In old and historic structures, foundations may or may not meet current construction standards. In the case of a building that has a brick foundation wall, for example, brick is extended into the soil. These kinds of foundation walls allow considerable amounts of moisture to penetrate the interior of the building below grade. Brick foundation walls often spall, which means that the exposed surfaces of the brick peel away due to moisture penetrating through the wall. Tuck pointing is also required for this kind of wall to assure the integrity of the wall as a whole (Figure 2.63).

Another kind of foundation system found in old and historic structures is made from stone. The same problems exist for stone foundation walls as exist for brick foundation walls. The tendency for the stone to spall would be less than with a brick foundation wall because stone is

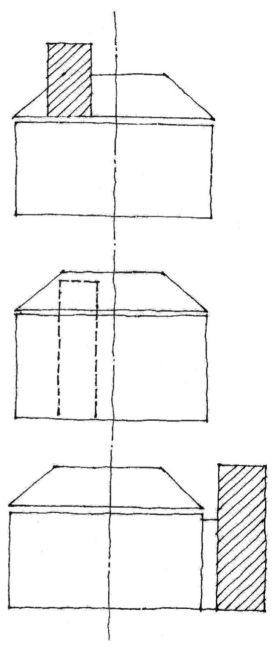

FIGURE 2.61 Top: diagram of elevator over-ride projecting beyond the existing roof line. Middle: elevator within the existing building perimeter. Bottom: elevator added to the exterior of a building.

FIGURE 2.62a Top row: elevator doors and associated ornament locations either connected to the elevator frame or kept isolated from the frame.

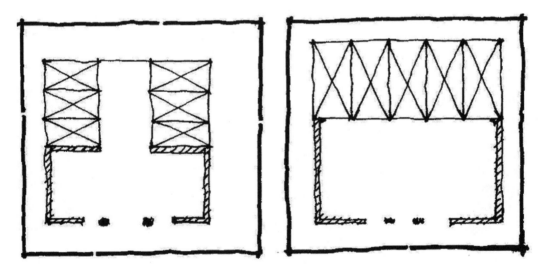

FIGURE 2.62b Traditional elevator locations adjacent to lobbies.

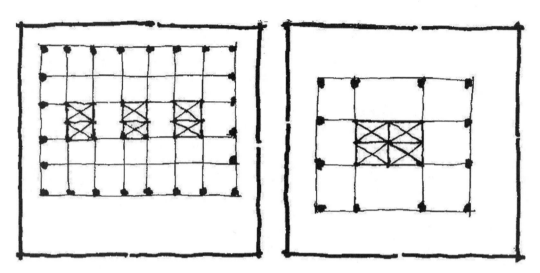

FIGURE 2.62c Elevator locations in Modernist buildings.

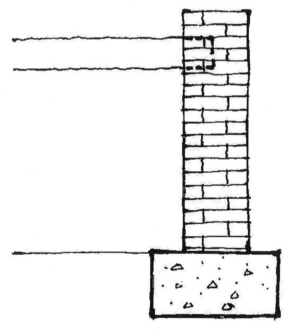

FIGURE 2.63 Detail showing brick foundation system.

more dense than brick, but moisture would still tend to work its way to the interior of a stone foundation wall system. As with brick systems, the footing below the wall would need to be verified prior to commencing with work above. Stone walls may or may not have consistent coursing that runs through the entire wall. The mortar joints on the exterior may or may not match those of the interior. By checking these, the size of the stones may be determined (Figure 2.64)

In current construction, foundation systems are typically made from reinforced concrete. Additionally, current practice is to provide moisture protection and drainage along the exterior portions of the foundation wall. With existing buildings, it is advisable to check with local building officials to verify local sub-surface conditions. In an existing building if there is no drainage around the perimeter of the building, a determination should be made as to whether or not a new drainage system should be installed. The advantage of installing a new system around an existing foundation wall is to remove moisture from the exterior of the foundation wall. The disadvantage, and this should be verified by local engineers and building officials, is that by removing moisture from the soil at the perimeter of a building, the load bearing capacity of the soil may change, creating the potential for the foundation to slip (Figure 2.65).

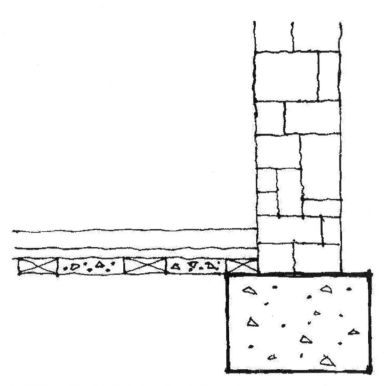

FIGURE 2.64 Detail of stone foundation system.

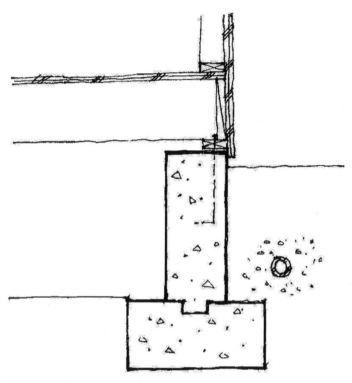

FIGURE 2.65 Detail showing foundation system with concrete wall and footing.

WALL SYSTEMS

A common misconception relating to wall framing is that balloon framing refers to all wood framed construction. Balloon framing, developed in the early 19th century in fact refers to a specific kind of wood framing. Balloon framing is evident in buildings where wood studs extend continuously from the first floor to the roof framing above (Figure 2.66). Second floor joists are nailed to the sides of the continuous stud and a gap exists from the first floor to the roof between the studs. This differs from current framing practice which is referred to as platform framing (Figure 2.67). Platform framing is evident in buildings where the wood studs extend only one floor at a time, and the second floor joists are placed above the first floor studs. Platform framing does not create a gap between the studs that extends the entire height of a building.

   In a building constructed with balloon framing, it is important to place wood
blocks at intermittent points in the wall to provide a fire stop in the event of a fire.
Filling in the gaps between the studs mitigates the potential for a fire to spread. The
load bearing capacity and spacing of the existing wood studs should be verified prior
to adding additional loads onto the existing wall structure.

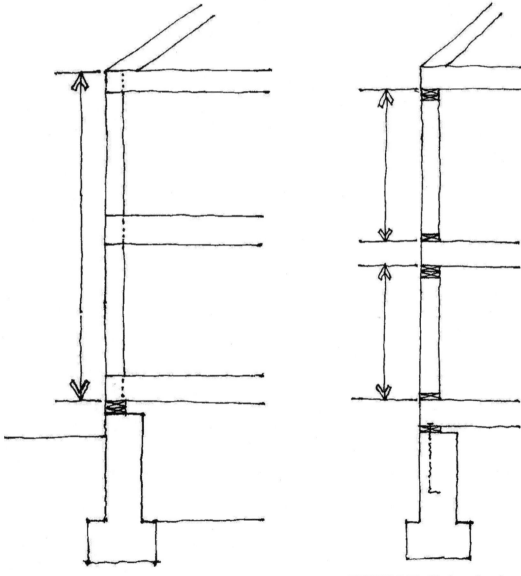

FIGURE 2.66 Balloon framing.   **FIGURE 2.67** Platform framing.

Curtain Walls

With Modernist steel and glass buildings, the exterior wall is often attached to a structural skeleton of steel and/or concrete. This is called curtain wall construction and presents several issues for historic preservation. Most curtain walls show evidence of sealant decay or failure at some point. Also, the rubber pieces that surround glass and create a waterproof seal become brittle and begin to fall away. Therefore, restoration of a steel and glass building most often involves the re-sealing of glass and the replacement of rubber components. Another factor to consider is the condition of the metals in the curtain wall system. If water penetrates the interior of a curtain wall, then it is possible that the components that attach the glass to the steel or concrete may be deteriorated and will require replacement [10]. Curtain wall deterioration could also be caused by the effects of dissimilar metals creating a corrosive effect. When a determination can be made that two dissimilar metals are in contact with each other and that the corrosion resulting from electrolysis is harming the stability of a wall system, then measures need to be undertaken to either separate the two metals, or to replace one of the metals with a metal similar to the other metal.

Plaster

In new construction, interior walls are made of gypsum wall board, sometimes referred to in the field as *gyp* or *rock*. Gypsum wall board is installed over wood or metal framing, then is finished with tape, a light coat of plaster and then paint. Gypsum board is not the same as plaster. Most interior construction in old buildings is comprised of wet plaster. The process of plastering involved applying a coat of wet plaster on a matrix of small wood slats called lath. The lath is attached to the underlying wood or masonry framing.

If patching is required in a restoration program, then wet plaster should be replaced with wet plaster, not simply filled in with gypsum wall board. The reason for this is that the texture of the final surface will be noticeably different. Also, the joint between the gypsum wall board and the wet plaster will not be achievable.

FLOOR SYSTEMS

The three common floor systems prevalent in old and historic buildings are wood, concrete, and tile. Wood framing has been discussed in relation to balloon framing. But with regard to wood floor framing, wood floor joists should be checked for deterioration due to termites, water infiltration, and holes that have been cut into the floor in the past and subsequently covered up. Concrete floors in historic buildings should be tested for consistency throughout the pour. In concrete construction from the early 20th century, the consistency of gravel and sand within the concrete is not up to current standards as seen in veins of gravel that run through the thickness of a pour. If additional load is to be placed on an existing concrete structure then the condition of the concrete should be verified so that any weaknesses in the existing slab may be corrected.

Another factor to be considered when working with old concrete is the location and condition of steel reinforcing bars within the concrete. Figure 2.68 shows an example of a building in an advanced state of decay. This building, although built in the 1950s, was not built correctly. The photograph shows a v-shaped crack just below the second floor column. Had this condition not been discovered, the column would have ultimately slipped off the concrete below it. The crack in this case was caused by loads placed on an unreinforced portion of concrete. Examination showed that the steel bars that were to have been placed within the slab and column simply did not exist in the correct configuration to resist the weight of the column and the roof structure above it. The solution to this problem was to anchor steel plates to the concrete to add additional load bearing capacity of the existing concrete.

Concrete restoration techniques are particularly important to the restoration of concrete Modernist structures. Many buildings of this kind are built of poured concrete that is left exposed to the exterior. This poses particular problems having to do with decay that can be caused by chemical, physical, or electrolytic factors, along with possible construction errors in the original construction [11].

Concrete floors are made of a thin top coat or leveling coat that is placed on top of a concrete subfloor. The concrete subfloor may be built of poured concrete or precast concrete. Pre-cast concrete floors are made from long planks of concrete with cylindrical cores within. With either precast concrete or poured concrete, if additional loads are added to a structure, or if the existing structure is to be removed or changed in anyway, the entire assembly should be verified and designed structurally prior to commencing construction. If concrete is to be cut it should be saw-cut and not jackhammered (Figure 2.69).

A third type of floor system is called clay-tile fireproof construction. Many institutional buildings made in the early 20th century have floors that are made in this way. In this type of construction, the floor is made by clay tile arches (Figure 2.70)

Hollow clay tiles span from steel beams and completely encase the steel providing a fireproof cover for the steel. If additional loads are placed on the clay tile exceeding the capacity of the clay tile, the arch will slip and large cracks will develop. The clay tile will not be evident from the top of the arches because the tiles will be covered with a top coat of concrete.

FIGURE 2.68 An example of concrete in an advanced state of decay caused by improper reinforcing.

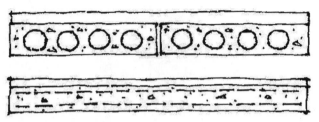

FIGURE 2.69a Diagram showing precast concrete planks with a top coat of concrete.

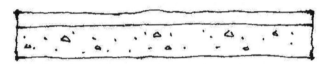

FIGURE 2.69b Poured concrete with a top coat of concrete.

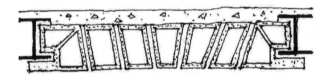

FIGURE 2.70 Clay tile arch system.

ROOF SYSTEMS

Roof systems may be made from clay tile fireproof construction or poured or precast concrete, as well as wood framing. When new roofing is added to an old or historic building, the prevention of moisture penetration becomes critical. In institutional and commercial buildings of a large scale, current practice is to install roofing materials that are a composite of bituminous asphalt, mineral fiber, and a polymer additive. The combination of these three components allows a roof to resist punctures and to regain its shape if stretched in multiple directions.

The connection between the roof and the wall is where moisture penetration is most likely, underscoring the importance of proper flashing and sealant.

POSTS

With urban residential structures dating from the early 20th century, the common method of construction was to place large wood columns in the center of the building supporting a center ridge beam running the entire length of the structure (Figure 2.71). Commonly, well-meaning homeowners will replace the existing wood columns with steel columns thinking that the steel is automatically stronger that the existing wood columns. If the wood columns need to be replaced because they have deteriorated due to moisture or termites, then replacing the wood is a proper tack to take. If replacement is necessary, then a footing should be poured if one does not exist already. Wood posts to match the existing may be installed, or an appropriately engineered steel post may be installed.

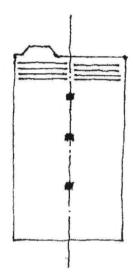

FIGURE 2.71 Plan showing location of central posts and framing in an urban residence.

ADDITIONS

Additions to existing residential structures should be designed in a manner that maintains the primary form of the main structure while distinguishing the addition as secondary. Very often, residential additions often include an expanded kitchen on the first floor with bedrooms and bathrooms above. Additions to large residences that are added to the back of the existing structure create a second front. While residences were originally designed to have a single front, usually at the street, social activity at present has shifted to the rear of the home. The addition of a kitchen and bedroom allows the home to be more accommodating to current patterns of use. By adding to the back of the house, the architect has an opportunity to design an elevation for a building that might not have had a designed elevation at the back.

The addition should be secondary to the main house. The roof line should not extend above the existing and the footprint or plan of the exterior wall should not extend beyond the existing width of the house if possible. Roof pitches should match, as should materials and color. The siding on the addition may be more cleanly constructed if an offset is created between the addition and the main house. (Figure 2.72).

For large-scale institutional additions, many of the same principles apply. Materials should match existing materials, the primary form of the existing structure should

FIGURE 2.72   Varieties of building additions.

be maintained, and a clear distinction between the addition and the original structure should be created by means of a reveal joint or by means of an offset. With institutional additions, the elevation of the original may provide the proportion and scale of the elevation of the addition. If horizontal lines are present in the original building, these are best extended in to the addition. The overall scale, proportion, and massing of the existing should be respected and extended if possible into the new structure.

Ornamental trim establishes scale in a building of any size and therefore plays a role in determining the primary and secondary massing of a building. An example of ornamental trim may be seen in Figure 2.73, which shows the top of a large residence. The ornament in this example is comprised of scalloped shingles directly under the eave and curved woodwork extending from the bottom of the scallops to the third floor windows.

FIGURE 2.73 An example of ornamental trim.

Figure 2.74 is another example of ornamental trim, with a slight variation. In this example, the original building has a series of brackets that extend from the outer most portion of the roof to the exterior wall. The brackets define the roof line of the third and second floors and provide a means of determining a visual scale for the building.

A more ornate example is shown in Figure 2.75. This Tudor style house includes a piece of trim called a barge board that follows the line of the roof at the front of the building. In between the wood trim is stucco that, if repaired, should be made of a consistent color and texture

Figure 2.76 shows an example of a smaller house that has wood brackets projecting from the front wall to the farthest extent of the roof. The top floor is defined ornamentally by a horizontal wood band that runs just beneath the sills of the upper level windows.

The house in Figure 2.77 is a variation of a Dutch gable roof. The trim runs horizontally at the top of the second floor and is expressed by an oversized dentil mold that extends about two feet from the edge of the roof.

FIGURE 2.74   An example of ornamental trim with brackets at the second and third ceiling lines.

FIGURE 2.75 Tudor-style home.

FIGURE 2.76 Bracket detail.

FIGURE 2.77   Dutch gable roof and oversized dentil mold.

In Figure 2.78, the opposite effect is achieved. A window is underscaled to give the eave a vertical emphasis. The small arch in the narrow window is repeated in the trim that forms the uppermost part of the gable.

In a second Dutch gable example, an arched window has a keystone that provides scale for the entire elevation. The arches are repeated within the window and visually create a delicate scale within a very large façade (Figure 2.79).

FIGURE 2.78 Underscaled arch window and wood trim.

Garages

Garages in historic areas are normally detached secondary structures currently used for storing automobiles. Garages are often accessed from an alley. There are two kinds of garages that exist in historic areas; first are structures made solely to store one automobile, and the second are larger structures made to store two automobiles and sometimes have living quarters above.

The first kind often are deteriorated and should be replaced. The second variety, sometimes called a coach house, should be kept. The first kind often has no area for storage beyond that of the automobile itself and sometimes even lacks space for doors to open on both sides at the same time. Coach houses are usually built large enough to accommodate two modern automobiles.

The living quarters above should be used as living quarters if allowable by code. Coach houses are often designed as small-scale versions of the larger buildings with which they are associated. If a coach house needs to be modified, the relationship of the character of the coach house to the main building should be maintained. The scale of the coach house should not be altered nor should its proportion, style, massing, or detailing.

If a new secondary structure needs to be built to replace an obsolete secondary structure, the new structure should be designed in the same architectural vocabulary as the

FIGURE 2.79 Dutch gable with keystone trim.

primary structure. For example, if the primary structure is a Prairie Style house, then the secondary structure should be designed in the Prairie Style. If the primary structure is an International Style Modernist house, then the secondary structure should be designed as an International Style Modernist Structure.

Garage doors are either eight feet wide for a single car, or 16 feet wide for a two-car opening. The single door is preferable because the eight foot wide dimension creates a better scale and massing for the structure. By doubling the single door with an intermediate pier, the structure may be built to accommodate two vehicles. Also, space should be provided adjacent to, or in front of, the vehicles to be used for storage.

Most new garages are designed with low-pitched roofs that usually clash with the character of historic neighborhoods. By increasing the roof pitch more space is made available for storage above. Most garages are pitched at 3.5:12 or 4:12, but what is most desirable in an historic district is a pitch of at least 6:12, which is a 45 degree angle. Also, the roof type and material should match that of the primary structure, along with the siding type and material.

If the pattern in a neighborhood is to have detached structures at the rear of a site accessible from an alley, then this should be continued. The addition of an attached garage would not be in keeping with the character of the community. If a home-owner had an existing structure that has decayed and needs to be replaced, the replacement structure should be free standing rather than attached (Figures 2.80 through 2.84).

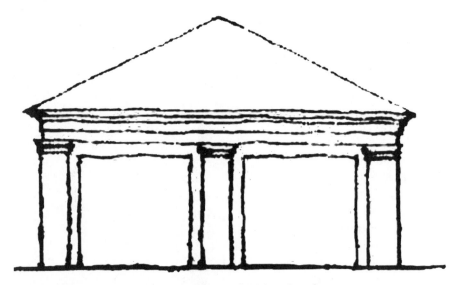

FIGURE 2.80   Diagram of two-car garage with hipped roof.

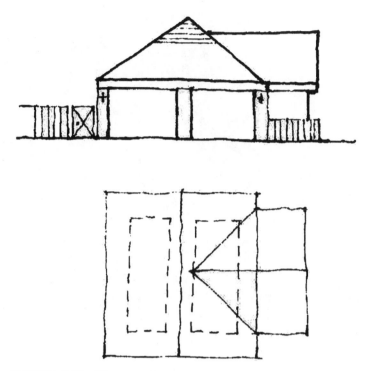

FIGURE 2.81 Diagram of garage. Two-car garage with storage above in gable and dormer.

FIGURE 2.82 Diagram of two-car garage with cupola and trim.

FIGURE 2.83 New garage out of scale with adjacent outbuilding.

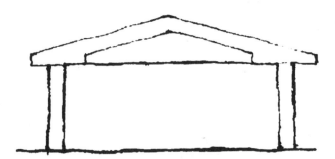

FIGURE 2.84 Diagram of poorly articulated garage.

Fences

Well-crafted fences not only make good neighbors but also make humane places in which to live. Fences should be made so that on a corner residential lot for example, the fence is low at the front of the house and high at the rear of the house. The height of the fence allowed by code will vary from place to place, but a recommended height for the rear part of the fence is five feet, with the front yard portion at three feet. The slats that make the middle portion of the fence should allow for some light to pass through. This may be accomplished by alternating the slats on the inside or outside of the horizontal-framing member, or the vertical slats could be placed with a gap between them. Fences should be placed about 18 inches in from sidewalks. This provides a place for landscaping or a flowerbed. Also, the 18 inch area allows space for bicycle handlebars to pass without scratching the fence. An additional advantage of the 18 inch space is that it allows elbows to pass without hitting the fence when two strollers pass one another on the sidewalk (Figures 2.85 through 2.94).

FIGURE 2.85 Fence detail. Fence with landscaping between sidewalk and fence showing center line of bike.

FIGURE 2.86   Varieties of wood fences.

FIGURE 2.87 Varieties of metal fences.

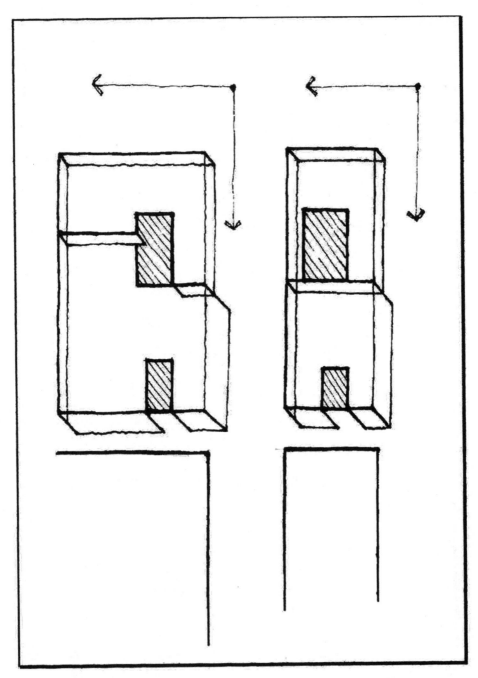

FIGURE 2.88 Diagram showing fencing at residential corner. High fence at rear, low fence at front.

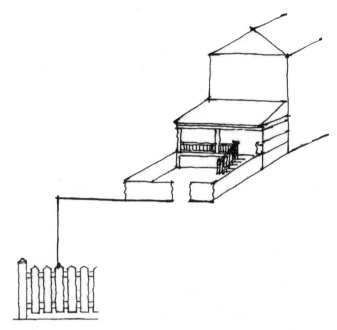

FIGURE 2.89 Diagram showing continuous picket fence as fencing material in relation to a front porch.

FIGURE 2.90 White picket fence.

FIGURE 2.91   Example of a metal fence with brick masonry base.

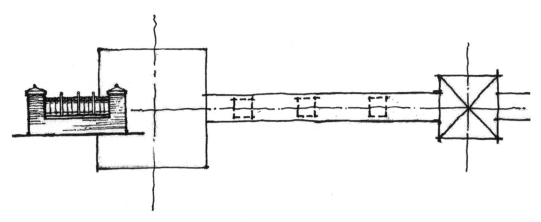

FIGURE 2.92   Metal fence.

FIGURE 2.93 Metal fence with intermediate brick piers.

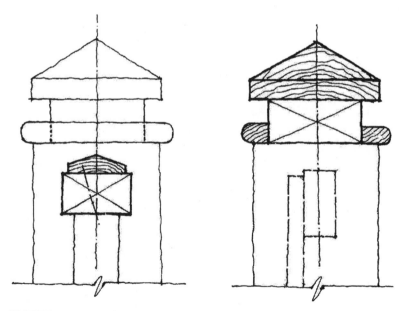

FIGURE 2.94 Diagram showing fence detail.

PUBLIC SPACE

How space is crafted is of significance for communities trying to reconstitute a sense of character and a set of spaces dedicated to public use. Understanding the relationship between primary and secondary structures, the relationship between institution, commercial, and residential buildings, and the way in which buildings relate to roads, streets, and alleys is critical to the preservation of character in historic communities.

A primary structure is one that is dominant on a site. A secondary structure is one that is of lesser importance relative to other buildings on a site. Examples of primary structures and secondary structures include large homes with free-standing outbuildings. Another example is that of a main building on a university campus that is larger and of a greater scale than the surrounding buildings. A third example is that of a church with ancillary chapels attached by means of arcaded walkways. It is absolutely critical from a preservation point of view that the relationships between primary and secondary buildings be maintained when adding onto or modifying in any other way an existing built context. If, for example, a university desires to add on to a building that is of a secondary scale to that of an adjacent primary building, the addition should be added without altering the scale of the secondary building. If a church desires to add more space to its main building, it should do so by making the addition part of the primary structure without altering the secondary structures around it. This is a matter of public space because the consistent pattern of primary and secondary structures is often one of the contributing factors in determining the merit of historic districts. If the pattern is disrupted, then the integrity of a district is disrupted and the establishment of character in the public realm will be put at risk.

Another example of public space exists in historic suburbs. In suburbs dating from the early 20th century and earlier, the space in between buildings shaped by porches, verandas, and terraces create the character of the public space. Public space such as this is given a human scale through the detailing of railings, balusters, urns, and overhead trellises. These elements of the suburban environment provide space that is both enclosed and outside, privately owned but visible from the public way (Figures 2.95, 2.96, and 2.97).

Figure 2.98 represents what can happen when public space is violated. The diagrams show a public square with incompatible subtractions and additions. Most often compatibility is thought of as a process of addition, and there are many examples of incompatible additions to existing contexts with which one is all too familiar. But with an urban square such as a courthouse square or a landscaped park that is clearly defined as a square, the very quality of the public space depends upon the definition of the perimeter of the space. So if someone removes a building as shown in the top of the diagram in Figure 2.98, the quality of the space is compromised. Conversely, if an addition is made to the square that projects into the square, the square is also compromised.

FIGURE 2.95 Diagram of public space. Public space including inhabited sidewalk and central fountain area.

FIGURE 2.96 An example of a residential porch as public/private space.

FIGURE 2.97 An example of a front porch as public/private space.

Often the integrity of the physical environment depends upon how well exterior space is crafted. Figure 2.99 represents a cross section from a public street through a front yard through a primary structure and through a backyard through a secondary structure and through an alley. Very often in settings such as this, there is a primary and secondary level of landscape that corresponds to the primary and secondary scale of houses and garages. The primary landscape is comprised of large trees and the secondary level of landscape is comprised of bushes, shrubs and smaller trees.

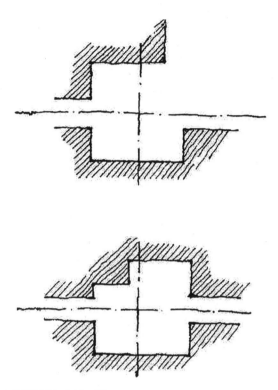

FIGURE 2.98 Diagram of public space. Incompatible alteration of urban form.

How institutional, commercial, civic, and residential buildings are defined is essential to the understanding of historic contexts. For preservation, the use of a building does not need to correspond with the building type. For example, a commercial building that was originally designed as an office structure with a warehouse facility could be changed into a residential unit. A school could be converted into offices, and an office could be converted into another use such as a hotel.

When architectural identity is defined with regard to building type, this refers to the building's original architectural expression, not the current use. For example, if a commercial building is to be changed into a residence, the preservation of the building should recognize the history of the building as a commercial structure. If a house is used as offices or for a commercial establishment, the preservation and definition of the house need to be understood within the context of residential architecture, not commercial architecture. Often, the architectural definition of a building as institutional, commercial, civic, or residential has to do with the use of massing

FIGURE 2.99 Diagram showing cross section from alley
to street with primary and secondary landscaping.

and scale in relation to style. An example of how this is accomplished is seen in
church architecture. In an American context, churches are typically placed within
residential neighborhoods rather than at the end of great vistas or placed as a focus
of a great urban space. What is of significance to preservation is the manipulation of
the scale of the church building to relate to the adjacent residential context. This is
seen in the extension of the nave roof to about 10 feet above grade in alignment with
the first floors of surrounding residences. A second example is from an urban context where a church is built in the context of commercial buildings. The Methodist
Temple in Chicago is approximately 15 stories tall, and unlike the previous example
which is scaled down to fit a residential context, the building is scaled up to fit a commercial context. The building is a Gothic style building but is scaled to hold its own
among its neighboring high rise office buildings (Figure 2.100).

The material quality of buildings, objects, and sites is represented through the
thoughtful and practical assembly of building materials and the spaces between the
materials. Recognizing the effective use of building materials and their proper detailing is a first essential step to the making and remaking of meaningful places.

FIGURE 2.100 Methodist Temple, Holabird and Root, Chicago.

REFERENCES

1. Witkower, Rudolf. 1974. *Palladio and English Palladianism.* Thames and Hudson, New York. Chapter 3, *The Renaissance Baluster and Palladio.*

2. Benjamin, Asher. 1969 (Reprint of the sixth edition, 1827). *The American Builder's Companion: Or, A System of Architecture Particularly Adapted to the Present Style of Building.* Dover, New York.

3. Scottish Lime Centre. 1995. *Preparation and Use of Lime Mortar, An Introduction to the Principles of Using Lime Mortars.* Edinburgh, Scotland.

Speweik, John P. 1995. *The History of Masonry Mortar.* National Lime Asociation, Arlington, Virginia.

4. Palladio, Andrea. 1997. *The Four Books on Architecture.* Trans. Robert Tavernor and Richard Schofield. MIT Press, Cambridge, Massachusetts. (Originally published as *I Quattro Libri dell' Architettura*, Book I, 1570.)

5. Benjamin.

6. Palladio, Book I.

7. Palladio, Book I.

8. Palladio, Book I.

9. Sheet Metal and Air Conditioning Contractors National Association, *Architectural Sheet Metal Manual.* Fifth edition, 1993.

10. Wessel de Jonge and Arjan Doolaar, eds. 1997. *Curtain Wall Refurbishment: A Challenge to Manage.* The Netherlands, DOCOMOMO International, Eindhoven University of Technology, Eindhoven.

11. DOCOMOMO.

PART
THREE

The previous chapters describe what should be preserved, and a method for observing and evaluating the physical material of historic preservation. This chapter addresses meaning in historic preservation. Meanings, as they relate to physical settings, result from the development of interpretations of buildings, objects, and sites that constitute any given place. In order to create meaningful places, careful consideration should be given to the interpretation of what comprises a place. Interpretation of buildings and sites fix buildings and sites within a particular time and place. Interpretations can be stories of the creation of a place or the people who live in a place, and it is through interpretation of these stories that history is made a part of historic preservation. Furthermore, when history is brought into historic preservation, the act of preserving buildings through the restoration and repair of building materials becomes a cultural concern more than a matter of utility.

INTERPRETATION

Just as floor plans are diagrams of the social relationships that occur within buildings, the exteriors of buildings, spaces between buildings, and the composition and character of a building's exterior are the cultural expressions of the people who live in and around those structures. This is evident in the buildings at Shaker Village in Lexington, Kentucky, where the architecture and landscape in which the architecture is set convey the aspirations and values of the people for whom the village was made. The elegant simplicity and the clear plain massing and proportion of each building regardless of use are a direct outcome of the belief system of the village's inhabitants (Figure 3.1).

The challenge for historic preservation is to create interpretations of other buildings and places that are inclusive in their scope in order to fully articulate the cultural impact of architecture. By doing this, historic preservation may take on a greater role in the making of public space, in particular by broadening its base and encompassing a wider range of buildings and places.

173

FIGURE 3.1 Shaker Village, Lexington, Kentucky.

One example of how this is being done is the inclusion of Modernist buildings into historic preservation. The Modern Movement developed in Europe in the early 20th century and was transported to the United States in the middle of the century. Some Modernist buildings are over 50 years old, and how these are interpreted is of great consequence because this requires a rethinking of approach.

Formerly, there was a clear stylistic differentiation between what was or was not historic, because Modernist buildings simply did not exceed the 50 year benchmark for consideration as historic structures. Today, there is not always a stylistic distinction that squares directly with merit and significance. For example, a Modernist building may be older and have a greater significance historically than a non-Modernist building that is not as old.

The buildings of Modernism should be viewed in the context of ideological positions of the architects of Modernism in order to provide a full historical accounting. Modernism as an ideology not only shaped the modern city, it shaped the attitudes of most architects, planners, and designers practicing today. However, their points of view are presented as history rather than current events when a Modernist building is considered for historic merit.

Another way in which historic preservation may expand its scope is by recognizing the multi-cultural context in which most architecture has developed. Embracing the cultural heritage of non-Western societies and people whose backgrounds are not European gives voice to other perspectives and will ensure that historic preservation is an activity that has a continued broad appeal.

One way to accomplish all this is to look at how human beings relate to physical places by examining the social and historical contexts of buildings and sites. By doing this one learns what it is about the people who lived in a particular place and what it is about the time in which they lived that may or may not be different from what one is familiar with in the present. Furthermore, learning about the social relationships among people or groups that may or may not be different from present social relationships may shed light on the development of neighborhoods and districts.

Bringing architecture to life by linking social and historic contexts to brick and mortar provides added insight to interpretive historic preservation. For example, many large late 19th century and early 20th century homes contain large, grandiose, beautifully detailed stairways directly accessible from their front doors. Also, many homes such as these have small parlors adjacent to the stairs where visitors would wait until the person they were visiting arrived from the upper levels of the home. Socially, what does this arrangement of space say about how people presented themselves to others a century ago? What does the arrangement of space say about the private lives of people a century ago and, more important to this study, what are the implications for the making of public space?

Another example from early in the 20th century is the existence of servant's rooms in apartment buildings. This is similar to the previous example in that the existence of a space dedicated to an archaic use speaks to the present about the way in which people lived decades ago. Many floor plans that include old servant's rooms are now sold as dens or home offices with adjacent small bathrooms, but these were originally rooms for paid help.

At the city scale, what public spaces currently exist if any and what happened in those spaces? Have any public spaces that were previously landscaped parks been turned into places for people to park their automobiles? Are the values that would allow this to occur prevalent in the community today or does this represent an attitude that has had its day? If there are public spaces in a community, and there are many that have none, what is the history of what happened in these spaces?

The ornamentation of buildings is another direct expression of people's connection to buildings. Ornamentation can literally tell the story of a place and its inhabitants. The relief sculpture from the State Street Bridge in Chicago tells the story of the making of the bridge. The State Street Bridge is a draw bridge and, as such, has towers located at either end that contain mechanisms for managing the periodic raising and lowering of the street to allow boats to pass. On the west side of one of the bridge towers, there is a relief sculpture with an inscription that says "First Bridge Built in 1864." Above the inscription is carved a sailing vessel passing through a drawbridge that is made to look heavier than the new bridge. On the south side of the same tower there is another inscription. This one says "Present Bridge built in 1949." Above this inscription is a carving of a vessel that is clearly not powered by the wind, and the bridge is represented in its present form. The relief sculptures and the manner in which they tell a story linking technological progress and architectural achievement serve as a clear example of the expressive possibilities existing within architecture not only today but in the past (Figures 3.2 and 3.3).

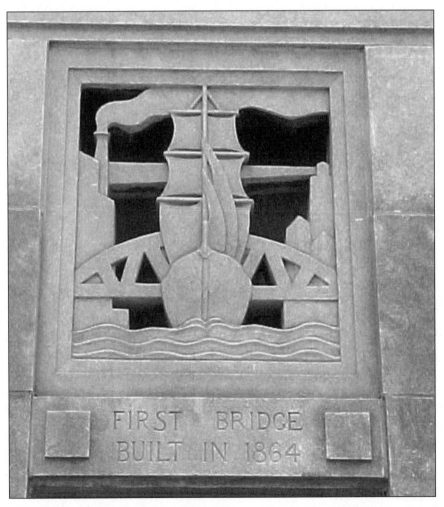

FIGURE 3.2 State Street Bridge, Chicago.

FIGURE 3.3   State Street Bridge, Chicago.

An additional example, also from Chicago, is the relief sculpture that exists at the end of LaSalle Street above the main entrance to the Chicago Board of Trade Building (Figure 3.4). On the right is a Native American holding ears of corn. On the left is a figure presumably of European descent holding stalks of grain. The implication is that they are trading with one another, both with natural resources. The question of how one treats this transaction as a piece of architectural history raises several important issues. Foremost is what happens when one finds material literally carved

into buildings or in the written history of architecture that does not represent currently accepted standards of social equity. While the examples of the building of the
bridges are innocuous, the trading motif on the Board of Trade building is not.
Should the building be changed to fit contemporary standards? Or should the motifs
remain and be interpreted in a statement saying, " We don't accept the racial stereo-
type represented in the sculpture, but keep the sculpture intact because it represents
a point of view that has passed." One can see how putting the history into historic
preservation can very quickly become a matter much more complex than fixing and
patching decayed pieces of buildings.

Architectural style is one way in which people may develop a sense of historical
time. Important to discussions of architectural style is the understanding that style is
an invented concept created for the purpose of classifying and categorizing architecture. Like any other concept, however, the understanding of style is fluid and what
someone today thinks about style may be very different than the point of view of
someone living at a different time.

FIGURE 3.4 Relief sculpture, Chicago Board of Trade, Holabird and Root, Chicago.

The issue of style is a key factor in deciding how to interpret buildings and places, yet style is sometimes considered without regard to the analysis of the building form that creates the style, or the discussion of style is taken out of context and provides an interpretation stripped of historical time. Style is sometimes treated as a commodity invented by architects rather than an idea about the classification and categorization of form. Also, style is sometimes viewed in a way that inaccurately implies qualitative progress where one style is succeeded by another and yet another, with each succeeding style considered better than the previous style. Stylistic analysis provides a common language for the description and classification of buildings and places and, when properly used, can provide a proper starting point for the designation process.

Defining the general stylistic features of a building or site in terms of broad stylistic categories gives an overall framework for defining the architecture of a proposed district or landmark. Gathering specific data within that framework, including dates of construction, architect's names, owner's names and the history of the structure, helps define the building in its local context. Another step is to continue the analysis of the building form and seek out any local variations of the broad stylistic categories. This approach produces a refined study and recognizes general trends, while specifically defining the architecture stylistically in the context of time and place.

An example of how the very idea of style itself can change may be seen by looking at preservation from the 18th century and comparing it to that of today. John Ruskin and his French contemporary Eugéne-Emmanuel Viollet-le-Duc are considered the founders of historic preservation. While people have always made repairs to buildings and rebuilt destroyed or decayed structures, Ruskin and Viollet established methods for restoration that took into account the historical contexts of that which was being restored. Significantly, both were concerned primarily with the restoration of Roman and Gothic antiquities in France and England and thus both worked within a clear stylistic paradigm. They knew that Roman architecture was different from Gothic architecture and that the two architectures differed from the buildings of the Renaissance in France and England, and differed from buildings built in their own time. Their historical paradigm was one of hundreds and even thousands of years, not an historical threshold of 50 years as is common today when discussing historic merit.

The idea of an ancient architecture and the idea of a modern architecture as distinct from one another originates in 17th century French architectural theoretical discourses that debated the merits of the two [1]. To early 21st century eyes, the architecture that illustrated the debate is singularly classical. Yet to the 17th century theorists and architects, the architecture representing the two points of view, one ancient and the other modern, had vast differences and could not be possibly be classified within one category. The distinctions they drew between the two approaches raise issues that still have relevance to historic preservation today. An ancient point of view says that there are universal, ideal, and mathematically defined forms best represented in the architecture of the ancients that cannot and should not change. The modern point of view, on the other hand, states that architecture is a matter of taste and fashion and, rather than being based upon universal laws, is based upon custom. This links to historic preservation in that many of the current public debates surrounding preservation also draw sharp distinctions like those articulated in the 17th century treatises. The "beauty is in the eye of the beholder" argument is common at public hearings, as is the opposite argument that advocates for a "standard of taste." Fortunately, preservation policy has been written to allow for the localized diversity of the former while providing for the idealistic purity of the latter.

POLICY

Policies enacted to guide people in conducting a public dialogue for the purpose of objectively establishing significance and merit should include standards for review, a definition of the scope of authority of the group conducting the dialogue, a means to determine the qualifications of those to whom authority is delegated, and an appeals process.

The powers and duties of the group conducting the review process should be clearly delineated. By extension, the process should be clear as to when and how the reviewing body will advocate for preservation, while maintaining neutrality in matters that require public debate and discourse.

Policies are the rules that are in place to frame and manage the designation of historic and cultural properties and sites. Policies should be commonly understood and agreed upon, and they should be responsive to local conditions while being consistent with national and international guidelines and laws. Policies enacted in local ordinances should have a means of measuring support for designation of properties and, conversely, have a means for measuring lack of support for preservation initiatives.

The Secretary of the Interior's Standards for Rehabilitation serve as the backbone of many historic preservation policies and ordinances. Developed by the United States federal government and overseen by the Department of the Interior, these standards may be adopted by local municipalities and applied to local circumstances [2]. They read as follows:

1. A property shall be used for its historic purpose or be placed in a new use that requires minimal change to the defining characteristics of the building and its site and environment.

2. The historical character of a property shall be retained and preserved. The removal of historical materials or alteration of features and spaces that characterize a property shall be avoided.

3. Each property shall be recognized as a physical record of its time, place, and use. Changes that create a false sense of historical development, such as adding conjectural features or architectural elements from other buildings shall not be undertaken.

4. Most properties change over time; those changes that have acquired historic significance in their own right shall be retained and preserved.

5. Distinctive features and construction techniques or examples of craftsmanship that characterize a historic property shall be preserved.

6. Deteriorated historic features shall be repaired rather than replaced. Where the severity of deterioration requires replacement of a distinctive feature, the new feature shall match the old in design, color, texture, and other visual qualities and, where possible, materials. Replacement of missing features shall be substantiated by documentary, physical, or pictorial evidence.

7. Chemical or physical treatments, such as sandblasting, that cause damage to historic materials shall not be used. The surface cleaning of structures, if appropriate, shall be undertaken using the gentlest means possible.

8. Significant archeological resources affected by a project shall be protected and preserved. If such resources must be disturbed, mitigation measures shall be undertaken.

9. New additions, exterior alterations, or related new construction shall not destroy historic materials that characterize the property. The new work shall be differentiated from the old and shall be compatible with the massing, size, scale, and architectural features to protect the historic integrity of the property and its environment.

10. New additions and adjacent or related new construction shall be undertaken in such a manner that if removed in the future, the essential form and integrity of the historic property and its environment would be unimpaired.

The Standards are an interpretive policy tool because they incorporate several concepts primary to the work of historic preservation. The first of these is compatibility. Chapter 1 showed in a theoretical sense ways in which buildings may or may not be compatible in size, scale, massing, and proportion. The building recently constructed at the corner of State and Randolph in Chicago serves to further illustrate these concepts (Figures 3.5 and 3.6).

This building is used primarily as a dormitory for art students at the School of the Art Institute of Chicago. A second use is for retail establishments which occupy the first several floors. A third use is the Gene Siskel Center for Film. The residential component of the building is above the retail, with the exception of a lobby space at grade. The building on the corner is entirely new. The Baroque style single story structure is an existing building, as is the northmost portion of the building on State

FIGURE 3.5   Dormitory, School of the Art Institute of Chicago, Randolph and State Streets, Booth Hansen, 2000, Chicago.

FIGURE 3.6 Dormitory, School of the Art Institute of Chicago, Randolph and State Streets, Booth Hansen, 2000, Chicago.

Street. The site faces the Reliance Building by D. H. Burnham and Company, which is one block to the south. Diagonally across from the building is the Marshall Field and Company Building, also designed by D.H. Burnham and Company. The architects made several decisions that merit discussion. First is that the design of the building appears to be four buildings in response to the urban context, while the floor plan of the building is a single *floor plate,* meaning that each floor is on the same level. The advantage of this approach is that the building is versatile with regard to its interior layout and may be changed to other uses in the future if need be. More important to this particular discussion is the response to the urban setting. The west part of the building incorporates the existing single story structure by recessing ten or so feet to allow the unique profile of the parapet to be noticed. Also, the color of the cladding at the recessed portion is slightly darker than the rest of the building, which works well with the darker building adjacent to the west. The corner portion refers directly to the Reliance Building (Figure 3.7).

The color and massing and proportion of the new design are clearly an extension of the paradigm set by Burnham and Company over one hundred years ago. The corner portion also relates to the massing of the existing structure to the north that is incorporated into the design. The tri-partite or base middle top composition of the corner is an extension of the proportions set in place by the existing structure to the north. The Film Center is located in this part of the building. The retail part of the building is contained cleanly within the base of the building. The residential part of the building is the middle and the top. The material used as cladding is called glass fiber reinforced concrete or GFRC. The GFRC panels may be formed into multiple profiles and shapes because the GFRC begins life as a slurry mixture that is poured into forms offsite, then allowed to harden. The panels are then attached to the underlying steel frame as if they were terra cotta or stone. The building is compatible with its context visually, socially, and, by virtue of its references to the historic context around it, historically as well.

A second concept is historical time. The Standards say that buildings change over time and that a "false sense of historic development" shall be avoided. This is an interesting part of the Standards and can be understood in several ways. The first is to understand the statement as having an underlying assumption that all new buildings will necessarily be a different stylistic expression than old buildings. While at one point in history this may have been the case, current architectural practice does not support a sharp differentiation based on style alone. There are architects who design neo-Classical buildings, there are architects who design Modernist buildings, and there are those who base their work on a study of traditional town and city planning, making the question of what constitutes historical development unclear in this interpretation of the standard.

Is the historical development of architecture and, thereby, the cultural identity of a place expressed through the progressive adaptation and growth of one style into

FIGURE 3.7 The Reliance Building, D.H. Burnham and Company, 1895, Chicago.

another culminating in the current style of the day? Or, as illustrated in the example of the dormitory building in Chicago, may a thoroughly modern building be designed to address current social and economic conditions but also reach into history for the basis of its design?

Standard three, which contains the language regarding a false sense of historical development, continues by describing false historical development as the addition of "...conjectural features or architectural elements from other buildings." Additionally, it says that buildings are a record of time, place, and use.

A distinction needs to be made here. Designing within a healthy urban context and interpreting other architecture in one's work is different than a false sense of historical development. False sense of historical development would be if the architects of the dormitory said, this *is* the Reliance Building, or this *is* the Santa Fe Building, completely obliterating any sense of time and place whatsoever. This fortunately is not what the architects did at the dormitory. Instead they intelligently chose the best parts of what was around them and wove a unified architectural tapestry with the pieces. Some of the pieces were found in history, others found in the present day.

Another example is the placement of the Mausoleum of Halicarnassus on the top of the Strauss Building in downtown Chicago (Figure 3.8). If Graham Anderson Probst and White said, "This really *is* the Mausoleum of Halicarnassus on the top of our building," then they would be creating a false sense of historical development. But instead they chose to interpret what was known at the time about the great ancient building to create an exotic and unique top to what was one of the largest buildings in Chicago at the time it was designed. It is rather certain that the top of the building is an interpretation of the Mausoleum for a few reasons. First, there is a central column on axis. The Mausoleum at Halicarnassus included a peristyle, or row of columns, of an odd number on each face. This means that there would have been a column centrally placed on each side of the building. The roof of the Mausoleum was a pyramid with a horse draw chariot placed on top (Figure 3.8).

The top of the Strauss Building has an odd number of columns, and includes a roof shaped like a pyramid. The new pyramid is topped not with a chariot but with a beehive lantern. At the time the Strauss Building was built, proper historical development included the lifting of building elements from one building to the next, such as the Mausoleum motif. During most of the 20th century, this practice was seen as inconsistent with proper historical development, but at other times in history, design had a broader historical reach and buildings were topped not only with mausoleums as with the Strauss Building, but with other motifs such as tempiettos, flying buttresses, and towers as seen in the London Guarantee Building (Figure 3.9), the Tribune Tower designed by Hood and Howells and the adjacent Wrigley Building by Graham Anderson Probst and White (Figure 3.10), and the Auditorium Building by

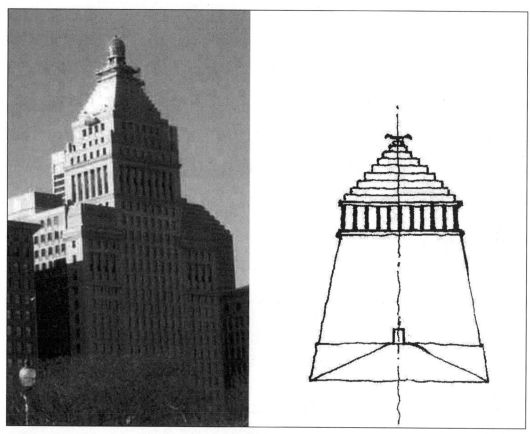

FIGURE 3.8 The Strauss Building, Graham Anderson Probst and White, Chicago. Conjectural sketch of the Mausoleum of Halicarnassus.

Adler and Sullivan (Figure 3.11). Broadly defined design metaphors such as beehives above mausoleums on top of office buildings and tempiettos on top of insurance company buildings create richness and diversity in the physical environment and should be encouraged.

Standard three prevents additions to buildings that are not cultural and formal extensions of what exists already. This standard may be applied to individual buildings that currently exist and require renovation, or it may be applied to the design of new buildings in historic contexts. In the past, the standard has been used as a way to impose stylistic predilections on historic preservation by limiting the historical reach of designers. But, as the previous analysis shows, Standard three, when interpreted in the manner described above, is a valuable resource for the making of meaningful communities.

FIGURE 3.9 The London Guarantee Building.

FIGURE 3.10 The Tribune Building, Hood and Howells, 1925, Chicago, and the Wrigley Building, Graham Anderson Probst and White, 1921, 1924, Chicago.

FIGURE 3.11 The Auditorium Building, Adler and Sullivan, 1889, Chicago.

Scope of Authority: Binding versus Advisory Review

Another helpful tool is binding review, which refers to a time when a preservation commission or board is granted legal authority over what is or is not built or demolished within an historic district or property. This is an interpretive tool, because the decisions of a group that has legal authority have permanence and the weight of law behind them. As such, they are required to be inclusive in their scope. A preservation commission with binding review has the authority to stop construction or demolition. Binding review, however, is different than advisory review. A commission with advisory review does not have the authority to stop construction or demolition in an historic district or property.

The advantage of binding review from the preservationist's perspective is that the effort that is put into reviewing property will have an effect on the community in which the commission is working. From the community's perspective, binding review authority provides an opportunity for citizens to participate in a dialogue about what is or is not built in their community. With binding review, citizens may stop unwanted growth or inappropriate design intervention. With advisory review there is no mechanism to manage the character of new development beyond imploring private individuals to accept another's point of view. With binding review the review process is set out with regard to a set of criteria that will most likely be related to the Secretary's Standards described above. Binding review mandates that a commission or board issue findings of fact based upon a set of criteria, usually based upon the Secretary's Standards. Findings of fact are the legal backbone of binding review, and provide the basis for establishing merit or significance. With advisory review, findings are not issued since there is no legal authority to do so. Only opinions are issued; these may or may not be based upon a reasoned and deliberative debate.

A community that decides to delegate binding review authority to a group of citizens for the purpose of debating matters concerning character, merit, and significance should first of all have a group of buildings and sites that show potential for various levels of historic designation. Second, the community should have within it a group of people who are qualified to make proper evaluations and judgments for the benefit of the community. Third, the community should have a clear idea as to its cultural identity.

What a community decides with regard to the constitution of its cultural identity will depend on the community's ability to articulate its values openly, and its ability to come to a consensus in a public forum. Architecturally, its cultural identity will depend upon the quality and character of its existing buildings and places. Furthermore, the cultural identity will depend upon the ability of the community to articulate a point of view with regard to its existing buildings and places.

A singular cultural expression may have multiple articulations within one community. For example, if a community decides to establish an historic district because of the number and quality of bungalow houses present in the community, then the identity would be based on the existence of the bungalows. Yet, there may be different kinds of bungalows within the district. They may vary with regard to who built them, or when. They may vary by virtue of who designed them. They may even vary in style, but the district's identity and thereby the identity of the community is based on the architecture of the bungalow.

Contributing and Non-Contributing Structures

Determining whether or not a building is a contributing or non-contributing structure is a way to decide what counts and to what extent in a district. A non-contributing structure is one whose characteristics do not define the characteristics of a district.

A contributing structure is the opposite. It is a building whose characteristics help to define a district. The main issue relating to contributing and non-contributing structures is that of consistency. An occasional non-contributing structure does not invalidate a district. If there are several non-contributing structures organized in a way in which the quality, size, scale, or massing of a group of buildings is interrupted, then the non-contributing buildings would be excluded from the district and a boundary for the district would be set at the non-contributing buildings. Figure 3.12 shows a grouping of several contributing structures. These are each of similar size, scale, massing, and quality. They are different styles, but they relate to the street and sidewalk in the same way. These show how different styles may exist compatibly within a district while maintaining the integrity of the district. Figure 3.13 shows an example of a district boundary. The bridge is a barrier and change in scale and use compared to the adjacent buildings.

FIGURE 3.12 A group of contributing buildings in a proposed historic district.

Other examples of a district boundary might be natural features such as a river or lake, or built features such as a change in building scale and massing. Boundaries create edges and a zone of inclusion and exclusion. Therefore, the interpretation of boundaries is critical. Preservation is best served when boundaries are defined by obvious features in the landscape that are clearly definable and comprehensible. Historic preservation policies should address the following architectural issues:

- General
- Public space
- Preservation of space for public use
- Preservation of areas between buildings and between buildings and streets.
- Preservation of streets and sidewalks.
- Preservation of consistent fenestration pattern.
- Preservation of quality building materials and details
- Preservation of size, scale, mass, and proportions when present.

FIGURE 3.13 A district boundary formed by a train bridge.

Figure 3.14 shows a group of buildings in Charleston, South Carolina, that are not identical but are of similar materials, proportion, and spatial configuration in relation to the exterior spaces around them. Each building has its own merits architecturally, but as a group of buildings, or as a district, they comprise an historical setting that has merit because of the manner in which the spaces in between the buildings are designed, and how they relate to sidewalks and streets.

Several questions should be asked about this grouping of buildings and the areas around them. These include:

- What kind of streets are present, and how did the urban pattern develop over time?
- Who developed it and why?
- How do they intersect?
- Do they form a grid?
- If so, what kind of grid, regular or irregular?
- Are there trees at the side of the streets?
- Are there trees in the center of the street or on the side and if so what kind are they?

FIGURE 3.14 Charleston, South Carolina.

Regarding the uses of these buildings and public spaces the following should be asked:

- What kind of public spaces are present?
- Are there parks?
- Are there boulevards?
- Are there urban plazas?
- Are there any monuments commemorating people or events?
- What kind of buildings are present?
- Are there buildings for commerce?
- Are there buildings for education?
- Are there buildings for domestic uses?
- Are there buildings for religious institutions?
- Are there buildings for entertainment?

Asking questions about the groups of buildings and about the specific uses of the buildings in the groups of buildings allows the story of this district to be told most comprehensively. Noting the placement of buildings in an urban or rural setting and taking into consideration their current or original use may help to interpret the story or meaning of a particular building or group of buildings. Also, taking building use into consideration demonstrates patterns of development that could not be evaluated by stylistic analysis alone.

The question of how people interact with buildings is important to understanding not only the relationship between building and street but can say something about the social context of a building in a particular setting. The location of doors, either on primary or secondary axes, becomes essential to understanding the way the building relates to the adjacent street.

- Where is the first floor?
- Is the first floor at grade?
- Is the first floor above grade?
- Is there an edge?
- Is there a center?
- What happens between the base of the building and the top?
- What is the window and door pattern (fenestration)?

There is a tendency for buildings with large windows and high ceilings to accommodate a change in use. An example of a building whose use changed but form did not is the Fisher Building (Figure 3.15) on Dearborn Street in Chicago between Van

Buren and Jackson. This building, originally designed by D. H. Burnham and Company as commercial offices, has recently been converted to a residential use. The exterior of the building is clad with Gothic details including gargoyles and collonnettes, yet the use of steel framing provides the opportunity to maximize the openings in the exterior walls (Figure 3.16 and 3.17). The windows therefore are extensive, as are the ceiling heights.

There are several other questions that should be asked in order to evaluate a building's relationship to its site or urban context. The example of Charleston provided an illustration of districts of buildings that are comprised of individual structures that may or may not have individual designation as landmarks. The Fisher Building is a landmark building but could also be considered a part of a significant historic context. How this building relates to its urban setting is of interest. Within one block of the Fisher Building is the first all steel framed high rise building, the Manhattan Building by William Le Baron Jenney. In the opposite direction is Mies van der Rohe's Federal Buildings and Loop Post Office. Directly across the street is the Monadnock Building, the north half of which is the largest bearing wall structure in Chicago. Across the street in the other direction is the Old Colony Building by Holabird and Roche. To the east are the Rothschild Building by Holabird and Roche, the second Leiter Building by Le Baron Jenney, the new Harold Washington Chicago Public Library Center by Hammond, Beeby and Babka, and the Chicago Bar Association by Stanley Tigerman. Several questions regarding urban context should be asked if attempting to tell the story of all of these buildings These are:

- How do the buildings relate to each other?
- Are the buildings similar in size?
- Are the buildings similar in material?
- Are the buildings different sizes but similar materials?
- Are the buildings different sizes but similar in proportion?
- Are the buildings made for the same original use or has the use changed?

With a well known body of work such as the Fisher Building and the buildings that are adjacent to it, volumes of archival material and secondary sources exist that will assist in the documentation of the buildings and the telling of their stories. A more common case is that large archives do not exist for a building or group of buildings, requiring research at a local level by contacting local historical associations or groups or identifying local archives of photographs and deed searches in the public records departments of local municipalities.

By applying commonly held principles of historic preservation to local needs and circumstances, historic preservation provides a basis for the re-establishment and continuation of a community's cultural and economic well being. By following a method

FIGURE 3.15   Fisher Building, D.H. Burnham and Company, 1896, Chicago.

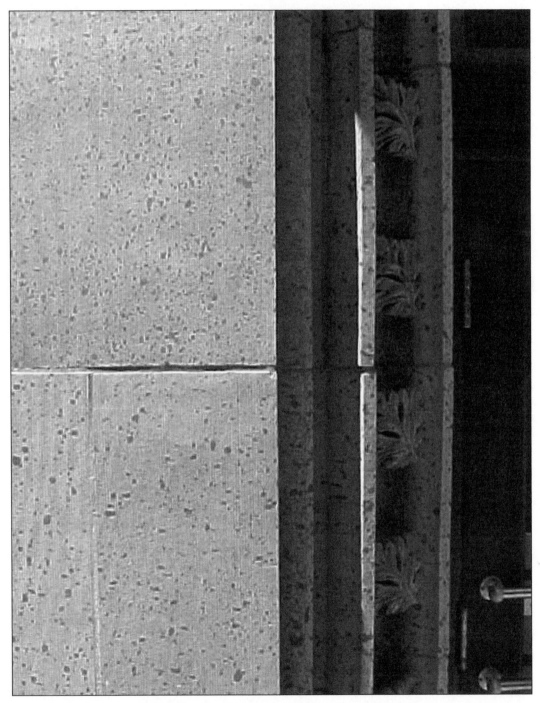

FIGURE 3.16　Detail, Fisher Building, D. H. Burnham and Company, 1896, Chicago.

FIGURE 3.17 Detail, Fisher Building, D. H. Burnham and Company, 1896, Chicago.

where style is understood within a context of a framework that includes an understanding of historical time and the social context of buildings and sites, historic preservation empowers communities in the making of meaningful communities.

How individuals understand themselves in relation to their property and the buildings that are on their property can range from the most intense expressions of individual license to a more developed sensibility that expresses a balance between the rights of property owners with the needs of the a community (Figure 3.18). The intensity of the property rights issue seems to vary regionally, and it has been noted that sometimes the most strongly held views in opposition to historic preservation come from the wealthiest sectors of the population. The rights of individual property owners should be respected and, indeed, these rights are respected in the laws and policies that regulate and limit the scope of historic preservation.

The need for historic preservation policy is summarized in Figures 3.19 and 3.20. Figure 3.19 shows a storefront pasted onto a bank building in Cincinnati with complete disregard for its context. Figure 3.20 shows an abandoned building in rural Ohio that, despite being left to decay naturally, fits its surroundings. The images represent, in very different ways, a hands-off approach to existing buildings and places.

FIGURE 3.18 Homemade "No Trespassing" sign, Bell County, Kentucky.

The building in the country remains virtually untouched while the building in the city remains scarred. Each building has its own history and story about the people who lived their lives within its walls. The decay of the building in the country is picturesque to modern eyes, while the addition to the bank building in the city is grotesque. The picturesque example remains in its original and pure form. It has simply decayed, while the bank building has obviously been changed for the worse. It has been subjected to a change that someone at some time thought was appropriate for some reason. Historic preservation policy exists for both cases. The building in the country should be restored in a way that does not add or take away to what is there already. The windows should not change, the shape of the building should not change, the color of the brick probably should not change. The use might change and there will be new heating and air conditioning systems, a new electrical system, and new lighting, but the building will essentially remain as it has for years. The example in the city will require a different approach. Restoration of this building will require changing the outside of the building. The addition needs to be taken away. The shape of the building needs to be changed back to the way the building appeared originally. The integrity of both buildings should be restored but in different ways.

FIGURE 3.19 Bank building in Cincinnati, Ohio.

FIGURE 3.20 Ruins in rural Ohio.

In the appendices following this chapter are several examples of historic preservation policies, ranging from local ordinances to international charters. Each has a way to determine significance and merit and each has its own point of view. For example, the Canadian charter takes the point of view that cultural heritage is a matter of national identity. The Charter for New Urbanism adopts the view that historic preservation serves the purpose of making livable communities. The Charleston Code, which is a part of the zoning ordinance for Charleston, South Carolina, enables a local community to manage its architectural heritage on a block-by-block, house-by-house basis.

The oldest document reproduced here is the Athens charter from the early 20th century which provides the basis upon which other charters and ordinances have been established. The international charters come from the International Council on Monuments and Sites (ICOMOS). The ICOMOS is an organization that maintains a World Heritage List of buildings and sites around the world that are protected under international treaties intended to protect cultural properties in the event of war or inappropriate development. ICOMOS is a part of UNESCO and is based in Paris. The Chapter 106 section is a federal document that outlines methods used by federal agencies when evaluating cultural property within the United States.

It is not the intent to critique each of these documents or to compare them to one another. They are presented here as a point of reference for the purpose of expanding the scope of historic preservation and strengthening the ability of local organizations to protect buildings, objects, and sites from inappropriate decay and destruction.

REFERENCES

1. Dora Wiebenson. 1993. *French Books: Seventeenth through Nineteenth Centuries.* George Braziller, New York.

2. U. S. Department of the Interior National Park Service Preservation Assistance Division. *The Secretary of the Interior's Standards for Rehabilitation: and Guidelines for Rehabilitating Historic Buildings.* U.S. Printing Office, Washington D.C.

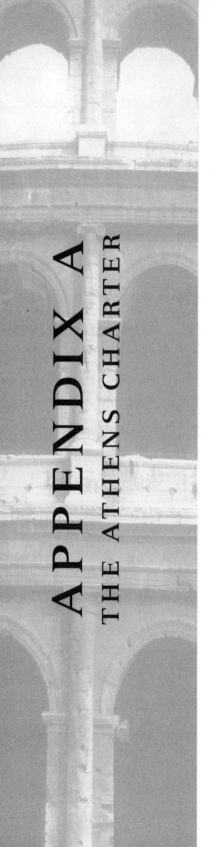

The Athens Charter for the Restoration of Historic Monuments. Adopted at the First International Congress of Architects and Technicians of Historic Monuments, Athens 1931. At the Congress in Athens the following seven main resolutions were made and called *Carta del Restauro*:

1. International organizations for Restoration on operational and advisory levels are to be established.

2. Proposed Restoration projects are to be subjected to knowledgeable criticism to prevent mistakes which will cause loss of character and historical values to the structures.

3. Problems of preservation of historic sites are to be solved by legislation at national level for all countries.

4. Excavated sites which are not subject to immediate restoration should be reburied for protection.

5. Modern techniques and materials may be used in restoration work.

6. Historical sites are to be given strict custodial protection.

7. Attention should be given to the dangers by initiating a system of regular and permanent maintenance calculated to ensure the preservation of the buildings.

I. DOCTRINES, GENERAL PRINCIPLES

The Conference heard the statement of the general principles and doctrines relating to the protection of monuments.

Whatever may be the variety of concrete cases, each of which are open to a different solution, the Conference noted that there predominates in the different countries represented a general tendency to abandon restorations *in toto* and to avoid the attendant dangers by initiating a system of regular and permanent maintenance calculated to ensure the preservation of the buildings.

When, as the result of decay or destruction, restoration appears to be indispensable, it recommends that the historic and artistic work of the past should be respected, without excluding the style of any given period.

The Conference recommends that the occupation of buildings, which ensures the continuity of their life, should be maintained but that they should be used for a purpose which respects their historic or artistic character.

II. ADMINISTRATIVE AND LEGISLATIVE MEASURES REGARDING HISTORICAL MONUMENTS

The Conference heard the statement of legislative measures devised to protect monuments of artistic, historic or scientific interest and belonging to the different countries. It unanimously approved the general tendency which, in this connection, recognises a certain right of the community in regard to private ownership. It noted that the differences existing between these legislative measures were due to the difficulty of reconciling public law with the rights of individuals.

Consequently, while approving the general tendency of these measures, the Conference is of opinion that they should be in keeping with local circumstances and with the trend of public opinion, so that the least possible opposition may be encountered, due allowance being made for the sacrifices which the owners of property may be called upon to make in the general interest. It recommends that the public authorities in each country be empowered to take conservatory measures in cases of emergency.

It earnestly hopes that the International Museums Office will publish a repertory and a comparative table of the legislative measures in force in the different countries and that this information will be kept up to date.

III. AESTHETIC ENHANCEMENT OF ANCIENT MONUMENTS

The Conference recommends that, in the construction of buildings, the character and external aspect of the cities in which they are to be erected should be respected, especially in the neighbourhood of ancient monuments, where the surroundings should be given special consideration. Even certain groupings and certain particularly picturesque perspective treatment should be preserved.

A study should also be made of the ornamental vegetation most suited to certain monuments or groups of monuments from the point of view of preserving their ancient character. It specially recommends the suppression of all forms of publicity, of the erection of unsightly telegraph poles and the exclusion of all noisy factories and even of tall shafts in the neighbourhood of artistic and historic monuments.

IV. RESTORATION OF MONUMENTS

The experts heard various communications concerning the use of modern materials for the consolidation of ancient monuments. They approved the judicious use of all the resources at the disposal of modern technique and more especially of reinforced concrete. They specified that this work of consolidation should whenever possible be concealed in order that the aspect and character of the restored monument may be preserved. They recommended their adoption more particularly in cases where their use makes it possible to avoid the dangers of dismantling and reinstating the portions to be preserved.

V. THE DETERIORATION OF ANCIENT MONUMENTS

The Conference noted that, in the conditions of present day life, monuments throughout the world were being threatened to an ever-increasing degree by atmospheric agents. Apart from the customary precautions and the methods successfully applied in the preservation of monumental statuary in current practice, it was impossible, in view of the complexity of cases and with the knowledge at present available, to formulate any general rules. The Conference recommends:

1. That, in each country, the architects and curators of monuments should collaborate with specialists in the physical, chemical, and natural sciences with a view to determining the methods to be adopted in specific cases;
2. That the International Museums Office should keep itself informed of the work being done in each country in this field and
3. that mention should be made thereof in the publications of the Office.

With regard to the preservation of monumental sculpture, the Conference is of opinion that the removal of works of art from the surroundings for which they were designed is, *in principle*, to be discouraged. It recommends, by way of precaution, the preservation of original models whenever these still exist or if this proves impossible, the taking of casts.

VI. THE TECHNIQUE OF CONSERVATION

The Conference is gratified to note that the principles and technical considerations set forth in the different detailed communications are inspired by the same idea, namely:

In the case of ruins, scrupulous conservation is necessary, and steps should be taken to reinstate any original fragments that may be recovered (anastylosis), whenever this is possible; the new materials used for this purpose should in all cases be recognisable. When the preservation of ruins brought to light in the course of excavations is found to be impossible, the Conference recommends that they be buried, accurate records being of course taken before filling-in operations are undertaken.

It should be unnecessary to mention that the technical work undertaken in connection with the excavation and preservation of ancient monuments calls for close collaboration between the archaeologist and the architect.

With regard to other monuments, the experts unanimously agreed that, before any consolidation or partial restoration is undertaken, a thorough analysis should be made of the defects and the nature of the decay of these monuments. They recognised that each case needed to be treated individually.

VII. THE CONSERVATION OF MONUMENTS AND INTERNATIONAL COLLABORATION

a) Technical and Moral Cooperation

The Conference, convinced that the question of the conservation of the artistic and archaeological property of mankind is one that interests the community of the States, which are wardens of civilisation:

Hopes that the States, acting in the spirit of the Covenant of the League of Nations, will collaborate with each other on an ever-increasing scale and in a more concrete manner with a view to furthering the preservation of artistic and historic monuments;

Considers it highly desirable that qualified institutions and associations should, without in any manner whatsoever prejudicing international public law, be given an opportunity of manifesting their interest in the protection of works of art in which civilisation has been expressed to the highest degree and which would seem to be threatened with destruction;

Expresses the wish that requests to attain this end, submitted to the Intellectual Cooperation Organisation of the League of Nations, be recommended to the earnest attention of the States.

It will be for the International Committee on Intellectual Cooperation, after an enquiry conducted by the International Museums Office and after having collected all relevant information, more particularly from the National Committee on Intellectual Cooperation concerned, to express an opinion on the expediency of the steps to be taken and on the procedure to be followed in each individual case.

The members of the Conference, after having visited in the course of their deliberations and during the study cruise which they were able to make on this occasion, a number of excavation sites and ancient Greek monuments, unanimously paid a tribute to the Greek Government, which, for many years past, has been itself responsible for extensive works and, at the same time, has accepted the collaboration of archaeologists and experts from every country.

The members of the Conference there saw an example of activity which can but contribute to the realisation of the aims of intellectual cooperation, the need for which manifested itself during their work.

b) The Role of Education in the Respect of Monuments

The Conference, firmly convinced that the best guarantee in the matter of the preservation of monuments and works of art derives from the respect and attachment of the peoples themselves;

Considering that these feelings can very largely be promoted by appropriate action on the part of public authorities;

Recommends that educators should urge children and young people to abstain from disfiguring monuments of every description and that they should teach them to take a greater and more general interest in the protection of these concrete testimonies of all ages of civilisation.

c) Value of International Documentation

The Conference expresses the wish that:

1. Each country, or the institutions created or recognised competent for this purpose, publish an inventory of ancient monuments, with photographs and explanatory notes;
2. Each country constitute official records which shall contain all documents relating to its historic monuments;
3. Each country deposit copies of its publications on artistic and historic monuments with the International Museums Office;
4. The Office devote a portion of its publications to articles on the general processes and methods employed in the preservation of historic monuments;
5. The Office study the best means of utilising the information so centralised.

PREAMBLE

Imbued with a message from the past, the historic monuments of generations of people remain to the present day as living witnesses of their age-old traditions. People are becoming more and more conscious of the unity of human values and regard ancient monuments as a common heritage. The common responsibility to safeguard them for future generations is recognized. It is our duty to hand them on in the full richness of their authenticity.

It is essential that the principles guiding the preservation and restoration of ancient buildings should be agreed and be laid down on an international basis, with each country being responsible for applying the plan within the framework of its own culture and traditions.

By defining these basic principles for the first time, the Athens Charter of 1931 contributed towards the development of an extensive international movement which has assumed concrete form in national documents, in the work of ICOM and UNESCO and in the establishment by the latter of the International Centre for the Study of the Preservation and the Restoration of Cultural Property. Increasing awareness and critical study have been brought to bear on problems which have continually become more complex and varied; now the time has come to examine the Charter afresh in order to make a thorough study of the principles involved and to enlarge its scope in a new document.

Accordingly, the 2nd International Congress of Architects and Technicians of Historic Monuments, which met in Venice from May 25th to 31st 1964, approved the following text.

DEFINITIONS

ARTICLE 1. The concept of an historic monument embraces not only the single architectural work but also the urban or rural setting in which is found the evidence of a particular civilization, a significant development or an historic event. This applies not only to great works of art but also to more modest works of the past which have acquired cultural significance with the passing of time.

ARTICLE 2. The conservation and restoration of monuments must have recourse to all the sciences and techniques which can contribute to the study and safeguarding of the architectural heritage.

AIM

ARTICLE 3. The intention in conserving and restoring monuments is to safeguard them no less as works of art than as historical evidence.

CONSERVATION

ARTICLE 4. It is essential to the conservation of monuments that they be maintained on a permanent basis.

ARTICLE 5. The conservation of monuments is always facilitated by making use of them for some socially useful purpose. Such use is therefore desirable but it must not change the lay-out or decoration of the building. It is within these limits only that modifications demanded by a change of function should be envisaged and may be permitted.

ARTICLE 6. The conservation of a monument implies preserving a setting which is not out of scale. Wherever the traditional setting exists, it must be kept. No new construction, demolition or modification which would alter the relations of mass and color must be allowed.

ARTICLE 7. A monument is inseparable from the history to which it bears witness and from the setting in which it occurs. The moving of all or part of a monument cannot be allowed except where the safeguarding of that monument demands it or where it is justified by national or international interest of paramount importance.

ARTICLE 8. Items of sculpture, painting or decoration which form an integral part of a monument may only be removed from it if this is the sole means of ensuring their preservation.

RESTORATION

ARTICLE 9. The process of restoration is a highly specialized operation. Its aim is to preserve and reveal the aesthetic and historic value of the monument and is based on respect for original material and authentic documents. It must stop at the point where conjecture begins, and in this case moreover any extra work which is indispensable must be distinct from the architectural composition and must bear a contemporary stamp. The restoration in any case must be preceded and followed by an archaeological and historical study of the monument.

ARTICLE 10. Where traditional techniques prove inadequate, the consolidation of a monument can be achieved by the use of any modern technique for conservation and construction, the efficacy of which has been shown by scientific data and proved by experience.

ARTICLE 11. The valid contributions of all periods to the building of a monument must be respected, since unity of style is not the aim of a restoration. When a building includes the superimposed work of different periods, the revealing of the underlying state can only be justified in exceptional circumstances and when what is removed is of little interest and the material which is brought to light is of great historical, archaeological or aesthetic value, and its state of preservation good enough to justify the action. Evaluation of the importance of the elements involved and the decision as to what may be destroyed cannot rest solely on the individual in charge of the work.

ARTICLE 12. Replacements of missing parts must integrate harmoniously with the whole, but at the same time must be distinguishable from the original so that restoration does not falsify the artistic or historic evidence.

ARTICLE 13. Additions cannot be allowed except in so far as they do not detract from the interesting parts of the building, its traditional setting, the balance of its composition and its relation with its surroundings.

HISTORIC SITES

ARTICLE 14. The sites of monuments must be the object of special care in order to safeguard their integrity and ensure that they are cleared and presented in a seemly manner. The work of conservation and restoration carried out in such places should be inspired by the principles set forth in the foregoing articles.

EXCAVATIONS

ARTICLE 15. Excavations should be carried out in accordance with scientific standards and the recommendation defining *international principles to be applied in the case of archaeological excavation* adopted by UNESCO in 1956.

Ruins must be maintained and measures necessary for the permanent conservation and protection of architectural features and of objects discovered must be taken. Furthermore, every means must be taken to facilitate the understanding of the monument and to reveal it without ever distorting its meaning.

All reconstruction work should however be ruled out *"a priori."* Only anastylosis, that is to say, the reassembling of existing but dismembered parts can be permitted. The material used for integration should always be recognizable and its use should be the least that will ensure the conservation of a monument and the reinstatement of its form.

PUBLICATION

ARTICLE 16. In all works of preservation, restoration or excavation, there should always be precise documentation in the form of analytical and critical reports, illustrated with drawings and photographs. Every stage of the work of clearing, consolidation, rearrangement and integration, as well as technical and formal features identified during the course of the work, should be included. This record should be placed in the archives of a public institution and made available to research workers. It is recommended that the report should be published.

The following persons took part in the work of the Committee for drafting the International Charter for the Conservation and Restoration of Monuments:

Piero Gazzola (Italy), Chairman
Raymond Lemaire (Belgium), Reporter
Jose Bassegoda-Nonell (Spain)
Luis Benavente (Portugal)
Djurdje Boskovic (Yugoslavia)
Hiroshi Daifuku (UNESCO)
P.L de Vrieze (Netherlands)
Harald Langberg (Demmark)
Mario Matteucci (Italy)
Jean Merlet (France)
Carlos Flores Marini (Mexico)
Roberto Pane (Italy)

S.C.J. Pavel (Czechoslovakia)
Paul Philippot (ICCROM)
Victor Pimentel (Peru)
Harold Plenderleith (ICCROM)
Deoclecio Redig de Campos (Vatican)
Jean Sonnier (France)
Francois Sorlin (France)
Eustathios Stikas (Greece)
Mrs. Gertrud Tripp (Austria)
Jan Zachwatovicz (Poland)
Mustafa S. Zbiss (Tunisia)

Published by ICOMOS Canada under the auspices of the English-Speaking Committee, Ottawa, Canada, August 1983.

A. PREAMBLE

This charter acknowledges The International Charter for the Conservation & Restoration of Monuments & Sites (Venice, 1964), the Australia ICOMOS Charter for the Conservation of Places of Cultural Significance (*the Burra Charter* of February 23, 1981), and the Charter for the Preservation of Quebec's Heritage (Declaration of Deschambault), without which it could not exist.

It further recognizes that the sound management of the built environment is an important cultural activity; and that conservation is an essential component of the management process.

B. FRAMEWORK

Intervention within the built environment may occur at many levels (from preservation to redevelopment), at many scales (from individual building elements to entire sites), and will be characterized by one or more activities, ranging from maintenance to addition.

Though any given project may combine intervention scales, levels and activities, projects should be characterized by a clearly stated goal against which small scale decisions may be measured. The appropriate level of intervention can only be chosen after careful consideration of the merits of the following:

- cultural significance,
- condition and integrity of the fabric,
- contextual value,
- appropriate use of available physical, social and economic resources.

Decisions concerning the relative importance of these factors must represent as broadly based a consensus as possible. Legitimate consensus will involve public participation and must precede initiation of work. The relationship between scales of intervention levels of intervention and intervention activities is summarized below.

ACTIVITY

Levels of Intervention:	Maintenance	Stabilization	Removal	Addition
Preservation	X	X		
Period Restoration	X	X	X	X
Rehabilitation	X	X	X	X
Period Reconstruction			X	
Redevelopment			X	

SCALES OF INTERVENTION

Levels of Intervention:	Bldg Elements	Bldgs	Groups of Buildings	Bldgs and Settings	Sites
Preservation	X	X	X	X	X
Period Restoration	X	X	X	X	X
Rehabilitation	X	X	X	X	X
Period Reconstruction	X	X	X	X	X
Redevelopment	X	X	X	X	X

Levels of Intervention

Preservation:
- retention of the existing form, material and integrity of site.

Period Restoration:
- recovery of an earlier form, material and integrity of a site.

Rehabilitation:
- modification of a resource to contemporary functional standards which may involve adaptation for new use.

Period Reconstruction:
- recreation of vanished or irreversibly deteriorated resources.

Redevelopment:
- insertion of contemporary structures or additions sympathetic to the setting.

Activities

Maintenance:

- continual activity to ensure the longevity of the resource without irreversible or damaging intervention.

Stabilization:

- a periodic activity to halt deterioration and to put the existing form and materials of a site into a state of equilibrium, with minimal change.

Removal:

- a periodic activity: modification which involves the subtraction of surfaces, layers, volumes and/or elements.

Addition:

- a periodic activity: modification which involves the introduction of new material.

C. PRINCIPLES

Respect for the existing fabric is fundamental to the activities of protection and enhancement. The process of protection and enhancement must recognize all interests and have recourse to all fields of expertise which can contribute to the study and safeguarding of a resource. In intervening at the scales, levels and activities described, measures in support of the protection and enhancement of the built environment will involve adherence to the following principles:

Protection

Protection may involve stabilization; it must involve a continuing programme of maintenance.

Artifactual Value

Sites of the highest cultural significance are to be considered primarily as artifacts, demanding protection as fragile and complex historical monuments.

Setting

Any element of the built environment is inseparable from the history to which it bears witness, and from the setting in which it occurs. Consequently, all interventions must deal with the whole as well as with the parts.

Relocation

Relocation and dismantling of an existing resource should be employed only as a last resort, if protection cannot be achieved by any other means.

Enhancement

The activities of removal or addition are characteristic of measures in support of enhancement of the heritage resource.

Use

A property should be used for its originally intended purpose. If this is not feasible, every reasonable effort shall be made to provide a compatible use which requires minimal alteration. Consideration of new use should begin with respect for existing and original traditional patterns of movement and layout.

Additions

New volumes, materials and finishes may be required to satisfy new uses or requirements. They should echo contemporary ideas but respect and enhance the spirit of the original.

Environmental Control

Systems of insulation, environmental control and other servicing should be upgraded in ways which respect the existing and traditional equilibria and do not set in motion processes of deterioration.

D. PRACTICE

Documentation

The better a resource is understood and interpreted, the better it will be protected and enhanced. In order to properly understand and interpret a site, there must be a comprehensive investigation of all those qualities which invest a structure with significance. This activity must precede activity at the site. Work on site must itself be documented and recorded.

Conjecture

Activities which involve the recovery or recreation of earlier forms must be limited to those forms which can be achieved without conjecture.

Distinguishability

New work should be identifiable on close inspection or to the trained eye, but should not impair the aesthetic integrity or coherence of the whole.

Materials and Techniques

Materials and techniques should respect traditional practice unless modern substitutes for which a firm scientific basis exists, which have been supported by a body of experience and which provide significant advantage can be identified.

Patina

Patina forms part of the historic integrity of a resource, and its destruction should be allowed only when essential to the protection of the fabric. Falsification of patina should be avoided.

Reversibility

The use of reversible processes is always to be preferred to allow the widest options for future development or the correction of unforeseen problems, or where the integrity of the resource could be affected.

Integrity

Structural and technological integrity must be respected and will require attention to performance as well as to appearance.

DESCHAMBAULT DECLARATION

Adopted by the Conseil des monuments et des sites du Québec, ICOMOS Canada French-Speaking Committee, April 1982.

1. WHY THE CHARTER?

The postwar period has witnessed the worldwide spread of various currents of thought that seem to adjust people's way of living to new socio-economic conditions, and to criticize the consequences of industrialization, of urbanization on a massive scale, of progress at all costs, and of the consumer society. Whether extreme or moderate, these ideologies have helped to make people aware of certain human values that merited preservation. These things of value include the architectural, artistic or simply material remains that our predecessors have bequeathed us.

The basic principles of heritage preservation were set forth in the Venice International Charter of 1964, which was signed by experts from many countries. The aim of this charter was to regulate and promote efforts to safeguard national heritages. Subsequently, at Amsterdam and Nairobi this initial undertaking was further developed by the addition of other basic principles that expressed an increased desire not only to pass on an accumulated heritage, but also to broaden the concept of heritage itself. Henceforth, people wanted to ensure the preservation of all aspects of national heritage.

This movement began to have a noticeable influence on Quebec from 1960 on. The Quebec government's first action in this field was to create a Ministry of Cultural Affairs which made it possible to pass the Cultural Properties Act in 1972. At that moment our heritage acquired value in the eyes of the law. However, even before this Act was passed, the community had organized itself into groups that differed in structure, but shared a common desire to become involved in safeguarding their environment and culture, and to develop strategies that would make the different levels of government aware of the issue.

This individual and collective commitment resulted in significant achievements in the areas of preservation, stimulation of community participation and development. Whether through municipal, provincial or federal programs, large-scale projects or more modest actions, the people of Quebec have shown that they are interested in their heritage and are determined to revive it.

The *Conseil des monuments et sites du Québec* offers this charter in support of these efforts. The Charter is intended as an orientation guide, a reference tool, a remedy and above all a code of ethics that we should adopt in dealing with our heritage. While this charter draws upon previous experience and on international currents of thought, the principles of preservation and development it contains may be applied by all individuals and organizations that are concerned with the protection of the natural, cultural and historical aspects of the Quebec heritage.

The first aim of this charter, which has been specifically drafted for Quebec, is to try to identify our cultural personality, and thereby define the special nature of our heritage. Secondly, the charter seeks to encourage people to think before they act; and finally, it proposes a framework for action that is positive and objective, that provides incentive, and that takes into account both the particular problems of Quebec and contemporary doctrines of heritage development.

2. THE QUEBEC CULTURAL CONTEXT

The experience of Quebec is similar to that of other nations in that the specific character of its culture has been determined by its history which has taken place in a particular environment. The main features of this environment are a harsh climate, a vast territory, the relatively recent establishment of a North American civilization that is European in origin, the French factor, Catholicism and a particular pattern of human settlement.

Wrested from the American Indians who were its original inhabitants, Quebec became first a French, then a British colony, and finally a part of the Canadian confederation. Quebec's political history has been marked by the struggle to preserve its French and Catholic roots on a North American continent where the majority of the population is and has been English-speaking.

Nevertheless, a variety of elements has contributed to the development of our social fabric. In the course of time, immigrants from different places have been added to the amalgam of the three peoples who originally fought over the territory of Quebec. Sometimes immigration occurred all at once, as in the case of the Loyalists and the Irish; and sometimes it was spread over time, as happened with the Italians and the Chinese. Little by little, the immigrant phenomenon has altered the physiognomy and mentality of Quebec's population.

Our material heritage has been marked not only by this mixture of cultural traits, but also by certain fashions that have had international currency. Of these, the Victorian influence is certainly the most important, but we also find traces of Art Nouveau, the skyscraper era and many other esthetic or technological vogues.

Economic life, that mainspring of societies, has probably had the greatest impact on the distribution of Quebec's population. From the very beginning, more or less densely populated communities were concentrated in areas that had acquired importance because of the fur trade. Seigniorial estates and English townships provided the framework for the development of agriculture. Many elements of our society were drawn northward by the forest products and mining industries. Finally, the spectacular growth of the United States had repercussions of the utmost importance on our economic model and our way of life: massive urbanization, high rate of consumption, establishment of large industrial centres and development of means of transportation for natural, human and energy resources.

Many other factors have contributed to the shaping of our image. The preponderance of Catholicism prompted the proliferation of churches and convents and gave rise to an art that was centered on the sacred. The rigors of the climate forced people to make adaptations in every aspect of their way of life. As for the distribution of population, it was for the most part determined by the waterways of the St. Lawrence basin.

It would be pointless to offer here an exhaustive list of all the geographic, social, historical and economic factors that have contributed to the development of our cultural fabric. Suffice it to say that this ferment of ideas, habits and customs, taking place as it did in a particular geographic context, has given rise to traditions, a folklore, a mentality, ways of doing things, and architecture, a social structure and, in sum, an art of living that is uniquely Quebecois. Though the elements that make up this culture have not all been integrated to the same degree, nor in the same way, their importance cannot be doubted. They constitute our heritage, which is nourished and strengthened by the past, and continues to flourish in the lives of the present generations. We cannot allow this dynamic growth to be cut off from its roots.

3. THE SITUATION TODAY

We felt the need to publish this charter because all too often our heritage is threatened, when it is not forgotten or destroyed. This problem, of course, is not peculiar to Quebec. Modernization and the pursuit of new lifestyles have, in fact, relentlessly imperiled national heritages everywhere. Such is the price of progress!

In Quebec, the great distances between population centres and the immensity of the territory have led to a more or less integrated development. All these factors have been unfavorable to the preservation of our national heritage. Consequently, we must show greater vigilance, enhance dialogue and consultation, and do more to mobilize the forces of the community.

The climate is also, at times, a menace to our architectural heritage and to the remains of former times. Frost, especially combined with thawing, has a serious effect on buildings in Quebec. Rapid and technologically competent action is necessary in this area.

Finally, our European and North American cultural heritage is threatened by a danger that is less perceptible but no less real than the others. Because this culture is of recent origin and only extends over a short span of time, it would be inappropriate to rely solely on chronological classification to determine the relative value of its different elements. One should not, for example, attribute greater value to the remains of the 18th century than to those of the 19th century. Of course, the older things are, the rarer and more valuable they generally are; however, one must use subtlety in judging these matters.

DEFINITION OF HERITAGE AND PRESERVATION

Heritage is defined as "the combined creations and products of nature and man, in their entirety, that make up the environment in which we live in space and time.

Heritage is a reality, a possession of the community, and a rich inheritance that may be passed on, which invites our recognition and our participation." (Quebec Association for the Interpretation of the National Heritage, Committee on Terminology, July 1980).

The concept of heritage as defined above is intended to cover much more than buildings erected in a more or less distant past. Neither in the past nor in the future is heritage limited in time. We use the heritage of yesterday to build the heritage of tomorrow, for culture is by its very nature dynamic and is constantly being renewed and enriched.

Heritage, in our view, is a very comprehensive term that includes three major entities: material culture (cultural properties) and the geographic and human environments. People are, of course, most familiar with the concept of cultural properties since these are defined by law. We should remember, however, that in addition to formal and popular architecture, these properties include all other forms of material evidence, such as archaeological and ethnographical objects, iconography, written archives, furniture, art objects and, in sum, the whole of the material environment in which we live. The geographical environment is nature as it manifests itself on the territory of Quebec in coast, mountain and plain. We wish to insist above all on the great importance of our landscapes and our natural sites, which have a unique esthetic and/or panoramic value. And let us note, finally, that the people in their environment, who have their own customs and traditions, whose memory is furnished with a particular folklore, and whose way of living is adapted to this specific setting, are a human and social treasure that also requires protection.

This broad definition of our national heritage includes, then, all the elements of our civilization, as they exist not only individually but also as components of larger historical, cultural and traditional unities or, to put it in simpler terms, as examples of man's adaptation to his environment. This concept of heritage includes the idea of a cultural landscape which may be defined as the result of the interaction of human society and nature.

Preservation of the national heritage may be viewed, in this light, as that combination of study, expertise and physical intervention which aims at conserving every element of this heritage in the best possible condition. This activity involves proper maintenance, consolidation, repair, safeguarding and restoration, to prevent the deterioration and, at worst, the destruction of the national heritage.

ARTICLE I

The citizens of Quebec are the foremost protectors of the national heritage.

Article I-A

The citizens of Quebec have, in the first place, an individual responsibility to protect their heritage. They must do all they can to appreciate its value, to strive to understand its full significance, and to contribute to its preservation.

Article I-B

This individual responsibility must also find expression in every decision that is made on behalf of the community, whether by elected representatives or by corporate or institutional managers.

ARTICLE II

The national heritage is a treasure that belongs to the community. It is precious and non-renewable.

Article II-A

The national heritage must be preserved, safeguarded and developed for the benefit of present and future generations. This treasure does not belong to us; it has been entrusted to us so we may pass it on to others. We must ensure its proper use and conservation.

Article II-B

All the laws and regulations as well as the fiscal, financial and administrative mechanisms in their entirety must further the preservation and development of the national heritage. This action must start at the municipal level, for the municipalities are the primary legal representatives of the community.

Article II-C

The national heritage must remain in the possession of the people of Quebec, and it must be recognized that cultural properties belong in their place of origin.

Article II-D

The greatest possible attention must be paid to authenticity in preserving and developing the national heritage, and in passing it on to future generations. When only certain elements of this heritage remain, these must be treated as integral wholes. Any action taken must be comprehensible and reversible.

ARTICLE III

Knowledge of the national heritage is an essential prerequisite for its preservation.

Article III-A

All the appropriate means for acquiring this knowledge must be provided. In particular, we must have up-to-date inventories and the specialized expertise that is required before any action can be taken.

ARTICLE IV

The national heritage must enjoy public and unconditional recognition.

Article IV-A

Interdisciplinary teams must assess the cultural, historical, natural, social and aesthetic importance of our heritage on the national, regional and local levels.

Article IV-B

Respect must be shown for the significant contribution of every historical period.

ARTICLE V

The preservation of the national heritage requires maintenance, protection and development.

Article V-A

Protection of our national heritage must be ensured, in the first place, by ongoing maintenance.

Article V-B

The development of cultural properties is of essential importance. This development includes all measures that serve to make them accessible and useful, and that, if necessary, make it possible to reintroduce them into the daily life of the people of Quebec.

Article V-C

Every action to preserve the national heritage should be designed to conserve as much as possible of the original, and to avoid reconstruction based on conjecture.

Article V-D

The development of cultural properties should be followed up by the dissemination of that practical knowledge that is required for passing on these properties to future generations and ensuring their permanent protection.

ARTICLE VI

The national heritage must be given priority in all areas.

Article VI-A

Legislation affecting the national heritage must take precedence over all other legislation.

Article VI-B

The principles of protection and development of the national heritage must have primacy in all development plans.

Article VI-C

When the importance, for our heritage, of a building or group of buildings or landscapes has been recognized, these must take precedence over the rest of the environment. This consideration must be a decisive factor in any alteration of that environment, and the adaption, integration and respect of the heritage material must be ensured.

Article VI-D

Any contemporary additions, which must be creative works in their own right, have to be integrated and harmonized with the surrounding context in regard to tonality, texture, proportions, pattern of filled and empty spaces, and overall composition.

It must not be forgotten that an archaeological analysis of all ground where new construction is planned is absolutely essential, to uncover the earlier remains of construction and habitation and, where necessary, to examine the possibilities of conservation in site.

ARTICLE VII

The public has a legitimate right to participate in any decision in regard to actions to preserve the national heritage.

Article VII-A

At all times, those who may become involved in actions to preserve our heritage have a responsibility to disseminate information on that heritage, to implement procedures ensuring the circulation of ideas, to further community participation, and to promote the preservation of our heritage.

Article VII-B

When the national heritage is affected by a particular action, those responsible for that action must consult with the citizens and inform them of the scope of that action. Documents relating to such actions must be made available to the public and must be prepared in such a way that non-specialists can understand them.

Furthermore, those involved in furthering these actions must develop adequate consultation procedures in order to take note of the opinions of the public. Such procedures will, in particular, include public hearings, information sessions and exhibitions.

ARTICLE VIII

The revival of our heritage must be compatible with the maintenance, and even the improvement, of its specific identity, integrity and cultural values.

Article VIII-A

Our heritage must be employed in such a way as to maintain or introduce functions that are useful to society and that are compatible with the structure and nature of the buildings, spaces and sites of which it is made up. In using our heritage, we must show consideration for its integration into the economic and social activities of the surrounding community.

Article VIII-B

We must promote the continuous use of our heritage, without any interruption of occupation.

Article VIII-C

Whenever we decide to make new use of heritage material, we must ensure the preservation of all the important characteristics of that material. Any changes that are made must, at all times, be reversible.

Article VIII-D

The selection of a new function for heritage material must avoid excessive use and the deterioration that would result from such use.

ARTICLE IX

The preservation of the dynamic and functional character of our heritage is ensured by local residents who are an integral part of that heritage and contribute to its protection and its vitality.

Article IX-A

In using our heritage, we must preserve or reintroduce everyday life rather than the artificial life of museums and tourist centres. Preference should be given to traditional occupations; and we must, in any case, respect the needs and legitimate aspirations of the inhabitants, even if this requires us to adopt uses that are different from the original uses.

Article IX-B

In other words, it is necessary to encourage respect for the established rights of the local population. The housing function should take precedence over all other uses and be given first priority.

ARTICLE X

Our educational institutions must promote the idea that everyone has to take responsibility for preserving the national heritage.

Article X-A

Our educational system must disseminate knowledge pertaining to our heritage, to make people aware of its value and of the need to preserve it.

Article X-B

The educational system must ensure that traditions are passed on, and thereby encourage the training of artisans, technicians and professionals who will be able to work to safeguard our heritage.

Article X-C

Other educational authorities (the family, newspapers and magazines, radio and TV, etc.) must also do their part in furthering heritage education. In particular, heritage practitioners and specialists increase awareness through the communication of their knowledge to the general public.

THE DECLARATION OF AMSTERDAM

The Congress of Amsterdam, the crowning event of European Architectural Heritage Year 1975, and composed of delegates from all parts of Europe, wholeheartedly welcomes the Charter promulgated by the Committee of Ministers of the Council of Europe, which recognizes that Europe's unique architecture is the common heritage of all her peoples and which declared the intention of the Member States to work with one another and with other European governments for its protection.

The Congress likewise affirms that Europe's architectural heritage is an integral part of the cultural heritage of the whole world and has noted with great satisfaction the mutual undertaking to promote cooperation and exchanges in the field of culture contained in the Final Act of the Congress on Security and Cooperation in Europe adopted at Helsinki in July of this year.

In so doing, the Congress emphasized the following basic considerations:

a. Apart from its priceless cultural value, Europe's architectural heritage gives to her peoples the consciousness of their common history and common future. Its preservation is, therefore, a matter of vital importance.

b. The architectural heritage includes not only individual. buildings of exceptional quality and their surroundings, but also all areas of towns or villages of historic or cultural interest.

c. Since these treasures are the joint possession of all the peoples of Europe, they have a joint responsibility to protect them against the growing dangers with which they are threatened—neglect and decay, deliberate demolition, incongruous new construction and excessive traffic.

d. Architectural conservation must be considered, not as a marginal issue, but as a major objective of town and country planning.

e. Local authorities, which whom most of the important planning decisions rest, have a special responsibility for the protection of the architectural heritage and should assist one another by the exchange of ideas and information.

f. The rehabilitation of old areas should be conceived and carried out in such a way as to ensure that, where possible, this does not necessitate a major change in the social composition of the residents, all sections of society should share in the benefits of restoration financed by public funds.

g. The legislative and administrative measures required should be strengthened and made more effective in all countries,

h. To help meet the cost oœ restoration, adaptation and maintenance of buildings and areas of architectural or historic interest, adequate financial assistance should be made available to local authorities and financial support and fiscal relief should likewise be made available to private owners.

i. The architectural heritage will survive only if it is appreciated by the public and in particular by the younger generation. Educational programmes for all ages should, therefore, give increased attention to this subject.

j. Encouragement should be given to independent organizations—international, national and local—which help to awake public interest.

k. Since the new buildings of today will be the heritage of tomorrow, every effort must be made to ensure that contemporary architecture is of a high quality.

In view of the recognition by the Committee of Ministers in the European Charter of the architectural heritage that it is the duty of the Council of Europe to ensure that the Member States pursue coherent policies in a spirit of solidarity, it is essential that periodic reports should be made on the progress of architectural conservation in all European countries in a way which will promote an exchange of experience.

The Congress calls upon governments, parliaments,spiritual and cultural institutions, professional institutes, commerce, industry, independent associations and all individual citizens to give their full support to the objectives of this Declaration and to do all in their power to secure their implementation.

Only in this way can Europe's irreplaceable architectural heritage be preserved, for the enrichment of the lives of all her peoples now and in the future.

Arising from its deliberations, the Congress submits its conclusions and recommendations, as set out below.

Unless a new policy of protection and integrated conservation is urgently implemented, our society will shortly find itself obliged to give up the heritage of buildings and sites which form its traditional environment. Protection is needed today for historic towns, the old quarters of cities, and towns and villages with a traditional character as well as historic parks and gardens, The conservation of these architectural complexes can only be conceived in a wide perspective, embracing all buildings of cultural value, from the greatest to the humblest—not forgetting those of our own day together with their surroundings. This overall protection will complement the piecemeal protection of individual and isolated monuments and sites.

The significance of the architectural heritage and justification for conserving it are now more clearly perceived. It is known that historical continuity must be preserved in the environment if we are to maintain or create surroundings which enable individuals to find their identity and feel secure despite abrupt social changes. A new type of town-planning is seeking to recover the enclosed spaces, the human dimensions, the inter-penetration of functions and the social and cultural diversity that characterized the urban fabric of old towns. But it is also being realized that the conservation of ancient buildings helps to economise resources and combat waste, one of the major preoccupations of present-day society. It has been proved that historic buildings can be given new functions which correspond to the needs of contemporary life. Furthermore, conservation calls for artists and highly-qualified craftsmen whose talents and know-how have to be kept alive and passed on. Lastly, the rehabilitation of existing housing helps to check encroachments on agricultural land and to obviate, or appreciably diminish, movements of population—a very important advantage of conservation policy.

Although, for all these reasons, there seems a stronger justification than ever today for the conservation of the architectural heritage, it must be placed on firm and lasting foundations. It must accordingly be made the subject of basis research and a feature of all educational courses *and cultural* development programmes.

The conservation of the architectural heritage: one of the major objectives of urban and regional planning

The conservation of the architectural heritage should become an integral part of urban and regional planning, instead of being treated as a secondary consideration or one requiring action here and there as has so often been the case in the recent past. A permanent dialogue between conservationists and those responsible for planning is thus indispensable.

Planners should recognize that not all areas are the same and that they should therefore be dealt with according to their individual characteristics. The recognition of the claims of the aesthetic and cultural values of the architectural heritage should lead to the adoption of specific aims and planning rules for old architectural complexes.

It is not enough to simply superimpose, although coordinating them, ordinary planning regulations and specific rules for protecting historic buildings.

To make the necessary integration possible, an inventory of buildings, architectural complexes and sites demarcating protected zones around them is required. It should be widely circulated, particularly among regional and local authorities and officials in charge of town and country planning, in order to draw their attention to the buildings and areas worthy of protection. Such an inventory will furnish a realistic basis for conservation as a fundamental qualitative factor in the management of space.

Regional planning policy must take account of the conservation of the architectural heritage and contribute to it. In particular it can induce new activities to establish themselves in economically declining areas in order to check depopulation and thereby prevent the deterioration of old buildings. In addition, decisions on the development of peripheral urban areas can be orientated in such a way as to reduce pressure on the older neighbourhoods; here transport and employment policies and a better distribution of the focal points of urban activity may have an important impact on the conservation of the architectural heritage.

The full development of a continuous policy of conservation requires a large measure of decentralization as well as a regard for local cultures. This means that there must be people responsible for conservation at all levels (central, regional and local) at which planning decisions are taken. The conservation of the architectural heritage, however, should not merely be a matter for experts. The support of public opinion is essential. The population, on the basis of full and objective information, should take a real part in every stage of the work, from the drawing up of inventories to the preparation of decisions,

Lastly, the conservation of the architectural heritage should become a feature of a new long-term approach which pays due attention to criteria of quality and just proportions and which should make it possible henceforth to reject options and aims which are too often governed by short-term considerations, narrow view of technology and, in short, an obsolete outlook.

Integrated conservation involves the responsibility of local authorities and calls for citizens' participation.

Local authorities should have specific and extensive responsibilities in the protection of the architectural heritage. In applying the principles of integrated conservation, they should take account of the continuity of existing social and physical realities in urban and rural communities. The future cannot and should not be built at the expense of the past.

To implement such a policy, which respects the man-made environment intelligently, sensitively and with economy, local authorities should:

- use as a basis the study of the texture of urban and rural areas, notably their structure, their complex functions, and the architectural and volumetric characteristics of their built-up and open spaces;

- afford functions to buildings which, whilst corresponding to the needs of contemporary life, respect their character and ensure their survival;

- be aware that long-term studies on the development of public services (educational, administrative, medical) indicate that excessive size impairs their quality and effectiveness;

- devote an appropriate part of their budget to such a policy. In this context, they should seek from governments the creation of funds specifically earmarked for such purposes. Local authority grants and loans made to private individuals and various associations should be aimed at stimulating their involvement and financial commitment:

- appoint representatives to deal with all matters concerning the architectural heritage and sites;
- set up special agencies to provide direct links between potential users of buildings and their owners;
- facilitate the formation and efficient functioning of voluntary associations for restoration and rehabilitation.

Local authorities should improve their techniques of consultation for ascertaining the opinions of interested parties on conservation plans and should take these opinions into account from the earliest stages of planning. As part of their efforts to inform the public the decisions of local authorities should be taken in the public eye, using a clear and universally understood language, so that the local inhabitants may learn, discuss and assess the grounds for them. Meeting places should be provided, in order to enable members of the public to consult together.

In this respect, methods such as public meetings, exhibitions, opinion polls, the use of the mass media and all other appropriate methods should become common practice.

The education of young people in environmental issues and their involvement with conservation tasks is one of the most important communal requirements.

Proposals or alternatives put forward by groups or individuals should be considered as an important contribution to planning.

Local authorities can benefit greatly from each other's experience. They should therefore establish a continuing exchange of information and ideas through all available channels.

The success of any policy of integrated conservation depends on taking social factors into consideration.

A policy of conservation also means the integration of the architectural heritage into social life.

The conservation effort to be made must be measured not only against the cultural value of the buildings but also against their use-value. The social problems of integrated conservation can be properly posed only by simultaneous reference to both those scales of values.

The rehabilitation of an architectural complex forming part of the heritage is not necessarily more costly than new building on an existing infrastructure or even than building a new complex on a previously undeveloped site. When therefore comparing the cost of these three solutions, whose social consequences are quite different, it is important not to overlook the social costs. These concern not only owners and tenants but also the craftsmen, tradespeople and building contractors on the spot who keep the district alive.

To avoid the laws of the market having free play in restored and rehabilitated districts, resulting in inhabitants who are unable to pay the increased rents being forced out, public authorities should intervene to reduce the effect of economic factors as they always do when it is a case of low-cost housing. Financial interventions should aim to strike a balance between restoration grants to owners, combined with the fixing of maximum rent, and housing allowances to tenants to cover, in part or in whole, the difference between the old and new rents.

In order to enable the population to participate in the drawing up of programmes they must be given the facts necessary to understand the situation, on the one hand through explaining the historic and architectural value of the buildings to be conserved and on the other hand by being given full details about permanent and temporary rehousing.

This participation is all the more important because it is a matter not only of restoring a few privileged buildings but of rehabilitating whole areas.

This practical way of interesting people in culture would be of considerable social benefit.

Integrated conservation necessitates the adaptation of legislative and administrative measures.

Because the concept of the architectural heritage has been gradually extended from the individual historic building to urban and rural architectural complexes, and to the built testimonies of recent periods, far-reaching legislative reform, in conjunction with an increase in administrative resources, is a pre-requisite to effective action.

This reform must be guided by the need to coordinate regional planning legislation with legislation on the protection of the architectural heritage.

This latter must give a new definition of the architectural heritage and the aims of integrated conservation.

In addition it must make special provision for special procedures with regard to:

- the designation and delineation of architectural complexes;
- the mapping out of protective peripheral zones and the limitations on use to be imposed therein in the public interest;
- the preparation of integrated conservation schemes and the inclusion of their provisions in regional planning policies;
- the approval of projects and authorization to carry out work.

In addition the necessary legislation should be enacted in order to :

- ensure a balanced allocation of budgetary resources between rehabilitation and redevelopment respectively;
- grant citizens who decide to rehabilitate an old building at least the same financial advantages as those which they enjoy for new construction;

- revise the system of state financial aid in the light of the new policy of integrated conservation.

As far as possible, the application of building codes, regulations and requirements should be relaxed to meet the needs of integrated conservation.

In order to increase the operational capacity of the authorities, it is necessary to review the structure of the administration to ensure that the departments responsible for the cultural heritage are organized at the appropriate levels and that sufficient qualified personnel and essential scientific, technical and financial resources are put at their disposal.

These departments should assist local authorities, cooperate with regional planning offices and keep in constant touch with public and private bodies.

Integrated conservation necessitates appropriate financial means.

It is difficult to define a financial policy applicable to all countries or to evaluate the consequences of the different measures involved in the planning process, because of their mutual repercussions.

Moreover, this process is itself governed by external factors resulting from the present structure of society.

It is accordingly for every state to devise its own financing methods and instruments.

It can be established with certainty however, that there is scarcely any country in Europe where the financial means allocated to conservation are sufficient.

It is further apparent that no European country has yet devised the ideal administrative machinery to meet the economic requirements of an integrated conservation policy. In order to solve the economic problems of integrated conservation, it is important—and this is a decisive factor—to draw up legislation subjecting new building to certain restrictions with regard to their volume and dimensions (height, coefficient of utilization etc.) that will make for harmony with its surroundings.

Planning regulations should discourage increased density and promote rehabilitation rather than redevelopment.

Methods must be devised to assess the extra cost occasioned by the constraints of conservation programmes. Where possible, sufficient funds should be available to help owners who are obliged to carry out this restoration work to meet the extra cost—no more and no less.

If the criteria of extra cost were accepted, care would need to be taken of course, to see that the benefit was not diminished by taxation.

The same principle should be applied to the rehabilitation of dilapidated complexes of historic or architectural interest. This would tend to restore the social balance.

The financial advantages and tax concessions available for new building should be accorded in the same proportion for the upkeep and conservation of old buildings, less, of course, any compensation for extra cost that may have been paid.

Authorities should set up Revolving Funds, or encourage them to be established, by providing local authorities or non-profit making associations with the necessary capital. This if particularly applicable to areas where such programmes can become self-financing in the short or the long term because of the rise in value accruing from the high demand for such attractive property.

It is vital, however, to encourage all private sources of finance, particularly coming from industry. Numerous private initiatives have shown the viable part that they can play in association with the authorities at either national or local level.

Integrated conservation requires the promotion of methods, techniques and skills for restoration and rehabilitation.

Methods and techniques of the restoration and rehabilitation of historic complexes should be better exploited and their range developed.

Specialized techniques which have been developed for the restoration of important historic complexes should be henceforth applied to the wide range of buildings and complexes of less outstanding artistic merit. Steps should be taken to ensure that traditional building materials remain available and that traditional crafts and techniques continue to be used. Permanent maintenance of the architectural heritage, will, in the long run, obviate costly rehabilitation operations.

Every rehabilitation scheme should be studied thoroughly before it is carried out. Comprehensive documentation should be assembled about materials and techniques and an analysis of costs should be made. This documentation should be collected and housed in appropriate centres. New materials and techniques should be used only after approval by independent scientific institutions.

Research should be undertaken to compile a catalogue of methods and techniques used for conservation and for this purpose scientific institutions should be created and should cooperate closely with each other. This catalogue should be made readily available and distributed to everyone concerned, thus stimulating the reform of restoration and rehabilitation practices.

There is a fundamental need for better training programme to produce qualified personnel. These programmes should be flexible, multi-disciplinary and should include courses where on-site practical experience can be gained.

International exchange of knowledge, experience and trainees an essential element in the training of all personnel concerned.

This should help to create the required pool of qualified planners, architects, technicians and craftsmen to prepare conservation programmes and help to ensure that particular crafts for restoration work, that are in danger of dying out, will be fostered.

The opportunity for qualifications, conditions of work, salary, employment security and social status should be sufficiently attractive to induce young people to take up and stay in disciplines connected with restoration and rehabilitation work.

Furthermore, the authorities responsible for educational programmes at all levels should endeavour to promote the interest of young people in conservation disciplines.

Adopted by the Council of Europe, October 1975

INTRODUCTION

Thanks to the Council of Europe's initiative in declaring 1975 European Architectural Year, considerable efforts were made in every European country to make the public more aware of the irreplaceable cultural, social and economic values represented by historic monuments, groups of old buildings and interesting sites in both town and country.

It was important to co-ordinate all these efforts at the European level, to work out a joint approach to the subject and, above all, to forge a common language to state the general principles on which concerted action by the authorities responsible and the general public must be based.

It was with this intention that the Council of Europe drafted the Charter which appears below.

It is, of course, not sufficient simply to formulate principles; they must also be applied.

In future, the Council of Europe will devote its efforts to a thorough study of ways and means of applying the principles in each different country, the steady improvement of existing laws and regulations and the development of vocational training in this field.

The European Charter of the Architectural Heritage has been adopted by the Committee of Ministers of the Council of Europe and was solemnly proclaimed at the Congress on the European Architectural Heritage held in Amsterdam from 21 to 25 October 1975.

THE COMMITTEE OF MINISTERS

Considering that the aim of the Council of Europe is to achieve a greater unity between its members for the purpose of safeguarding and realizing the ideals and principles which are their common heritage;

Considering that the member states of the Council of Europe which have adhered to the European Cultural

Convention of 19 December 1954 committed themselves, under Article 1 of that convention, to take appropriate measures to safeguard and to encourage the development of their national contributions to the common cultural heritage of Europe;

Recognizing that the architectural heritage, an irreplaceable expression of the wealth and diversity of European culture, is shared by all people and that all the European States must show real solidarity in preserving that heritage;

Considering that the future of the architectural heritage depends largely upon its integration into the context of people's lives and upon the weight given to it in regional and town planning and development schemes;

Having regard to the Recommendation of the European Conference of Ministers responsible for the preservation and rehabilitation of the cultural heritage of monuments and sites held in Brussels in 1969, and to Recommendation 589 (1970) of the Consultative Assembly of the Council of Europe calling for a charter relating to the architectural heritage;

Asserts its determination to promote a common European policy and concerted action to protect the architectural heritage based on the principles of integrated conservation;

Recommends that the governments of member states should take the necessary legislative, administrative, financial and educational steps to implement a policy of integrated conservation for the architectural heritage, and to arouse public interest in such a policy, taking into account the results of the European Architectural Heritage Year campaign organized in 1975 under the auspices of the Council of Europe;

Adopts and proclaims the principles of the following charter, drawn up by the Council of Europe Committee on Monuments and Sites:

1. *The European architectural heritage consists not only of our most important monuments: it also includes the groups of lesser buildings in our old towns and characteristic villages in their natural or manmade settings.*

For many years, only major monuments were protected and restored and then without reference to their surroundings. More recently it was realized that, if the surroundings are impaired, even those monuments can lose much of their character.

Today it is recognized that entire groups of buildings, even if they do not include any example of outstanding merit, may have an atmosphere that gives them the quality of works of art, welding different periods and styles into a harmonious whole. Such groups should also be preserved.

The architectural heritage is an expression of history and helps us to understand the relevance of the past to contemporary life.

2. *The past as embodied in the architectural heritage provides the sort of environment indispensable to a balanced and complete life.*

In the face of a rapidly changing civilization, in which brilliant successes are accompanied by grave perils, people today have an instinctive feeling for the value of this heritage.

This heritage should be passed on to future generations in its authentic state and in all its variety as an essential part of the memory of the human race. Otherwise, part of man's awareness of his own continuity will be destroyed.

3. *The architectural heritage is a capital of irreplaceable spiritual, cultural, social and economic value.*

Each generation places a different interpretation on the past and derives new inspiration from it. This capital has been built up over the centuries; the destruction of any part of it leaves us poorer since nothing new that we create, however fine, will make good the loss.

Our society now has to husband its resources. Far from being a luxury this heritage is an economic asset which can be used to save community resources.

4. *The structure of historic centres and sites is conducive to a harmonious social balance.*

By offering the right conditions for the development of a wide range of activities our old towns and villages favoured social integration. They can once again lend themselves to a beneficial spread of activities and to a more satisfactory social mix.

5. *The architectural heritage has an important part to play in education.*

The architectural heritage provides a wealth of material for explaining and comparing forms and styles and their applications. Today when visual appreciation and first-hand experience play a decisive role in education, it is essential to keep alive the evidence of different periods and their achievements.

The survival of this evidence will be assured only if the need to protect it is understood by the greatest number, particularly by the younger generation who will be its future guardians.

6. *This heritage is in danger.*

It is threatened by ignorance, obsolescence, deterioration of every kind and neglect. Urban planning can be destructive when authorities yield too readily to economic pressures and to the demands of motor traffic. Misapplied contemporary technology and ill-considered restoration may be disastrous to old structures. Above all, land and property speculation feeds upon all errors and omissions and brings to nought the most carefully laid plans.

7. *Integrated conservation averts these dangers.*

Integrated conservation is achieved by the application of sensitive restoration techniques and the correct choice of appropriate functions. In the course of history the hearts of towns and sometimes villages have been left to deteriorate and have turned into areas of substandard housing. Their deterioration must be undertaken in a spirit of social justice and should not cause the departure of the poorer inhabitants. Because of this, conservation must be one of the first considerations in all urban and regional planning.

It should be noted that integrated conservation does not rule out the introduction of modern architecture into areas containing old buildings provided that the existing context, proportions, forms, sizes and scale are fully respected and traditional materials are used.

8. *Integrated conservation depends on legal, administrative, financial and technical support.*

Legal

Integrated conservation should make full use of all existing laws and regulations that can contribute to the protection and preservation of the architectural heritage. Where such laws and regulations are insufficient for the purpose they should be supplemented by appropriate legal instruments at national, regional and local levels.

Administrative

In order to carry out a policy of integrated conservation, properly staffed administrative services should be established.

Financial

Where necessary the maintenance and restoration of the architectural heritage and individual parts thereof should be encouraged by suitable forms of financial aid and incentives, including tax measures.

It is essential that the financial resources made available by public authorities for the restoration of historic centres should be at least equal to those allocated for new construction.

Technical

There are today too few architects, technicians of all kinds, specialized firms and skilled craftsmen to respond to all the needs of restoration.

It is necessary to develop training facilities and increase prospects of employment for the relevant managerial, technical and manual skills. The building industry should be urged to adapt itself to these needs. Traditional crafts should be fostered rather than allowed to die out.

9. *Integrated conservation cannot succeed without the cooperation of all.*

Although the architectural heritage belongs to everyone, each of its parts is nevertheless at the mercy of any individual.

The public should be properly informed because citizens are entitled to participate in decisions affecting their environment.

Each generation has only a life interest in this heritage and is responsible for passing it on to future generations.

10. *The European architectural heritage is the common property of our continent.*

Conservation problems are not peculiar to any one country. They are common to the whole of Europe and should be dealt with in a coordinated manner. It lies with the Council of Europe to ensure that member states pursue coherent policies in a spirit of solidari.

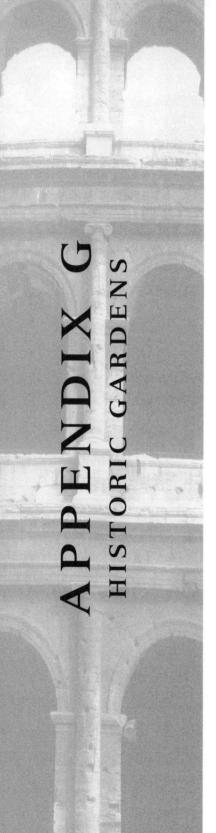

The ICOMOS-IFLA International Committee for Historic Gardens, meeting in Florence on 21 May 1981, decided to draw up a charter on the preservation of historic gardens which would bear the name of that town. The present Florence Charter was drafted by the Committee and registered by ICOMOS on 15 December 1982 as an addendum to the Venice Charter covering the specific field concerned.

DEFINITIONS AND OBJECTIVES

Art. 1. "An historic garden is an architectural and horticultural composition of interest to the public from the historical or artistic point of view." As such, it is to be considered as a monument.

Art. 2. "The historic garden is an architectural composition whose constituents are primarily vegetal and therefore living, which means that they are perishable and renewable." Thus its appearance reflects the perpetual balance between the cycle of the seasons, the growth and decay of nature and the desire of the artist and craftsman to keep it permanently unchanged.

Art. 3. As a monument, the historic garden must be preserved in accordance with the spirit of the Venice Charter. However, since it is a living monument, its preservation must be governed by specific rules which are the subject of the Present charter.

Art. 4. The architectural composition of the historic garden includes:

- Its plan and its topography.
- Its vegetation, including its species, proportions, colour schemes, spacing and respective heights.
- Its structural and decorative features.
- Its water, running or still, reflecting the sky.

Art. 5. As the expression of the direct affinity between civilization and nature, and as a place of enjoyment suited to meditation or repose, the garden thus acquires the cosmic significance of an idealized image of the world, a "paradise" in the etymological sense of the term, and yet a testimony to a culture, a style, an age, and often to the originality of a creative artist.

Art. 6. The term, "historic garden," is equally applicable to small gardens and to large parks, whether formal or "landscape."

Art. 7. Whether or not it is associated with a building in which case it is an inseparable complement, the historic garden cannot be isolated from its own particular environment, whether urban or rural, artificial or natural.

Art. 8. An historic site is a specific landscape associated with a memorable act, as, for example, a major historic event; a well-known myth; an epic combat; or the subject of a famous picture.

Art. 9. The preservation of historic gardens depends on their identification and listing. They require several kinds of action, namely maintenance, conservation and restoration. In certain cases, reconstruction may be recommended. The authenticity of an historic garden depends as much on the design and scale of its various parts as on its decorative features and on the choice of plant or inorganic materials adopted for each of its parts.

MAINTENANCE, CONSERVATION, RESTORATION, RECONSTRUCTION

Art. 10. In any work of maintenance, conservation, restoration or reconstruction of an historic garden, or of any part of it, all its constituent features must be dealt with simultaneously. To isolate the various operations would damage the unity of the whole.

MAINTENANCE AND CONSERVATION

Art. 11. Continuous maintenance of historic gardens is of paramount importance. Since the principal material is vegetal, the preservation of the garden in an unchanged condition requires both prompt replacements when required and a long-term programme of periodic renewal (clear felling and replanting with mature specimens).

Art. 12. Those species of trees, shrubs, plants and flowers to be replaced periodically must be selected with regard for established and recognized practice in each botanical and horticultural region, an with the aim to determine the species initially grown and to preserve them.

Art. 13. The permanent or movable architectural, sculptural or decorative features which form an integral part of the historic garden must be removed or displaced only insofar as this is essential for their conservation or restoration. The replacement or restoration of any such jeopardized features must be effected in accordance with the principles of the Venice Charter, and the date of any complete replacement must be indicated.

Art. 14. The historic garden must be preserved in appropriate surroundings. Any alteration to the physical environment which will endanger the ecological equilibrium must be prohibited. These applications are applicable to all aspects of the infrastructure, whether internal or external (drainage works, irrigation systems, roads, car parks, fences, caretaking facilities, visitors' amenities, etc.).

RESTORATION AND RECONSTRUCTION

Art. 15. No restoration work and, above all, no reconstruction work on an historic garden shall be undertaken without thorough prior research to ensure that such work is scientifically executed and which will involve everything from excavation to the assembling of records relating to the garden in question and to similar gardens. Before any practical work starts, a project must be prepared on the basis of said research and must be submitted to a group of experts for joint examination and approval.

Art. 16. Restoration work must respect the successive stages of evolution of the garden concerned. In principle, no one period should be given precedence over any other, except in exceptional cases where the degree of damage or destruction affecting certain parts of a garden may be such that it is decided to reconstruct it on the basis of the traces that survive or of unimpeachable documentary evidence. Such reconstruction work might be undertaken more particularly on the parts of the garden nearest to the building it contains in order to bring out their significance in the design.

Art. 17. Where a garden has completely disappeared or there exists no more than conjectural evidence of its successive stages a reconstruction could not be considered an historic garden.

USE

Art. 18. While any historic garden is designed to be seen and walked about in, access to it must be restricted to the extent demanded by its size and vulnerability, so that its physical fabric and cultural message may be preserved.

Art. 19. By reason of its nature and purpose, an historic garden is a peaceful place conducive to human contacts, silence and awareness of nature. This conception of its everyday use must contrast with its role on those rare occasions when it accomodates a festivity. Thus, the conditions of such occasional use of an historic garden should be clearly defined, in order that any such festivity may itself serve to enhance the visual effect of the garden instead of perverting or damaging it.

Art. 20. While historic gardens may be suitable for quiet games as a daily occurrence, separate areas appropriate for active and lively games and sports should also be laid out adjacent to the historic garden, so that the needs of the public may be satisfied in this respect without prejudice to the conservation of the gardens and landscapes.

Art. 21. The work of maintenance and conservation, the timing of which is determined by season and brief operations which serve to restore the garden's authenticity, must always take precedence over the requirements of public use. All arrangements for visits to historic gardens must be subjected to regulations that ensure the spirit of the place is preserved.

Art. 22. If a garden is walled, its walls may not be removed without prior examination of all the possible consequences liable to lead to changes in its atmosphere and to affect its preservation.

LEGAL AND ADMINISTRATIVE PROTECTION

Art. 23. It is the task of the responsible authorities to adopt, on the advice of qualified experts, the appropriate legal and administrative measures for the identification, listing and protection of historic gardens. The preservation of such gardens must be provided for within the framework of land-use plans and such provision must be duly mentioned in documents relating to regional and local planning. It is also the task of the responsible authorities to adopt, with the advice of qualified experts, the financial measures which will facilitate the maintenance, conservation and restoration, and, where necessary, the reconstruction of historic gardens.

Art. 24. The historic garden is one of the features of the patrimony whose survival, by reason of its nature, requires intensive, continuous care by trained experts. Suitable provision should therefore be made for the training of such persons, whether historians, architects, landscape architects, gardeners or botanists. Care should also be taken to ensure that there is regular propagation of the plant varieties necessary for maintenance or restoration.

Art. 25. Interest in historic gardens should be stimulated by every kind of activity capable of emphasizing their true value as Part of the patrimony and making for improved knowledge and appreciation of them: promotion of scientific research; international exchange and circulation of information; publications, including works designed for the general public; the encouragement of public access under suitable control and use of the media to develop awareness of the need for due respect for nature and the historic heritage. The most outstanding of the historic gardens shall be proposed for inclusion in the World Heritage List.

NOTA BENE

The above recommendations are applicable to all the historic gardens in the world. Additional clauses applicable to specific types of gardens may be subsequently appended to the present Charter with brief descriptions of the said types.

The ICOMOS Charter for the Conservation of Historic Towns and Urban Areas is the result of 12 years of study and development by international specialists. The document was adopted at the October 1987 meeting of the ICOMOS General Assembly in Washington, DC, and is known commonly as the *"Washington Charter."* The terms of the Charter are purposefully broad; internationally, there are many methods of planning and protection for historic urban areas, many ways that urban development may impact on the patterns of post-industrial societies, and this diversity is addressed in the Charter. The text of the Charter follows.

PREAMBLE AND DEFINITIONS

1. All urban communities, whether they have developed gradually over time or have been created deliberately, are an expression of the diversity of societies throughout history.

2. This charter concerns historic urban areas, large and small, including cities, towns and historic centres or quarters, together with their natural and man-made environments. Beyond their role as historical documents, these areas embody the values of traditional urban cultures. Today many such areas are being threatened, physically degraded, damaged or even destroyed, by the impact of the urban development that follows industrialization in societies everywhere.

3. Faced with this dramatic situation, which often leads to irreversible cultural, social and even economic losses, the International Council on Monuments and Sites (ICOMOS) deems it necessary to draw up an international charter for historic towns and urban areas that will complement the "International Charter for the Conservation and Restoration of Monuments and Sites," usually referred to as "The Venice Charter." This new text defines the principles, objectives, and methods necessary for the conservation of historic towns and urban areas. It also seeks to promote

the harmony of both private and community life in these areas and to encourage the preservation of those cultural properties, however modest in scale, that constitute the memory of mankind.

4. As set out in the UNESCO "Recommendation Concerning the Safeguarding and Contemporary Role of Historic Areas" (Warsaw-Nairobi, 1976), and also in various other international instruments, "the conservation of historic towns and urban areas" is understood to mean those steps necessary for the protection, conservation and restoration of such towns and areas as well as their development and harmonious adaptation to contemporary life.

PRINCIPLES AND OBJECTIVES

1. In order to be most effective, the conservation of historic towns and other historic urban areas should be an integral part of coherent policies of economic and social development and of urban and regional planning at every level.

2. Qualities to be preserved include the historic character of the town or urban area and all those material and spiritual elements that express this character, especially:

   a) urban patterns as defined by lots and streets;

   b) relationships between buildings and green and open spaces;

   c) the formal appearance, interior and exterior, of buildings as defined by scale, size, style, construction, materials, colour and decoration;

   d) the relationship between the town or urban area and its surrounding setting, both natural and man-made; and

   e) the various functions that the town or urban area has acquired over time.

   Any threat to these qualities would compromise the authenticity of the historic town or urban area.

3. The participation and the involvement of the residents are essential for the success of the conservation programme and should be encouraged. The conservation of historic towns and urban areas concerns their residents first of all.

4. Conservation in an historic town or urban area demands prudence, a systematic approach and discipline. Rigidity should be avoided since individual cases may present specific problems.

Methods and instruments

5. Planning for the conservation of historic towns and urban areas should be preceded by multidisciplinary studies.

- Conservation plans must address all relevant factors including archaeology, history, architecture, techniques, sociology and economics.
- The principal objectives of the conservation plan should be clearly stated as should the legal, administrative and financial measures necessary to attain them.
- The conservation plan should aim at ensuring a harmonious relationship between the historic urban areas and the town as a whole.
- The conservation plan should determine which buildings must be preserved, which should be preserved under certain circumstances and which, under quite exceptional circumstances, might be expendable.
- Before any intervention, existing conditions in the area should be thoroughly documented.
- The conservation plan should be supported by the residents of the historic area.

6. Until a conservation plan has been adopted, any necessary conservation activity should be carried out in accordance with the principles and the aims of this Charter and the Venice Charter.

7. Continuing maintenance is crucial to the effective conservation of an historic town or urban area.

8. New functions and activities should be compatible with the character of the historic town or urban area.

   Adaptation of these areas to contemporary life requires the careful installation or improvement of public service facilities.

9. The improvement of housing should be one of the basic objectives of conservation.

10. When it is necessary to construct new buildings or adapt existing ones, the existing spatial layout should be respected, especially in terms of scale and lot size.

   The introduction of contemporary elements in harmony with the surroundings should not be discouraged since such features can contribute to the enrichment of an area.

11. Knowledge of the history of an historic town or urban area should be expanded through archaeological investigation and appropriate preservation of archaeological findings.

12. Traffic inside an historic town or urban area must be controlled and parking areas must be planned so that they do not damage the historic fabric or its environment.

13. When urban or regional planning provides for the construction of major motorways, they must not penetrate an historic town or urban area, but they should Improve access to them.

14. Historic towns should be protected against natural disasters and nuisances such as pollution and vibrations in order to safeguard the heritage and for the security and well-being of the residents.

    Whatever the nature of a disaster affecting an historic town or urban area, preventative and repair measures must be adapted to the specific character of the properties concerned.

15. In order to encourage their participation and involvement, a general information programme should be set up for all residents, beginning with children of school age.

16. Specialized training should be provided for all those professions concerned with conservation.

The Congress for the New Urbanism views disinvestment in central cities, the spread of placeless sprawl, increasing separation by race and income, environmental deterioration, loss of agricultural lands and wilderness, and the erosion of society's built heritage as one interrelated community-building challenge.

We stand for the restoration of existing urban centers and towns within coherent metropolitan regions, the reconfiguration of sprawling suburbs into communities of real neighborhoods and diverse districts, the conservation of natural environments, and the preservation of our built legacy.

We recognize that physical solutions by themselves will not solve social and economic problems, but neither can economic vitality, community stability, and environmental health be sustained without a coherent and supportive physical framework.

We advocate the restructuring of public policy and development practices to support the following principles: neighborhoods should be diverse in use and population; communities should be designed for the pedestrian and transit as well as the car; cities and towns should be shaped by physically defined and universally accessible public spaces and community institutions; urban places should be framed by architecture and landscape design that celebrate local history, climate, ecology, and building practice.

We represent a broad-based citizenry, composed of public and private sector leaders, community activists, and multidisciplinary professionals. We are committed to reestablishing the relationship between the art of building and the making of community, through citizen-based participatory planning and design.

We dedicate ourselves to reclaiming our homes, blocks, streets, parks, neighborhoods, districts, towns, cities, regions, and environment.

We assert the following principles to guide public policy, development practice, urban planning, and design:

METROPOLIS, CITY, AND TOWN

1. Metropolitan regions are finite places with geographic boundaries derived from topography, watersheds, coastlines, farmlands, regional parks, and river basins. The metropolis is made of multiple centers that are cities, towns, and villages, each with its own identifiable center and edges.

2. The metropolitan region is a fundamental economic unit of the contemporary world. Governmental cooperation, public policy, physical planning, and economic strategies must reflect this new reality.

3. The metropolis has a necessary and fragile relationship to its agrarian hinterland and natural landscapes. The relationship is environmental, economic, and cultural. Farmland and nature are as important to the metropolis as the garden is to the house.

4. Development patterns should not blur or eradicate the edges of the metropolis. Infill development within existing urban areas conserves environmental resources, economic investment, and social fabric, while reclaiming marginal and abandoned areas. Metropolitan regions should develop strategies to encourage such infill development over peripheral expansion.

5. Where appropriate, new development contiguous to urban boundaries should be   organized as neighborhoods and districts, and be integrated with the existing urban pattern. Noncontiguous development should be organized as towns and villages with their own urban edges, and planned for a jobs/housing balance, not as bedroom suburbs.

6. The development and redevelopment of towns and cities should respect historical patterns, precedents, and boundaries.

7. Cities and towns should bring into proximity a broad spectrum of public and private uses to support a regional economy that benefits people of all incomes. Affordable housing should be distributed throughout the region to match job opportunities and to avoid concentrations of poverty.

8. The physical organization of the region should be supported by a framework of transportation alternatives. Transit, pedestrian, and bicycle systems should maximize access and mobility throughout the region while reducing dependence upon the automobile.

9. Revenues and resources can be shared more cooperatively among the municipalities and centers within regions to avoid destructive competition for tax base and to promote rational coordination of transportation, recreation, public services, housing, and community institutions.

THE DISTRICT AND THE CORRIDOR

10. The neighborhood, the district, and the corridor are the essential elements of development and redevelopment in the metropolis. They form identifiable areas that encourage citizens to take responsibility for their maintenance and evolution.

11. Neighborhoods should be compact, pedestrian-friendly, and mixed-use. Districts generally emphasize a special single use, and should follow the principles of neighborhood design when possible. Corridors are regional connectors of neighborhoods and districts; they range from boulevards and rail lines to rivers and parkways.

12. Many activities of daily living should occur within walking distance, allowing independence to those who do not drive, especially the elderly and the young. Interconnected networks of streets should be designed to encourage walking, reduce the number and length of automobile trips, and conserve energy.

13. Within neighborhoods, a broad range of housing types and price levels can bring people of diverse ages, races, and incomes into daily interaction, strengthening the personal and civic bonds essential to an authentic community.

14. Transit corridors, when properly planned and coordinated, can help organize metropolitan structure and revitalize urban centers. In contrast, highway corridors should not displace investment from existing centers.

15. Appropriate building densities and land uses should be within walking distance of transit stops, permitting public transit to become a viable alternative to the automobile.

16. Concentrations of civic, institutional, and commercial activity should be embedded in neighborhoods and districts, not isolated in remote, single-use complexes. Schools should be sized and located to enable children to walk or bicycle to them.

17. The economic health and harmonious evolution of neighborhoods, districts, and corridors can be improved through graphic urban design codes that serve as predictable guides for change.

18. A range of parks, from tot-lots and village greens to ballfields and community gardens, should be distributed within neighborhoods. Conservation areas and open lands should be used to define and connect different neighborhoods and districts.

19. A primary task of all urban architecture and landscape design is the physical definition of streets and public spaces as places of shared use.

20. Individual architectural projects should be seamlessly linked to their surroundings. This issue transcends style.

21. The revitalization of urban places depends on safety and security. The design of streets and buildings should reinforce safe environments, but not at the expense of accessibility and openness.

22. In the contemporary metropolis, development must adequately accommodate automobiles. It should do so in ways that respect the pedestrian and the form of public space.

23. Streets and squares should be safe, comfortable, and interesting to the pedestrian. Properly configured, they encourage walking and enable neighbors to know each other and protect their communities.

24. Architecture and landscape design should grow from local climate, topography, history, and building practice.

25. Civic buildings and public gathering places require important sites to reinforce community identity and the culture of democracy. They deserve distinctive form, because their role is different from that of other buildings and places that constitute the fabric of the city.

26. All buildings should provide their inhabitants with a clear sense of location, weather and time. Natural methods of heating and cooling can be more resource-efficient than mechanical systems.

27. Preservation and renewal of historic buildings, districts, and landscapes affirm the continuity and evolution of urban society.

PART 6

Old and Historic District and Old City District Regulations

Sec. 54-230: Purpose of Creating Districts

In order to promote the economic and general welfare of the city and of the public generally, and to insure the harmonious, orderly and efficient growth and development of the municipality, it is deemed essential by the city council of the city that the qualities relating to the history of the city and a harmonious outward appearance of structures which preserve property values and attract tourist and residents alike be preserved; some of these qualities being the continued existence and *preservation* of historic areas and buildings; continued construction of buildings in the historic styles and a general harmony as to style, form, color, proportion, texture and material between buildings of historic design and those of more modern design; that such purpose is advanced through the *preservation* and protection of the old historic or architecturally worthy structures and quaint neighborhoods which impart a district aspect to the city and which serve as visible reminders of the historical and cultural heritage of the city, the state, and the nation.

Sec. 54-231: Designation of Old City District and Old and Historic Districts; Definitions

a. For the purpose of this article, two types of special districts are established, as follows:

1. The old city. The boundaries of the Old City District shall include the entire peninsula city of the city, south of Line Street and south of lines projected from the eastern and western ends of Line Street, in easterly and westerly directions to the Ashley and Cooper Rivers, excluding the Old and Historic District.

2. Old and Historic Districts. The boundaries of the Old and Historic Districts are as delineated upon the zone map, a part of the zoning ordinance of the city.

b. For the purposes of this article, "exterior architectural appearance" shall included architectural character, general composition and general arrangement of the exterior of a structure, including the kind, color and texture of the building material and type and character of all windows, doors, light fixtures, signs and appurtenant elements, visible from a street or public thoroughfare.

c. For the purposes of this article, "structure" shall include walls, fences, signs, light fixtures, steps or appurtenant elements thereof.

Sec. 54-232: Construction or Demolition of Building in Districts; Permit Required; Certificate of Approval

a.   No structure which is within the Old and Historic District shall be erected, demolished or removed in whole or in part, nor shall the exterior architectural appearance of any structure which is visible from the public right-of-way be altered until after an application for a permit has been submitted to and approved by the Board of Architectural Review.

b.   No structure, either more than 75 years old or listed in groups 1, 2, and 3 on the historic inventory map adopted by 54-235, which is within the Old City District but outside of an Old and Historic Charleston District shall be demolished, removed in whole or part, or relocated until after an application for a permit has been submitted to the Board of Architectural Review and either has been approved by it or the period of postponement in the case of application for partial or total demolition hereafter provided for in 54-240, d., has expired.

c.   The exterior architectural appearance of any structure, either more than one hundred years old or listed in Groups 1, 2, and 3 on the historic inventory map adopted by 54-235, which is within the Old City District but outside of an Old and Historic District, and which is visible from the public right-of-way, shall not be changed until after an application for a permit has been submitted to and approved by the Board of Architectural Review.

d.   Within the Old City District no new building which will be visible from a public right-of-way upon its completion shall be erected until after an application for a permit has been submitted to and approved by the Board of Architectural Review.

e.   Evidence of the approval required above shall be a certificate of appropriateness issued by the Board of Architectural Review as created herein. Such certificate shall be a statement signed by the chairman of the Board of Architectural Review stating that the demolition or the changes in the exterior architectural appearance of the proposed construction, reconstruction, alteration or restoration for which application has been made are approved by the Board of Architectural Review. Provided, however, that repairs and renovations to existing buildings which do not alter the exterior appearance and are so exempted by the administrative officer as herein provided need not be approved by the Board of Architectural Review.

f.   Any person requesting a permit under this section and article shall be entitled to a hearing on such request before the Board of Architectural Review.

Sec. 54-233: Board of Architectural Review Created; Composition; Appointment and Terms of Office

a.   A Board of Architectural Review is hereby established.

b.   The Board of Architectural Review shall consist of seven (7) citizen members who do not hold any other public office or position in the City of Charleston and are appointed by City Council. Of the members appointed, two (2) shall be architects, one (1) an engineer, and one (1) an attorney, all of whom must be residents of the City of Charleston.

c.   The initial terms of three (3) of seven (7) members first appointed shall expire on the date of the first regular City Council meeting in January following their appointment, and initial terms of the other four (4) of the seven (7) members first appointed shall expire on the date of the first regular City Council meeting in January two years thereafter. Following the initial term, the terms of all members shall be four years. No member shall serve more than two successive four-year terms. An appointment to fill a vacancy shall be only for the unexpired portion of the term.

d.   The board shall elect one of its members chairman, who shall serve for one year or until he is re-elected or his successor is elected and qualified. The board shall appoint a secretary who may be an officer of the governing authority or of the Board of Architectural Review. The board shall adopt rules of procedure in accordance with the provisions of any ordinance adopted pursuant to this chapter.

e.   Meetings of the board must be held at the call of the chairman and at such other times as the board may determine. The chairman or, in his or her absence, the acting chairman, may administer oaths and compel the attendance of witnesses by subpoena. The board shall keep minutes of its proceedings, showing the vote of each member upon each question, or if absent or failing to vote, indicating the fact, and shall keep records of its examinations and other official actions, all of which immediately must be filed in the office of the board and must be a public record.

(Ord. No. 1999-54, § 2A, 4-27-99; Ord. No. 2000-35, § 1, 3-14-00)

Sec. 54-234: Meeting of Board

a. The Board of Architectural Review may meet at any time upon call of the chairman and, in addition, shall within fifteen (15) days after notification by the administrative officer of the filing of an application for a permit to demolish any building in whole or in part, hold a public hearing upon each application. At least three (3) days notice of the time and place of each such hearing shall be given by the administrative officer as follows:

1. In writing to the applicant.

2. In writing to all persons or organizations who have filed an annual written request for such notices and have paid an annual fee, not to exceed twenty-five dollars ($25), to cover the costs involved.

3. By publication in the form of an advertisement in a newspaper of general circulation within the city.

Sec. 54-235: Adoption of Inventory Map; Procedure for Revision

In order to identify structures within peninsula Charleston south of Highway 17 which should be preserved, maintained and protected in the public interest and to provide guidance for the Board of Architectural Review there hereby is adopted as an official public document the inventory map entitled "Historic Architecture Inventory, 1972-73, Peninsula City, Charleston, S.C.," prepared for the city by Carl Feiss, FAIA, AIP, City Planning and Architectural Associates, and Russell Wright, AIP, consisting of peninsula Charleston south of Highway 17, said additional sheets being dated September 4, 1973, with revisions September 11, 1973, October 16, 1973, November 14, 1973, February 20, 1974 and March 27, 1974, and as amended by the inventory map entitled "South Carolina Inventory of Historic Places Survey Report, City of Charleston, S.C." prepared for the city by Geier Brown Renfrow Architects and dated August 1985. The original of the said inventory map shall be filed in the Department of Planning and Urban Development as a public record and shall be available for public inspection during normal business hours. Based on changed conditions, the Board of Architectural Review from time to time may recommend to the City Council additional revisions of said inventory map, but none shall become effective until the Zoning Ordinance has been appropriately amended.

Sec. 54-236: Guidance Standards; Maintenance of Consistent Policy

In order to provide guidance and insight into desirable goals and objectives for the Old City District and the old and historic Charleston districts or for desirable types of development, and for the maintenance of consistent policies in guiding the building public toward better standards of design, the Board of Architectural Review shall maintain a file containing records of all applications brought before the board for review, the action taken by the board, drawings submitted and amendments of drawings approved pertaining thereto, and drawings and photographs or reproductions thereof showing structures in authentic Charleston character which, in its opinion, may serve as general guides to appropriateness or as expression of objectives to prospective developers or property owners. Such documents shall remain the property of the city but be held in the custody of the Board of Architectural Review.

Sec. 54-237: Preapplication Review of Plans by Board Required; Procedure

Prior to the preparation of working drawings and specifications or calling for proposals or bids from contractors, prospective property developers, owners or agents shall prepare preliminary scale drawings and outline specifications, including color samples for outside work, for review and informal discussion with the Board of Architectural Review. The purpose of this review shall be to acquaint the developer, owner or agent with standards of appropriateness of design that are required of his proposed development.

The required preapplication review shall not require formal application but does require notice to be given to the administrative officer and subsequent notification of the chairman of the Board of Architectural Review at least ten (10) days before the date of the meeting at which the preliminary drawings are to be discussed. All documents submitted at this meeting shall be in triplicate prepared in a form suitable for filing in a standard size office filing cabinet.

In the case of very minor projects involving repair or alterations to existing buildings, the Board of Architectural Review, if the preliminary drawings and other data are sufficiently clear and explicit, may grant preliminary and final approval at one review session. Should said data indicate alterations, remodeling, or repairs not changing the exterior appearance, the administrative officer may exempt the application from provisions of this section and approve a permit.

Sec. 54-238: Contents of Application

a.   Drawings required for alterations and/or additions to existing structures or for new construction. Every application or review involving (a) alterations and/or additions to existing structures in an Old and Historic Charleston District, or (b) existing structures over one hundred years old in the Old City District, or (c) the erection of any new structure within an Old and Historic Charleston district shall be accompanied by drawings signed by the architect or draftsman and submitted in triplicate for the proposed alterations, additions or changes and for new construction of buildings or property use.

As used herein, drawings shall mean plans and exterior elevations drawn to scale, with sufficient detail to show, as far as they relate to exterior appearances, the architectural design of buildings, including proposed materials, textures, and colors, including samples of materials or color samples, and the plot plan or site layout, including all improvements affecting appearances such as walls, walks, terraces, planting, accessory buildings, signs, lights and other elements. Such document shall be filed with the administrative officer, and the administrative officer shall cause such documents to be made available to the Board of Architectural Review.

b. Photographs required with application for the demolition of existing structures. In the case of application for the demolition of structures within the jurisdiction of the Board of Architectural Review, the applicant shall submit legible photographs of all sides of the building under consideration and photographs showing contiguous properties.

c. Photographs required with applications for repair, alterations, and/or additions to existing structures. In the case of application to repair, alter or make additions to a structure within the Old City District and over one hundred years old, or to structures situated within the Old and Historic Charleston Districts, regardless of age, the application shall be accompanied by legible photographs of all sides of the structure.

d. Photographs required with applications for new construction. In the case of application to construct a new building situated within the Old and Historic Charleston Districts the application shall be accompanied by legible photographs of the adjoining properties.

e. All of the above mentioned data shall be filed with the administrative officer and the administrative officer shall cause said date to be made available to the Board of Architectural Review.

Sec. 54-239: Public Notice Requirements

Upon the filing of an application for with the Board of Architectural Review for property within the corporate limits of the city of Charleston, the property to which such application applies shall be posted with a sign at least five (5) days prior to any public hearing when the application will be considered and said sign shall specify the appropriate city department to contact concerning information regarding the application. The Board of Architectural Review shall adopt and implement rules of procedure by which the posting of signing shall be conducted, and may make recommendations to City Council of fees to be charged therefore. Any fee schedule established hereunder shall be approved by City Council.

Sec. 54-240: Board of Architectural Review; Powers and Duties

a. In passing upon an application to demolish, or demolish in part, or remove, or alter the exterior architectural appearance of any existing structure, the Board of Architectural Review shall consider, among other things, the historic, architectural and aesthetic features of such structure, the nature and character of the surrounding area, the use of such structure and the importance to the city.

b. In passing upon an application for new construction in an old and historic district, the Board of Architectural Review shall consider, among other things, the general design, the character and appropriateness of design, scale of buildings, arrangement, texture, materials and color of the structure in question, and the relation of such elements to similar features of structures in the immediate surroundings. The Board of Architectural Review shall not consider interior arrangement or interior design; nor shall it make requirements except for the purpose of preventing developments which are not in harmony with the prevailing character of Charleston, or which are obviously incongruous with this character.

c. The Board of Architectural Review may refuse a permit or Certificate of Appropriateness for the erection, reconstruction, alteration, demolition, partial demolition, or removal of any structure within the old and historic district, which in the opinion of the Board of Architectural Review, would be detrimental to the interests of the old and historic district and against the public interests of the city.

d. Upon receiving an application concerning the demolition or removal of a building or structure over seventy-five years old and within the limits of the old city district and outside of the old and historic districts, the Board of Architectural Review within forty-five (45) days after receipt of the application shall either approve or deny such application, or find that the preservation and protection of historic places and the public interest will best be served by postponing the demolition or alteration for a designated period, which shall not exceed one hundred eighty (180) days from the receipt of the application, and notify the applicant of such postponement.

e. In all applications involving the demolition or partial demolition of a structure, provision shall be made for a public hearing as set forth in this article.

f. In any case involving the demolition or partial demolition of a structure, before granting approval or requiring a postponement, the Board of Architecture Review may call on the city engineer to provide them with a report on the state of repair and structural stability of the structure under consideration.

g. Within the period of postponement of such demolition or alteration of any building, the Board of Architectural Review shall take steps to ascertain what the City Council can or may do to preserve such building, including consultation with private civic groups, interested private citizens and other public boards or agencies and including investigation of the potential use of the power of eminent domain when the preservation of a given building is clearly in the interest of the general welfare of the community and of certain historic and architectural significance. The Board of Architectural Review shall then make such recommendations thereabout to the City Council as the board may determine to submit.

h. In case of disapproval, the Board of Architectural Review shall state the reasons therefor in a written statement to the applicant and make recommendations in regard to appropriateness of design, arrangement, texture, material, color and the like of the property involved.

i. Among other grounds for considering a design inappropriate and requiring disapproval and resubmission are the following defects: Arresting and spectacular effects, violent contrasts of materials or colors and intense or lurid colors, a multiplicity or incongruity of details resulting in a restless and disturbing appearance, the absence of unity and coherence in composition not in consonance with the dignity and character of the present structure in the case of repair, remodeling or enlargement of an existing building or with the prevailing character of the neighborhood in the case of a new building.

j. The Board of Architectural Review may refuse to approve a permit for demolition, removal or alteration of any structure within the old and historic districts or within the old city district, if it deems the structure of such architectural or historical interest that the removal will be detrimental to the public interest.

k. The Board of Architectural Review shall have the power to delay for a period of 180 days or deny outright the demolition or removal of a building or structure over 75 years old in the area bounded to the north by Mount Pleasant Street or the extensions thereof into the waters of the Ashley and Cooper Rivers, to the east by the waters of the Cooper River to the south by the Old City District and to the west by the waters of the Ashley River.

l. The approval of an application for the use of land by the Board of Zoning Appeals—Zoning or the Board of Zoning Appeals—Site Design shall not deprive the Board of Architectural Review of any power granted to it in this ordinance, or in any manner diminish such powers.

(Ord. No. 1998-148, § 1, 8-18-98; Ord. No. 1999-54, § 4, 4-27-99)

Sec. 54-241: Powers of Board to Require Repair of Structures

The Board of Architectural Review, on its own initiative, may file a petition with the public safety and housing officer requesting that said officer proceed under the public safety and housing ordinance to require correction of defects or repairs to any structure covered by this article so that such structure shall be preserved and protected in consonance with the purpose of this article and the public safety and housing ordinance.

Sec. 54-242: Exemptions from Article

Nothing in this article shall be construed to prevent the ordinary maintenance or repair of any exterior elements of any building or structure described in section 54-232; nor shall anything in this article be construed to prevent the construction, reconstruction, alteration or demolition of any such elements which the authorized municipal officers shall certify as required by public safety.

Sec. 54-243: Report to Administrative Officer; Issuance of Certificate of Appropriateness

Upon approval of the plans or the granting of a permit, the Board of Architectural Review shall forthwith transmit a report to the administrative officer stating the basis upon which such approval was made and cause a certificate of appropriateness to be issued to the applicant. If the Board of Architectural Review shall fail to take final action upon any case within forty-five (45) days after the receipt of application for permit, the application shall be deemed to be disapproved, except where mutual agreement has been made for an extension of time limit.

When a certificate of appropriateness has been issued, a copy thereof shall be transmitted to the city building inspector, who shall from time to time inspect the alteration or construction approved by such certificate and shall make a weekly report of such inspection to the Board of Architectural Review listing all work inspected and reporting any work not in accordance with such certificate or violating any ordinances of the city.

Sec. 54-244: Time Limitations on Certificates of Appropriateness

Certificates of appropriateness issued before, on, or after March 10, 1999, will remain valid for one year from the date of issuance for demolitions and three years from the date of issuance for all other approvals, provided however, all non-demolition certificates of appropriateness in effect as of March 1, 1999, shall remain valid if within 180 days a building permit is issued. A new application for approval must be submitted after such time has elapsed if work has not commenced.
(Ord. No. 1999-24, § 1, 3-10-99)

Sec. 54-245: Appeals to Board of Architectural Review

Appeals to the Board of Architectural Review may be taken by any person aggrieved or by any officer, department, Board or bureau of the city. Such appeal shall be taken within a reasonable time as provided by the rules of the Board by filing with the officer from whom the appeal is taken and with the Board of Architectural Review a notice of appeal specifying the grounds thereof. The officer from whom the appeal is taken shall forthwith transmit to the Board all the papers constituting the record upon which the action appealed from was taken.
(Ord. No. 1999-54, § 2B, 4-27-99)

Sec. 54-246: Effect of an Appeal

An appeal stays all proceedings in furtherance of the action appealed from, unless the officer from whom the appeal is taken certifies to the Board, after the notice of appeal shall have been filed with him, that by reason of facts stated in the certificate a stay would, in his opinion, cause imminent peril to life or property. In such case proceedings shall not be stayed otherwise than by a restraining order which may be granted by the Board of Architectural Review or a court of record on application, on notice to the officer from whom the appeal is taken, and on due cause shown.
(Ord. No. 1999-54, § 2B, 4-27-99)

Sec. 54-247: Hearing an Appeal

The Board shall fix a reasonable time for the hearing of the appeal, or other matter referred to it, and give public notice of it, as well as due notice to the parties in interest, and decide the same within a reasonable time. At the hearing any party may appear in person or by agent or by attorney.
(Ord. No. 1999-54, § 2B, 4-27-99)

Sec. 54-248: Appeal from Board of Architectural Review to Circuit Court

A person who may have a substantial interest in any decision of the Board or any officer or agent of the appropriate governing authority may appeal from a decision of the Board to the circuit court in the county by filing with the clerk of court a petition in writing setting forth plainly, fully, and distinctly why the decision is contrary to law. The appeal must be filed within thirty days after the affected party receives actual notice of the decision of the Board.

SUBPART A—PURPOSES AND PARTICIPANTS

Section 800.1 Purposes

(a) Purposes of the section 106 process. Section 106 of the National Historic Preservation Act requires Federal agencies to take into account the effects of their undertakings on historic properties and afford the Council a reasonable opportunity to comment on such undertakings. The procedures in this part define how Federal agencies meet these statutory responsibilities. The section 106 process seeks to accommodate historic preservation concerns with the needs of Federal undertakings through consultation among the agency official and other parties with an interest in the effects of the undertaking on historic properties, commencing at the early stages of project planning. The goal of consultation is to identify historic properties potentially affected by the undertaking, assess its effects and seek ways to avoid, minimize or mitigate any adverse effects on historic properties.

(b) Relation to other provisions of the act. Section 106 is related to other provisions of the act designed to further the national policy of historic preservation. References to those provisions are included in this part to identify circumstances where they may affect actions taken to meet section 106 requirements. Such provisions may have their own implementing regulations or guidelines and are not intended to be implemented by the procedures in this part except insofar as they relate to the section 106 process. Guidelines, policies, and procedures issued by other agencies, including the Secretary, have been cited in this part for ease of access and are not incorporated by reference.

(c) *Timing.* The agency official must complete the section 106 process "prior to the approval of the expenditure of any Federal funds on the undertaking or prior to the issuance of any license." This does not prohibit agency official from conducting or authorizing nondestructive project planning activities before completing compliance with section 106, provided that such actions do not restrict the subsequent consideration of alternatives to avoid, minimize or mitigate the undertaking's adverse effects on historic properties. The agency official shall ensure that the section 106 process is initiated early in the undertaking's planning, so that a broad range of alternatives may be considered during the planning process for the undertaking.

Section 800.2 Participants in the Section 106 Process

(a) Agency official. It is the statutory obligation of the Federal agency to fulfill the requirements of section 106 and to ensure that an agency official with jurisdiction over an undertaking takes legal and financial responsibility for section 106 compliance in accordance with subpart B of this part. The agency official has approval authority for the undertaking and can commit the Federal agency to take appropriate action for a specific undertaking as a result of section 106 compliance. For the purposes of subpart C of this part, the agency official has the authority to commit the Federal agency to any obligation it may assume in the implementation of a program alternative. The agency official may be a State, local, or tribal government official who has been delegated legal responsibility for compliance with section 106 in accordance with Federal law.

(1) Professional standards. Section 112(a)(1)(A) of the act requires each Federal agency responsible for the protection of historic resources, including archeological resources, to ensure that all actions taken by employees or contractors of the agency shall meet professional standards under regulations developed by the Secretary.

(2) Lead Federal agency. If more than one Federal agency is involved in an undertaking, some or all the agencies may designate a lead Federal agency, which shall identify the appropriate official to serve as the agency official who shall act on their behalf, fulfilling their collective responsibilities under section 106. Those Federal agencies that do not designate a lead Federal agency remain individually responsible for their compliance with this part.

(3) Use of contractors. Consistent with applicable conflict of interest laws, the agency official may use the services of applicants, consultants, or designees to prepare information, analyses and recommendations under this part. The agency official remains legally responsible for all required findings and determinations. If a document or study is prepared by a non-Federal party, the agency official is responsible for ensuring that its content meets applicable standards and guidelines.

(4) *Consultation.* The agency official shall involve the consulting parties described in paragraph (c) of this section in findings and determinations made during the section 106 process. The agency official should plan consultations appropriate to the scale of the undertaking and the scope of Federal involvement and coordinated with other requirements of other statutes, as applicable, such as the National Environmental Policy Act, the Native American Graves Protection and Repatriation Act, the American Indian Religious Freedom Act, the Archeological Resources Protection Act, and agency-specific legislation. The Council encourages the agency official to use to the extent possible existing agency procedures and mechanisms to fulfill the consultation requirements of this part.

(b) *Council.* The Council issues regulations to implement section 106, provides guidance and advice on the application of the procedures in this part, and generally oversees the operation of the section 106 process. The Council also consults with and comments to agency officials on individual undertakings and programs that affect historic properties.

(1) Council entry into the section 106 process. When the Council determines that its involvement is necessary to ensure that the purposes of section 106 and the act are met, the Council may enter the section 106 process. Criteria guiding Council decisions to enter the section 106 process are found in appendix A to this part. The Council will document that the criteria have been met and notify the parties to the section 106 process as required by this part.

(2) Council assistance. Participants in the section 106 process may seek advice, guidance and assistance from the Council on the application of this part to specific undertakings, including the resolution of disagreements, whether or not the Council is formally involved in the review of the undertaking. If questions arise regarding the conduct of the section 106 process, participants are encouraged to obtain the Council's advice on completing the process.

(c) *Consulting parties.* The following parties have consultative roles in the section 106 process.

(1) State historic preservation officer.

(i) The State historic preservation officer (SHPO) reflects the interests of the State and its citizens in the preservation of their cultural heritage. In accordance with section 101(b)(3) of the act, the SHPO advises and assists Federal agencies in carrying out their section 106 responsibilities and cooperates with such agencies, local governments and organizations and individuals to ensure that historic properties are taking into consideration at all levels of planning and development.

(ii) If an Indian tribe has assumed the functions of the SHPO in the section 106 process for undertakings on tribal lands, the SHPO shall participate as a consulting party if the undertaking takes place on tribal lands but affects historic properties off tribal lands, if requested in accordance with Sec. 800.3(c)(1), or if the Indian tribe agrees to include the SHPO pursuant to Sec. 800.3(f)(3).

(2) Indian tribes and Native Hawaiian organizations.

(i) Consultation on tribal lands.

(A) Tribal historic preservation officer. For a tribe that has assumed the responsibilities of the SHPO for section 106 on tribal lands under section 101(d)(2) of the act, the tribal historic preservation officer (THPO) appointed or designated in accordance with the act is the official representative for the purposes of section 106. The agency official shall consult with the THPO in lieu of the SHPO regarding undertakings occurring on or affecting historic properties on tribal lands.

(B) Tribes that have not assumed SHPO functions. When an Indian tribe has not assumed the responsibilities of the SHPO for section 106 on tribal lands under section 101(d)(2) of the act, the agency official shall consult with a representative designated by such Indian tribe in addition to the SHPO regarding undertakings occurring on or affecting historic properties on its tribal lands. Such Indian tribes have the same rights of consultation and concurrence that the THPOs are given throughout subpart B of this part, except that such consultations shall be in addition to and on the same basis as consultation with the SHPO.

(ii) Consultation on historic properties of significance to Indian tribes and Native Hawaiian organizations. Section 101(d)(6)(B) of the act requires the agency official to consult with any Indian tribe or Native Hawaiian organization that attaches religious and cultural significance to historic properties that may be affected by an undertaking. This requirement applies regardless of the location of the historic property. Such Indian tribe or Native Hawaiian organization shall be a consulting party.

(A) The agency official shall ensure that consultation in the section 106 process provides the Indian tribe or Native Hawaiian organization a reasonable opportunity to identify its concerns about historic properties, advise on the identification and evaluation of historic properties, including those of traditional religious and cultural importance, articulate its views on the undertaking's effects on such properties, and participate in the resolution of adverse effects. It is the responsibility of the agency official to make a reasonable and good faith effort to identify Indian tribes and Native Hawaiian organizations that shall be consulted in the section 106 process. Consultation should commence early in the planning process, in order to identify and discuss relevant preservation issues and resolve concerns about the confidentiality of information on historic properties.

(B) The Federal Government has a unique legal relationship with Indian tribes set forth in the Constitution of the United States, treaties, statutes, and court decisions. Consultation with Indian tribes should be conducted in a sensitive manner respectful of tribal sovereignty. Nothing in this part alters, amends, repeals, interprets, or modifies tribal sovereignty, any treaty rights, or other rights of an Indian tribe, or preempts, modifies, or limits the exercise of any such rights.

(C) Consultation with an Indian tribe must recognize the government-to-government relationship between the Federal Government and Indian tribes. The agency official shall consult with representatives designated or identified by the tribal government or the governing body of a Native Hawaiian organization. Consultation with Indian tribes and Native Hawaiian organizations should be conducted in a manner sensitive to the concerns and needs of the Indian tribe or Native Hawaiian organization.

(D) When Indian tribes and Native Hawaiian organizations attach religious and cultural significance to historic properties off tribal lands, section 101(d)(6)(B) of the act requires Federal agencies to consult with such Indian tribes and Native Hawaiian organizations in the section 106 process. Federal agencies should be aware that frequently historic properties of religious and cultural significance are located on ancestral, aboriginal, or ceded lands of Indian tribes and Native Hawaiian organizations and should consider that when complying with the procedures in this part.

(E) An Indian tribe or a Native Hawaiian organization may enter into an agreement with an agency official that specifies how they will carry out responsibilities under this part, including concerns over the confidentiality of information. An agreement may cover all aspects of tribal participation in the section 106 process, provided that no modification may be made in the roles of other parties to the section 106 process without their consent. An agreement may grant the Indian tribe or Native Hawaiian organization additional rights to participate or concur in agency decisions in the section 106 process beyond those specified in subpart B of this part. The agency official shall provide a copy of any such agreement to the Council and the appropriate SHPOs.

(F) An Indian tribe that has not assumed the responsibilities of the SHPO for section 106 on tribal lands under section 101(d)(2) of the act may notify the agency official in writing that it is waiving its rights under Sec. 800.6(c)(1) to execute a memorandum of agreement.

(3) *Representatives of local governments.* A representative of a local government with jurisdiction over the area in which the effects of an undertaking may occur is entitled to participate as a consulting party. Under other provisions of Federal law, the local government may be authorized to act as the agency official for purposes of section 106.

(4) *Applicants for Federal assistance, permits, licenses, and other approvals.* An applicant for Federal assistance or for a Federal permit, license, or other approval is entitled to participate as a consulting party as defined in this part. The agency official may authorize an applicant or group of applicants to initiate consultation with the SHPO/THPO and others, but remains legally responsible for all findings and determinations charged to the agency official. The agency official shall notify the SHPO/THPO when an applicant or group of applicants is so authorized. A Federal agency may authorize all applicants in a specific program pursuant to this section by providing notice to all SHPO/THPOs. Federal agencies that provide authorizations to applicants remain responsible for their government-to-government relationships with Indian tribes.

(5) *Additional consulting parties.* Certain individuals and organizations with a demonstrated interest in the undertaking may participate as consulting parties due to the nature of their legal or economic relation to the undertaking or affected properties, or their concern with the undertaking's effects on historic properties.

(d) *The public.*

(1) *Nature of involvement.* The views of the public are essential to informed Federal decisionmaking in the section 106 process. The agency official shall seek and consider the views of the public in a manner that reflects the nature and complexity of the undertaking and its effects on historic properties, the likely interest of the public in the effects on historic properties, confidentiality concerns of private individuals and businesses, and the relationship of the Federal involvement to the undertaking.

(2) *Providing notice and information.* The agency official must, except where appropriate to protect confidentiality concerns of affected parties, provide the public with information about an undertaking and its effects on historic properties and seek public comment and input. Members of the public may also provide views on their own initiative for the agency official to consider in decisionmaking.

(3) *Use of agency procedures.* The agency official may use the agency's procedures for public involvement under the National Environmental Policy Act or

other program requirements in lieu of public involvement requirements in subpart B of this part, if they provide adequate opportunities for public involvement consistent with this subpart.

SUBPART B—THE SECTION 106 PROCESS

Section 800.3 Initiation of the Section 106 Process

(a) *Establish undertaking.* The agency official shall determine whether the proposed Federal action is an undertaking as defined in Sec. 800.16(y) and, if so, whether it is a type of activity that has the potential to cause effects on historic properties.

(1) *No potential to cause effects.* If the undertaking is a type of activity that does not have the potential to cause effects on historic properties, assuming such historic properties were present, the agency official has no further obligations under section 106 or this part.

(2) *Program alternatives.* If the review of the undertaking is governed by a Federal agency program alternative established under Sec. 800.14 or a programmatic agreement in existence before January 11, 2001, the agency official shall follow the program alternative.

(b) *Coordinate with other reviews.* The agency official should coordinate the steps of the section 106 process, as appropriate, with the overall planning schedule for the undertaking and with any reviews required under other authorities such as the National Environmental Policy Act, the Native American Graves Protection and Repatriation Act, the American Indian Religious Freedom Act, the Archeological Resources Protection Act, and agency-specific legislation, such as section 4(f) of the Department of Transportation Act. Where consistent with the procedures in this subpart, the agency official may use information developed for other reviews under Federal, State, or tribal law to meet the requirements of section 106.

(c) *Identify the appropriate SHPO and/or THPO.* As part of its initial planning, the agency official shall determine the appropriate SHPO or SHPOs to be involved in the section 106 process. The agency official shall also determine whether the undertaking may occur on or affect historic properties on any tribal lands and, if so, whether a THPO has assumed the duties of the SHPO. The agency official shall then initiate consultation with the appropriate officer or officers.

(1) *Tribal assumption of SHPO responsibilities.* Where an Indian tribe has assumed the section 106 responsibilities of the SHPO on tribal lands pursuant

to section 101(d)(2) of the act, consultation for undertakings occurring on tribal land or for effects on tribal land is with the THPO for the Indian tribe in lieu of the SHPO. Section 101(d)(2)(D)(iii) of the act authorizes owners of properties on tribal lands which are neither owned by a member of the tribe nor held in trust by the Secretary for the benefit of the tribe to request the SHPO to participate in the section 106 process in addition to the THPO.

(2) *Undertakings involving more than one State.* If more than one State is involved in an undertaking, the involved SHPOs may agree to designate a lead SHPO to act on their behalf in the section 106 process, including taking actions that would conclude the section 106 process under this subpart.

(3) *Conducting consultation.* The agency official should consult with the SHPO/THPO in a manner appropriate to the agency planning process for the undertaking and to the nature of the undertaking and its effects on historic properties.

(4) *Failure of the SHPO/THPO to respond.* If the SHPO/THPO fails to respond within 30 days of receipt of a request for review of a finding or determination, the agency official may either proceed to the next step in the process based on the finding or determination or consult with the Council in lieu of the SHPO/THPO. If the SHPO/THPO re-enters the Section 106 process, the agency official shall continue the consultation without being required to reconsider previous findings or determinations.

(d) *Consultation on tribal lands.* Where the Indian tribe has not assumed the responsibilities of the SHPO on tribal lands, consultation with the Indian tribe regarding undertakings occurring on such tribe's lands or effects on such tribal lands shall be in addition to and on the same basis as consultation with the SHPO. If the SHPO has withdrawn from the process, the agency official may complete the section 106 process with the Indian tribe and the Council, as appropriate. An Indian tribe may enter into an agreement with a SHPO or SHPOs specifying the SHPO's participation in the section 106 process for undertakings occurring on or affecting historic properties on tribal lands.

(e) *Plan to involve the public.* In consultation with the SHPO/THPO, the agency official shall plan for involving the public in the section 106 process. The agency official shall identify the appropriate points for seeking public input and for notifying the public of proposed actions, consistent with Sec. 800.2(d).

(f) *Identify other consulting parties.* In consultation with the SHPO/THPO, the agency official shall identify any other parties entitled to be consulting parties and invite them to participate as such in the section 106 process. The agency official may invite others to participate as consulting parties as the section 106 process moves forward.

(1) *Involving local governments and applicants.* The agency official shall invite any local governments or applicants that are entitled to be consulting parties under Sec. 800.2(c).

(2) *Involving Indian tribes and Native Hawaiian organizations.* The agency official shall make a reasonable and good faith effort to identify any Indian tribes or Native Hawaiian organizations that might attach religious and cultural significance to historic properties in the area of potential effects and invite them to be consulting parties. Such Indian tribe or Native Hawaiian organization that requests in writing to be a consulting party shall be one.

(3) *Requests to be consulting parties.* The agency official shall consider all written requests of individuals and organizations to participate as consulting parties and, in consultation with the SHPO/ THPO and any Indian tribe upon whose tribal lands an undertaking occurs or affects historic properties, determine which should be consulting parties.

(g) *Expediting consultation.* A consultation by the agency official with the SHPO/THPO and other consulting parties may address multiple steps in Secs. 800.3 through 800.6 where the agency official and the SHPO/THPO agree it is appropriate as long as the consulting parties and the public have an adequate opportunity to express their views as provided in Sec. 800.2(d).

Section 800.4 Identification of historic properties.

(a) *Determine scope of identification efforts.* In consultation with the SHPO/THPO, the agency official shall:

(1) Determine and document the area of potential effects, as defined in Sec. 800.16(d);

(2) Review existing information on historic properties within the area of potential effects, including any data concerning possible historic properties not yet identified;

(3) Seek information, as appropriate, from consulting parties, and other individuals and organizations likely to have knowledge of, or concerns with, historic properties in the area, and identify issues relating to the undertaking's potential effects on historic properties; and

(4) Gather information from any Indian tribe or Native Hawaiian organization identified pursuant to Sec. 800.3(f) to assist in identifying properties, including

those located off tribal lands, which may be of religious and cultural significance to them and may be eligible for the National Register, recognizing that an Indian tribe or Native Hawaiian organization may be reluctant to divulge specific information regarding the location, nature, and activities associated with such sites. The agency official should address concerns raised about confidentiality pursuant to Sec. 800.11(c).

(b) *Identify historic properties.* Based on the information gathered under paragraph (a) of this section, and in consultation with the SHPO/ THPO and any Indian tribe or Native Hawaiian organization that might attach religious and cultural significance to properties within the area of potential effects, the agency official shall take the steps necessary to identify historic properties within the area of potential effects.

(1) *Level of effort.* The agency official shall make a reasonable and good faith effort to carry out appropriate identification efforts, which may include background research, consultation, oral history interviews, sample field investigation, and field survey. The agency official shall take into account past planning, research and studies, the magnitude and nature of the undertaking and the degree of Federal involvement, the nature and extent of potential effects on historic properties, and the likely nature and location of historic properties within the area of potential effects. The Secretary's standards and guidelines for identification provide guidance on this subject. The agency official should also consider other applicable professional, State, tribal, and local laws, standards, and guidelines. The agency official shall take into account any confidentiality concerns raised by Indian tribes or Native Hawaiian organizations during the identification process.

(2) *Phased identification and evaluation.* Where alternatives under consideration consist of corridors or large land areas, or where access to properties is restricted, the agency official may use a phased process to conduct identification and evaluation efforts. The agency official may also defer final identification and evaluation of historic properties if it is specifically provided for in a memorandum of agreement executed pursuant to Sec. 800.6, a programmatic agreement executed pursuant to Sec. 800.14(b), or the documents used by an agency official to comply with the National Environmental Policy Act pursuant to Sec. 800.8. The process should establish the likely presence of historic properties within the area of potential effects for each alternative or inaccessible area through background research, consultation and an appropriate level of field investigation, taking into account the number of alternatives under consideration, the magnitude of the undertaking and its likely effects, and the views of the SHPO/THPO and any other consulting parties. As specific aspects

or locations of an alternative are refined or access is gained, the agency official shall proceed with the identification and evaluation of historic properties in accordance with paragraphs (b)(1) and (c) of this section.

(c) *Evaluate historic significance.*

(1) Apply National Register criteria. In consultation with the SHPO/THPO and any Indian tribe or Native Hawaiian organization that attaches religious and cultural significance to identified properties and guided by the Secretary's standards and guidelines for evaluation, the agency official shall apply the National Register criteria (36 CFR part 63) to properties identified within the area of potential effects that have not been previously evaluated for National Register eligibility. The passage of time, changing perceptions of significance, or incomplete prior evaluations may require the agency official to reevaluate properties previously determined eligible or ineligible. The agency official shall acknowledge that Indian tribes and Native Hawaiian organizations possess special expertise in assessing the eligibility of historic properties that may possess religious and cultural significance to them.

(2) *Determine whether a property is eligible.* If the agency official determines any of the National Register criteria are met and the SHPO/THPO agrees, the property shall be considered eligible for the National Register for section 106 purposes. If the agency official determines the criteria are not met and the SHPO/THPO agrees, the property shall be considered not eligible. If the agency official and the SHPO/THPO do not agree, or if the Council or the Secretary so request, the agency official shall obtain a determination of eligibility from the Secretary pursuant to 36 CFR part 63. If an Indian tribe or Native Hawaiian organization that attaches religious and cultural significance to a property off tribal lands does not agree, it may ask the Council to request the agency official to obtain a determination of eligibility.

(d) *Results of identification and evaluation.*

(1) *No historic properties affected.* If the agency official finds that either there are no historic properties present or there are historic properties present but the undertaking will have no effect upon them as defined in Sec. 800.16(i), the agency official shall provide documentation of this finding, as set forth in Sec. 800.11(d), to the SHPO/THPO. The agency official shall notify all consulting parties, including Indian tribes and Native Hawaiian organizations, and make the documentation available for public inspection prior to approving the undertaking. If the SHPO/THPO, or the Council if it has entered the section 106 process, does not object within 30 days of receipt of an adequately documented finding, the agency official's responsibilities under section 106 are fulfilled.

(2) *Historic properties affected.* If the agency official finds that there are historic properties which may be affected by the undertaking or the SHPO/THPO or the Council objects to the agency official's finding under paragraph (d)(1) of this section, the agency official shall notify all consulting parties, including Indian tribes or Native Hawaiian organizations, invite their views on the effects and assess adverse effects, if any, in accordance with Sec. 800.5.

Section 800.5 Assessment of Adverse Effects

(a) *Apply criteria of adverse effect.* In consultation with the SHPO/THPO and any Indian tribe or Native Hawaiian organization that attaches religious and cultural significance to identified historic properties, the agency official shall apply the criteria of adverse effect to historic properties within the area of potential effects. The agency official shall consider any views concerning such effects which have been provided by consulting parties and the public.

(1) *Criteria of adverse effect.* An adverse effect is found when an undertaking may alter, directly or indirectly, any of the characteristics of a historic property that qualify the property for inclusion in the National Register in a manner that would diminish the integrity of the property's location, design, setting, materials, workmanship, feeling, or association. Consideration shall be given to all qualifying characteristics of a historic property, including those that may have been identified subsequent to the original evaluation of the property's eligibility for the National Register. Adverse effects may include reasonably foreseeable effects caused by the undertaking that may occur later in time, be farther removed in distance or be cumulative.

(2) *Examples of adverse effects.* Adverse effects on historic properties include, but are not limited to:

(i) Physical destruction of or damage to all or part of the property;

(ii) Alteration of a property, including restoration, rehabilitation, repair, maintenance, stabilization, hazardous material remediation, and provision of handicapped access, that is not consistent with the Secretary's standards for the treatment of historic properties (36 CFR part 68) and applicable guidelines;

(iii) Removal of the property from its historic location;

(iv) Change of the character of the property's use or of physical features within the property's setting that contribute to its historic significance;

(v) Introduction of visual, atmospheric or audible elements that diminish the integrity of the property's significant historic features;

(vi) Neglect of a property which causes its deterioration, except where such neglect and deterioration are recognized qualities of a property of religious and cultural significance to an Indian tribe or Native Hawaiian organization; and

(vii) Transfer, lease, or sale of property out of Federal ownership or control without adequate and legally enforceable restrictions or conditions to ensure long-term preservation of the property's historic significance.

(3) *Phased application of criteria.* Where alternatives under consideration consist of corridors or large land areas, or where access to properties is restricted, the agency official may use a phased process in applying the criteria of adverse effect consistent with phased identification and evaluation efforts conducted pursuant to Sec. 800.4(b)(2).

(b) *Finding of no adverse effect.* The agency official, in consultation with the SHPO/THPO, may propose a finding of no adverse effect when the undertaking's effects do not meet the criteria of paragraph (a)(1) of this section or the undertaking is modified or conditions are imposed, such as the subsequent review of plans for rehabilitation by the SHPO/THPO to ensure consistency with the Secretary's standards for the treatment of historic properties (36 CFR part 68) and applicable guidelines, to avoid adverse effects.

(c) *Consulting party review.* If the agency official proposes a finding of no adverse effect, the agency official shall notify all consulting parties of the finding and provide them with the documentation specified in Sec. 800.11(e). The SHPO/THPO shall have 30 days from receipt to review the finding.

(1) *Agreement with finding.* Unless the Council is reviewing the finding pursuant to Sec. 800.5(c)(3), the agency official may proceed if the SHPO/THPO agrees with the finding. The agency official shall carry out the undertaking in accordance with Sec. 800.5(d)(1). Failure of the SHPO/THPO to respond within 30 days from receipt of the finding shall be considered agreement of the SHPO/THPO with the finding.

(2) *Disagreement with finding.*

(i) If the SHPO/THPO or any consulting party disagrees within the 30-day review period, it shall specify the reasons for disagreeing with the finding. The agency official shall either consult with the party to resolve the disagreement, or request the Council to review the finding pursuant to paragraph (c)(3) of this section.

(ii) The agency official should seek the concurrence of any Indian tribe or Native Hawaiian organization that has made known to the agency official that it attaches religious and cultural significance to a historic property subject to the finding. If such Indian tribe or Native Hawaiian organization disagrees with the finding, it may within the 30-day review period specify the reasons for disagreeing with the finding and request the Council to review the finding pursuant to paragraph (c)(3) of this section.

(iii) If the Council on its own initiative so requests within the 30-day review period, the agency official shall submit the finding, along with the documentation specified in Sec. 800.11(e), for review pursuant to paragraph (c)(3) of this section. A Council decision to make such a request shall be guided by the criteria in appendix A to this part.

(3) *Council review of findings.* When a finding is submitted to the Council pursuant to paragraph (c)(2) of this section, the agency official shall include the documentation specified in Sec. 800.11(e). The Council shall review the finding and notify the agency official of its determination as to whether the adverse effect criteria have been correctly applied within 15 days of receiving the documented finding from the agency official. The Council shall specify the basis for its determination. The agency official shall proceed in accordance with the Council's determination. If the Council does not respond within 15 days of receipt of the finding, the agency official may assume concurrence with the agency official's findings and proceed accordingly.

(d) *Results of assessment.*

(1) *No adverse effect.* The agency official shall maintain a record of the finding and provide information on the finding to the public on request, consistent with the confidentiality provisions of Sec. 800.11(c). Implementation of the undertaking in accordance with the finding as documented fulfills the agency official's responsibilities under section 106 and this part. If the agency official will not conduct the undertaking as proposed in the finding, the agency official shall reopen consultation under paragraph (a) of this section.

(2) *Adverse effect.* If an adverse effect is found, the agency official shall consult further to resolve the adverse effect pursuant to Sec. 800.6.

Section 800.6 Resolution of Adverse Effects

(a) *Continue consultation.* The agency official shall consult with the SHPO/THPO and other consulting parties, including Indian tribes and Native Hawaiian organizations, to develop and evaluate alternatives or modifications to the undertaking that could avoid, minimize, or mitigate adverse effects on historic properties.

(1) *Notify the Council and determine Council participation.* The agency official shall notify the Council of the adverse effect finding by providing the documentation specified in Sec. 800.11(e).

(i) The notice shall invite the Council to participate in the consultation when:

(A) The agency official wants the Council to participate;

(B) The undertaking has an adverse effect upon a National Historic Landmark; or

(C) A programmatic agreement under Sec. 800.14(b) will be prepared;

(ii) The SHPO/THPO, an Indian tribe or Native Hawaiian organization, or any other consulting party may at any time independently request the Council to participate in the consultation.

(iii) The Council shall advise the agency official and all consulting parties whether it will participate within 15 days of receipt of notice or other request. Prior to entering the process, the Council shall provide written notice to the agency official and the consulting parties that its decision to participate meets the criteria set forth in appendix A to this part. The Council shall also advise the head of the agency of its decision to enter the process. Consultation is conducted in accordance with paragraph (b)(2) of this section.

(iv) If the Council does not join the consultation, the agency official shall proceed with consultation in accordance with paragraph (b)(1) of this section.

(2) *Involve consulting parties.* In addition to the consulting parties identified under Sec. 800.3(f), the agency official, the SHPO/ THPO and the Council, if participating, may agree to invite other individuals or organizations to become consulting parties. The agency official shall invite any individual or organization that will assume a specific role or responsibility in a memorandum of agreement to participate as a consulting party.

(3) *Provide documentation.* The agency official shall provide to all consulting parties the documentation specified in Sec. 800.11(e), subject to the confidentiality provisions of Sec. 800.11(c), and such other documentation as may be developed during the consultation to resolve adverse effects.

(4) *Involve the public.* The agency official shall make information available to the public, including the documentation specified in Sec. 800.11(e), subject to the confidentiality provisions of Sec. 800.11(c). The agency official shall provide

an opportunity for members of the public to express their views on resolving adverse effects of the undertaking. The agency official should use appropriate mechanisms, taking into account the magnitude of the undertaking and the nature of its effects upon historic properties, the likely effects on historic properties, and the relationship of the Federal involvement to the undertaking to ensure that the public's views are considered in the consultation. The agency official should also consider the extent of notice and information concerning historic preservation issues afforded the public at earlier steps in the section 106 process to determine the appropriate level of public involvement when resolving adverse effects so that the standards of Sec. 800.2(d) are met.

(5) *Restrictions on disclosure of information.* Section 304 of the act and other authorities may limit the disclosure of information under paragraphs (a)(3) and (a)(4) of this section. If an Indian tribe or Native Hawaiian organization objects to the disclosure of information or if the agency official believes that there are other reasons to withhold information, the agency official shall comply with Sec. 800.11(c) regarding the disclosure of such information.

(b) *Resolve adverse effects.*

(1) *Resolution without the Council.*

(i) The agency official shall consult with the SHPO/THPO and other consulting parties to seek ways to avoid, minimize or mitigate the adverse effects.

(ii) The agency official may use standard treatments established by the Council under Sec. 800.14(d) as a basis for a memorandum of agreement.

(iii) If the Council decides to join the consultation, the agency official shall follow paragraph (b)(2) of this section.

(iv) If the agency official and the SHPO/THPO agree on how the adverse effects will be resolved, they shall execute a memorandum of agreement. The agency official must submit a copy of the executed memorandum of agreement, along with the documentation specified in Sec. 800.11(f), to the Council prior to approving the undertaking in order to meet the requirements of section 106 and this subpart.

(v) If the agency official, and the SHPO/THPO fail to agree on the terms of a memorandum of agreement, the agency official shall request the Council to join the consultation and provide the Council with the documentation set forth in Sec. 800.11(g). If the Council decides to join the consultation, the agency official shall proceed in accordance with paragraph (b)(2) of this section. If the Council decides not to join the consultation, the Council will notify the agency and proceed to comment in accordance with Sec. 800.7(c).

(2) *Resolution with Council participation.* If the Council decides to participate in the consultation, the agency official shall consult with the SHPO/THPO, the Council, and other consulting parties, including Indian tribes and Native Hawaiian organizations under Sec. 800.2(c)(3), to seek ways to avoid, minimize or mitigate the adverse effects. If the agency official, the SHPO/THPO, and the Council agree on how the adverse effects will be resolved, they shall execute a memorandum of agreement.

(c) *Memorandum of agreement.* A memorandum of agreement executed and implemented pursuant to this section evidences the agency official's compliance with section 106 and this part and shall govern the undertaking and all of its parts. The agency official shall ensure that the undertaking is carried out in accordance with the memorandum of agreement.

(1) *Signatories.* The signatories have sole authority to execute, amend or terminate the agreement in accordance with this subpart.

(i) The agency official and the SHPO/THPO are the signatories to a memorandum of agreement executed pursuant to paragraph (b)(1) of this section.

(ii) The agency official, the SHPO/THPO, and the Council are the signatories to a memorandum of agreement executed pursuant to paragraph (b)(2) of this section.

(iii) The agency official and the Council are signatories to a memorandum of agreement executed pursuant to Sec. 800.7(a)(2).

(2) *Invited signatories.*

(i) The agency official may invite additional parties to be signatories to a memorandum of agreement. Any such party that signs the memorandum of agreement shall have the same rights with regard to seeking amendment or termination of the memorandum of agreement as other signatories.

(ii) The agency official may invite an Indian tribe or Native Hawaiian organization that attaches religious and cultural significance to historic properties located off tribal lands to be a signatory to a memorandum of agreement concerning such properties.

(iii) The agency official should invite any party that assumes a responsibility under a memorandum of agreement to be a signatory.

(iv) The refusal of any party invited to become a signatory to a memorandum of agreement pursuant to paragraph (c)(2) of this section does not invalidate the memorandum of agreement.

(3) *Concurrence by others.* The agency official may invite all consulting parties to concur in the memorandum of agreement. The signatories may agree to invite others to concur. The refusal of any party invited to concur in the memorandum of agreement does not invalidate the memorandum of agreement.

(4) Reports on implementation. Where the signatories agree it is appropriate, a memorandum of agreement shall include a provision for monitoring and reporting on its implementation.

(5) Duration. A memorandum of agreement shall include provisions for termination and for reconsideration of terms if the undertaking has not been implemented within a specified time.

(6) Discoveries. Where the signatories agree it is appropriate, a memorandum of agreement shall include provisions to deal with the subsequent discovery or identification of additional historic properties affected by the undertaking.

(7) Amendments. The signatories to a memorandum of agreement may amend it. If the Council was not a signatory to the original agreement and the signatories execute an amended agreement, the agency official shall file It with the Council.

(8) Termination. If any signatory determines that the terms of a memorandum of agreement cannot be or are not being carried out, the signatories shall consult to seek amendment of the agreement. If the agreement is not amended, any signatory may terminate it. The agency official shall either execute a memorandum of agreement with signatories under paragraph (c)(1) of this section or request the comments of the Council under Sec. 800.7(a).

(9) Copies. The agency official shall provide each consulting party with a copy of any memorandum of agreement executed pursuant to this subpart.

Section 800.7 Failure to Resolve Adverse Effects

(a) Termination of consultation. After consulting to resolve adverse effects pursuant to Sec. 800.6(b)(2), the agency official, the SHPO/THPO, or the Council may determine that further consultation will not be productive and terminate consultation. Any party that terminates consultation shall notify the other consulting parties and provide them the reasons for terminating in writing.

(1) If the agency official terminates consultation, the head of the agency or an Assistant Secretary or other officer with major department-wide or agency-wide responsibilities shall request that the Council comment pursuant to paragraph (c) of this section and shall notify all consulting parties of the request.

(2) If the SHPO terminates consultation, the agency official and the Council may execute a memorandum of agreement without the SHPO's involvement.

(3) If a THPO terminates consultation regarding an undertaking occurring on or affecting historic properties on its tribal lands, the Council shall comment pursuant to paragraph (c) of this section.

(4) If the Council terminates consultation, the Council shall notify the agency official, the agency's Federal preservation officer and all consulting parties of the termination and comment under paragraph (c) of this section. The Council may consult with the agency's Federal preservation officer prior to terminating consultation to seek to resolve issues concerning the undertaking and its effects on historic properties.

(b) Comments without termination. The Council may determine that it is appropriate to provide additional advisory comments upon an undertaking for which a memorandum of agreement will be executed. The Council shall provide them to the agency official when it executes the memorandum of agreement.

(c) Comments by the Council.

(1) Preparation. The Council shall provide an opportunity for the agency official, all consulting parties, and the public to provide their views within the time frame for developing its comments. Upon request of the Council, the agency official shall provide additional existing information concerning the undertaking and assist the Council in arranging an onsite inspection and an opportunity for public participation.

(2) Timing. The Council shall transmit its comments within 45 days of receipt of a request under paragraph (a)(1) or (a)(3) of this section or Sec. 800.8(c)(3), or termination by the Council under Sec. 800.6(b)(1)(v) or paragraph (a)(4) of this section, unless otherwise agreed to by the agency official.

(3) Transmittal. The Council shall provide its comments to the head of the agency requesting comment with copies to the agency official, the agency's Federal preservation officer, all consulting parties, and others as appropriate.

(4) Response to Council comment. The head of the agency shall take into account the Council's comments in reaching a final decision on the undertaking. Section 110(l) of the act directs that the head of the agency shall document this decision and may not delegate his or her responsibilities pursuant to section 106. Documenting the agency head's decision shall include:

(i) Preparing a summary of the decision that contains the rationale for the decision and evidence of consideration of the Council's comments and providing it to the Council prior to approval of the undertaking;

(ii) Providing a copy of the summary to all consulting parties; and

(iii) Notifying the public and making the record available for public inspection.

Section 800.8 Coordination With the National Environmental Policy Act

(a) General principles.

(1) Early coordination. Federal agencies are encouraged to coordinate compliance with section 106 and the procedures in this part with any steps taken to meet the requirements of the National Environmental Policy Act

(NEPA). Agencies should consider their section 106 responsibilities as early as possible in the NEPA process, and plan their public participation, analysis, and review in such a way that they can meet the purposes and requirements of both statutes in a timely and efficient manner. The determination of whether an undertaking is a "major Federal action significantly affecting the quality of the human environment," and therefore requires preparation of an environmental impact statement (EIS) under NEPA, should include consideration of the undertaking's likely effects on historic properties. A finding of adverse effect on a historic property does not necessarily require an EIS under NEPA.

(2) Consulting party roles. SHPO/THPOs, Indian tribes, and Native Hawaiian organizations, other consulting parties, and organizations and individuals who may be concerned with the possible effects of an agency action on historic properties should be prepared to consult with agencies early in the NEPA process, when the purpose of and need for the proposed action as well as the widest possible range of alternatives are under consideration.

(3) Inclusion of historic preservation issues. Agency officials should ensure that preparation of an environmental assessment (EA) and finding of no significant impact (FONSI) or an EIS and record of decision (ROD) includes appropriate scoping, identification of historic properties, assessment of effects upon them, and consultation leading to resolution of any adverse effects.

(b) Actions categorically excluded under NEPA. If a project, activity or program is categorically excluded from NEPA review under an agency's NEPA procedures, the agency official shall determine if it still qualifies as an undertaking requiring review under section 106 pursuant to Sec. 800.3(a). If so, the agency official shall proceed with section 106 review in accordance with the procedures in this subpart.

(c) Use of the NEPA process for section 106 purposes. An agency official may use the process and documentation required for the preparation of an EA/FONSI or an EIS/ROD to comply with section 106 in lieu of the procedures set forth in Secs. 800.3 through 800.6 if the agency official has notified in advance the SHPO/THPO and the Council that it intends to do so and the following standards are met.

(1) Standards for developing environmental documents to comply with Section 106. During preparation of the EA or draft EIS (DEIS) the agency official shall:

(i) Identify consulting parties either pursuant to Sec. 800.3(f) or through the NEPA scoping process with results consistent with Sec. 800.3(f);

(ii) Identify historic properties and assess the effects of the undertaking on such properties in a manner consistent with the standards and criteria of Secs. 800.4 through 800.5, provided that the scope and timing of these steps may be phased to reflect the agency official's consideration of project alternatives in the NEPA process and the effort is commensurate with the assessment of other environmental factors;

(iii) Consult regarding the effects of the undertaking on historic properties with the SHPO/THPO, Indian tribes, and Native Hawaiian organizations that might attach religious and cultural significance to affected historic properties, other consulting parties, and the Council, where appropriate, during NEPA scoping, environmental analysis, and the preparation of NEPA documents;

(iv) Involve the public in accordance with the agency's published NEPA procedures; and

(v) Develop in consultation with identified consulting parties alternatives and proposed measures that might avoid, minimize or mitigate any adverse effects of the undertaking on historic properties and describe them in the EA or DEIS.

(2) Review of environmental documents.

(i) The agency official shall submit the EA, DEIS, or EIS to the SHPO/THPO, Indian tribes, and Native Hawaiian organizations that might attach religious and cultural significance to affected historic properties, and other consulting parties prior to or when making the document available for public comment. If the document being prepared is a DEIS or EIS, the agency official shall also submit it to the Council.

(ii) Prior to or within the time allowed for public comment on the document, a SHPO/THPO, an Indian tribe or Native Hawaiian organization, another consulting party or the Council may object to the agency official that preparation of the EA, DEIS, or EIS has not met the standards set forth in paragraph (c)(1) of this section or that the substantive resolution of the effects on historic properties proposed in an EA, DEIS, or EIS is inadequate. If the agency official receives such an objection, the agency official shall refer the matter to the Council.

(3) Resolution of objections. Within 30 days of the agency official's referral of an objection under paragraph (c)(2)(ii) of this section, the Council shall notify the agency official either that it agrees with the objection, in which case the agency official shall enter into consultation in accordance with Sec. 800.6(b)(2) or seek Council comments in accordance with Sec. 800.7(a), or that it disagrees with the objection, in which case the agency official shall continue its compliance with this section. Failure of the Council to respond within the 30 day period shall be considered disagreement with the objection.

(4) Approval of the undertaking. If the agency official has found, during the preparation of an EA or EIS that the effects of an undertaking on historic properties are adverse, the agency official shall develop measures in the EA, DEIS, or EIS to avoid, minimize, or mitigate such effects in accordance with paragraph (c)(1)(v) of this section. The agency official's responsibilities under section 106 and the procedures in this subpart shall then be satisfied when either:

(i) A binding commitment to such proposed measures is incorporated in:

(A) The ROD, if such measures were proposed in a DEIS or EIS; or

(B) An MOA drafted in compliance with Sec. 800.6(c); or

(ii) The Council has commented under Sec. 800.7 and received the agency's response to such comments.

(5) Modification of the undertaking. If the undertaking is modified after approval of the FONSI or the ROD in a manner that changes the undertaking oralters its effects on historic properties, or if the agency official fails to ensure that the measures to avoid, minimize or mitigate adverse effects (as specified in either the FONSI or the ROD, or in the binding commitment adopted pursuant to paragraph (c)(4) of this section) are carried out, the agency official shall notify the Council and all consulting parties that supplemental environmental documents will be prepared in compliance with NEPA or that the procedures in Secs. 800.3 through 800.6 will be followed as necessary.

Section 800.9 Council review of section 106 compliance.

(a) Assessment of agency official compliance for individual undertakings. The Council may provide to the agency official its advisory opinion regarding the substance of any finding, determination or decision or regarding the adequacy of the agency official's compliance with the procedures under this part. The Council may provide such advice at any time at the request of any individual, agency or organization or on its own initiative. The agency official shall consider the views of the Council in reaching a decision on the matter in question.

(b) Agency foreclosure of the Council's opportunity to comment. Where an agency official has failed to complete the requirements of section 106 in accordance with the procedures in this part prior to the approval of an undertaking, the Council's opportunity to comment may be foreclosed. The Council may review a case to determine whether a foreclosure has occurred. The Council shall notify the agency official and the agency's Federal preservation officer and allow 30 days for the agency official to provide information as to whether foreclosure has occurred. If the Council determines foreclosure has occurred, the Council shall transmit the determination to the agency official and the head of the agency. The Council shall also make the determination available to the public and any parties known to be interested in the undertaking and its effects upon historic properties.

(c) Intentional adverse effects by applicants.

(1) Agency responsibility. Section 110(k) of the act prohibits a Federal agency from granting a loan, loan guarantee, permit, license or other assistance to an applicant who, with intent to avoid the requirements of section 106, has intentionally significantly adversely affected a historic property to which the grant would relate, or having legal power to prevent it, has allowed such significant adverse effect to occur, unless the agency, after consultation with the Council, determines that circumstances justify granting such assistance despite the adverse effect created or permitted by the applicant. Guidance issued by the Secretary pursuant to section 110 of the act governs its implementation.

(2) Consultation with the Council. When an agency official determines, based on the actions of an applicant, that section 110(k) is applicable and that circumstances may justify granting the assistance, the agency official shall notify the Council and provide documentation specifying the circumstances under which the adverse effects to the historic property occurred and the degree of damage to the integrity of the property. This documentation shall include any views obtained from the applicant, SHPO/THPO, an Indian tribe if the undertaking occurs on or affects historic properties on tribal lands, and other parties known to be interested in the undertaking.

(i) Within thirty days of receiving the agency official's notification, unless otherwise agreed to by the agency official, the Council shall provide the agency official with its opinion as to whether circumstances justify granting assistance to the applicant and any possible mitigation of the adverse effects.

(ii) The agency official shall consider the Council's opinion in making a decision on whether to grant assistance to the applicant, and shall notify the Council, the SHPO/THPO, and other parties known to be interested in the undertaking prior to granting the assistance.

(3) Compliance with Section 106. If an agency official, after consulting with the Council, determines to grant the assistance, the agency official shall comply with Secs. 800.3 through 800.6 to take into account the effects of the undertaking on any historic properties.

(d) Evaluation of Section 106 operations. The Council may evaluate the operation of the section 106 process by periodic reviews of how participants have fulfilled their legal responsibilities and how effectively the outcomes reached advance the purposes of the act.

(1) Information from participants. Section 203 of the act authorizes the Council to obtain information from Federal agencies necessary to conduct evaluation of the section 106 process. The agency official shall make documentation of agency policies, operating procedures and actions taken to comply with section 106 available to the Council upon request. The Council may request available information and documentation from other participants in the section 106 process.

(2) Improving the operation of section 106. Based upon any evaluation of the section 106 process, the Council may make recommendations to participants, the heads of Federal agencies, and the Secretary of actions to improve the efficiency and effectiveness of the process. Where the Council determines that an agency official or a SHPO/THPO has failed to properly carry out the responsibilities assigned under the process in this part, the Council may participate in individual case reviews conducted under such process in addition to the SHPO/THPO for such period that it determines is necessary to improve performance or correct deficiencies. If the Council finds a pattern of failure by a Federal agency in carrying out its responsibilities under section 106, the Council may review the policies and programs of the agency related to historic preservation pursuant to section 202(a)(6) of the act and recommend methods to improve the effectiveness, coordination, and consistency of those policies and programs with section 106.

Section 800.10 Special Requirements for Protecting National Historic Landmarks

(a) Statutory requirement. Section 110(f) of the act requires that the agency official, to the maximum extent possible, undertake such planning and actions as may be necessary to minimize harm to any National Historic Landmark that may be directly and adversely affected by an undertaking. When commenting on such undertakings, the Council shall use the process set forth in Secs. 800.6 through 800.7 and give special consideration to protecting National Historic Landmarks as specified in this section.

(b) Resolution of adverse effects. The agency official shall request the Council to participate in any consultation to resolve adverse effects on National Historic Landmarks conducted under Sec. 800.6.

(c) Involvement of the Secretary. The agency official shall notify the Secretary of any consultation involving a National Historic Landmark and invite the Secretary to participate in the consultation where there may be an adverse effect. The Council may request a report from the Secretary under section 213 of the act to assist in the consultation.

(d) Report of outcome. When the Council participates in consultation under this section, it shall report the outcome of the section 106 process, providing its written comments or any memoranda of agreement to which it is a signatory, to the Secretary and the head of the agency responsible for the undertaking.

Section 800.11 Documentation Standards

(a) Adequacy of documentation. The agency official shall ensure that a determination, finding, or agreement under the procedures in this subpart is supported by sufficient documentation to enable any reviewing parties to understand its basis. The agency official shall provide such documentation to the extent permitted by law and within available funds. When an agency official is conducting phased identification or evaluation under this subpart, the documentation standards regarding description of historic properties may be applied flexibly. If the Council, or the SHPO/THPO when the Council is not involved, determines the applicable documentation standards are not met, the Council or the SHPO/THPO, as appropriate, shall notify the agency official and specify the information needed to meet the standard. At the request of the agency official or any of the consulting parties, the Council shall review any disputes over whether documentation standards are met and provide its views to the agency official and the consulting parties.

(b) Format. The agency official may use documentation prepared to comply with other laws to fulfill the requirements of the procedures in this subpart, if that documentation meets the standards of this section.

(c) Confidentiality.

(1) Authority to withhold information. Section 304 of the act provides that the head of a Federal agency or other public official receiving grant assistance pursuant to the act, after consultation with the Secretary, shall withhold from public disclosure information about the location, character, or ownership of a historic property when disclosure may cause a significant invasion of privacy; risk harm to the historic property; or impede the use of a traditional religious site by practitioners. When the head of a Federal agency or other public official has determined that information should be withheld from the public pursuant to these criteria, the Secretary, in consultation with such Federal agency head or official, shall determine who may have access to the information for the purposes of carrying out the act.

(2) Consultation with the Council. When the information in question has been developed in the course of an agency's compliance with this part, the Secretary shall consult with the Council in reaching determinations on the withholding and release of information. The Federal agency shall provide the Council with available information, including views of the SHPO/THPO, Indian tribes and Native Hawaiian organizations, related to the confidentiality concern. The Council shall advise the Secretary and the Federal agency within 30 days of receipt of adequate documentation.

(3) Other authorities affecting confidentiality. Other Federal laws and program requirements may limit public access to information concerning an undertaking and its effects on historic properties. Where applicable, those authorities shall govern public access to information developed in the section 106 process and may authorize the agency official to protect the privacy of non-governmental applicants.

(d) Finding of no historic properties affected. Documentation shall include:

(1) A description of the undertaking, specifying the Federal involvement, and its area of potential effects, including photographs, maps, drawings, as necessary;

(2) A description of the steps taken to identify historic properties, including, as appropriate, efforts to seek information pursuant to Sec. 800.4(b); and

(3) The basis for determining that no historic properties are present or affected.

(e) Finding of no adverse effect or adverse effect. Documentation shall include:

(1) A description of the undertaking, specifying the Federal involvement, and its area of potential effects, including photographs, maps, and drawings, as necessary;

(2) A description of the steps taken to identify historic properties;

(3) A description of the affected historic properties, including information on the characteristics that qualify them for the National Register;

(4) A description of the undertaking's effects on historic properties;

(5) An explanation of why the criteria of adverse effect were found applicable or inapplicable, including any conditions or future actions to avoid, minimize or mitigate adverse effects; and

(6) Copies or summaries of any views provided by consulting parties and the public.

(f) Memorandum of agreement. When a memorandum of agreement is filed with the Council, the documentation shall include, any substantive revisions or additions to the documentation provided the Council pursuant to Sec. 800.6(a)(1), an evaluation of any measures considered to avoid or minimize the undertaking's adverse effects and a summary of the views of consulting parties and the public.

(g) Requests for comment without a memorandum of agreement. Documentation shall include:

(1) A description and evaluation of any alternatives or mitigation measures that the agency official proposes to resolve the undertaking's adverse effects;

(2) A description of any reasonable alternatives or mitigation measures that were considered but not chosen, and the reasons for their rejection;

(3) Copies or summaries of any views submitted to the agency official concerning the adverse effects of the undertaking on historic properties and alternatives to reduce or avoid those effects; and

(4) Any substantive revisions or additions to the documentation provided the Council pursuant to Sec. 800.6(a)(1).

Section 800.12 Emergency Situations

(a) Agency procedures. The agency official, in consultation with the appropriate SHPOs/THPOs, affected Indian tribes and Native Hawaiian organizations, and the Council, is encouraged to develop procedures for taking historic properties into account during operations which respond to a disaster or emergency declared by the President, a tribal government, or the Governor of a State or which respond to other immediate threats to life or property. If approved by the Council, the procedures shall govern the agency's historic preservation responsibilities during any disaster or emergency in lieu of Secs. 800.3 through 800.6.

(b) Alternatives to agency procedures. In the event an agency official proposes an emergency undertaking as an essential and immediate response to a disaster or emergency declared by the President, a tribal government, or the Governor of a State or another immediate threat to life or property, and the agency has not developed procedures pursuant to paragraph (a) of this section, the agency official may comply with section 106 by:

(1) Following a programmatic agreement developed pursuant to Sec. 800.14(b) that contains specific provisions for dealing with historic properties in emergency situations; or

(2) Notifying the Council, the appropriate SHPO/THPO and any Indian tribe or Native Hawaiian organization that may attach religious and cultural significance to historic properties likely to be affected prior to the undertaking and affording them an opportunity to comment within seven days of notification. If the agency official determines that circumstances do not permit seven days for comment, the agency official shall notify the Council, the SHPO/THPO and the Indian tribe or Native Hawaiian organization and invite any comments within the time available.

(c) Local governments responsible for section 106 compliance. When a local government official serves as the agency official for section 106 compliance, paragraphs (a) and (b) of this section also apply to an imminent threat to public health or safety as a result of a natural disaster or emergency declared by a local government's chief executive officer or legislative body, provided that if the Council or SHPO/THPO objects to the proposed action within seven days, the agency official shall comply with Secs. 800.3 through 800.6.

(d) Applicability. This section applies only to undertakings that will be implemented within 30 days after the disaster or emergency has been formally declared by the appropriate authority. An agency may request an extension of the period of applicability from the Council prior to the expiration of the 30 days. Immediate rescue and salvage operations conducted to preserve life or property are exempt from the provisions of section 106 and this part.

Sec. 800.13 Post-Review Discoveries

(a) Planning for subsequent discoveries.

(1) Using a programmatic agreement. An agency official may develop a programmatic agreement pursuant to Sec. 800.14(b) to govern the actions to be taken when historic properties are discovered during the implementation of an undertaking.

(2) Using agreement documents. When the agency official's identification efforts in accordance with Sec. 800.4 indicate that historic properties are likely to be discovered during implementation of an undertaking and no programmatic agreement has been developed pursuant to paragraph (a)(1) of this section, the agency official shall include in any finding of no adverse effect or memorandum of agreement a process to resolve any adverse effects upon such properties. Actions in conformance with the process satisfy the agency official's responsibilities under section 106 and this part.

(b) Discoveries without prior planning. If historic properties are discovered or unanticipated effects on historic properties found after the agency official has completed the section 106 process without establishing a process under paragraph (a) of this section, the agency official shall make reasonable efforts to avoid, minimize or mitigate adverse effects to such properties and:

(1) If the agency official has not approved the undertaking or if construction on an approved undertaking has not commenced, consult to resolve adverse effects pursuant to Sec. 800.6; or

(2) If the agency official, the SHPO/THPO and any Indian tribe or Native Hawaiian organization that might attach religious and cultural significance to the affected property agree that such property is of value solely for its scientific, prehistoric, historic or archeological data, the agency official may comply with the Archeological and Historic Preservation Act instead of the procedures in this part and provide the Council, the SHPO/THPO, and the Indian tribe or Native Hawaiian organization with a report on the actions within a reasonable time after they are completed; or

(3) If the agency official has approved the undertaking and construction has commenced, determine actions that the agency official can take to resolve

adverse effects, and notify the SHPO/THPO, any Indian tribe or Native Hawaiian organization that might attach religious and cultural significance to the affected property, and the Council within 48 hours of the discovery. The notification shall describe the agency official's assessment of National Register eligibility of the property and proposed actions to resolve the adverse effects. The SHPO/THPO, the Indian tribe or Native Hawaiian organization and the Council shall respond within 48 hours of the notification. The agency official shall take into account their recommendations regarding National Register eligibility and proposed actions, and then carry out appropriate actions. The agency official shall provide the SHPO/THPO, the Indian tribe or Native Hawaiian organization and the Council a report of the actions when they are completed.

(c) Eligibility of properties. The agency official, in consultation with the SHPO/THPO, may assume a newly-discovered property to be eligible for the National Register for purposes of section 106. The agency official shall specify the National Register criteria used to assume the property's eligibility so that information can be used in the resolution of adverse effects.

(d) Discoveries on tribal lands. If historic properties are discovered on tribal lands, or there are unanticipated effects on historic properties found on tribal lands, after the agency official has completed the section 106 process without establishing a process under paragraph (a) of this section and construction has commenced, the agency official shall comply with applicable tribal regulations and procedures and obtain the concurrence of the Indian tribe on the proposed action.

SUBPART C—PROGRAM ALTERNATIVES

Section 800.14 Federal Agency Program Alternatives

(a) Alternate procedures. An agency official may develop procedures to implement section 106 and substitute them for all or part of subpart B of this part if they are consistent with the Council's regulations pursuant to section 110(a)(2)(E) of the act.

(1) Development of procedures. The agency official shall consult with the Council, the National Conference of State Historic Preservation Officers, or individual SHPO/THPOs, as appropriate, and Indian tribes and Native Hawaiian organizations, as specified in paragraph (f) of this section, in the development of alternate procedures, publish notice of the availability of proposed alternate procedures in the Federal Register and take other appropriate steps to seek public input during the development of alternate procedures.

(2) Council review. The agency official shall submit the proposed alternate procedures to the Council for a 60-day review period. If the Council finds the procedures to be consistent with this part, it shall notify the agency official and the agency official may adopt them as final alternate procedures.

(3) Notice. The agency official shall notify the parties with which it has consulted and publish notice of final alternate procedures in the Federal Register.

(4) Legal effect. Alternate procedures adopted pursuant to this subpart substitute for the Council's regulations for the purposes of the agency's compliance with section 106, except that where an Indian tribe has entered into an agreement with the Council to substitute tribal historic preservation regulations for the Council's regulations under section 101(d)(5) of the act, the agency shall follow those regulations in lieu of the agency's procedures regarding undertakings on tribal lands. Prior to the Council entering into such agreements, the Council will provide Federal agencies notice and opportunity to comment on the proposed substitute tribal regulations.

(b) Programmatic agreements. The Council and the agency official may negotiate a programmatic agreement to govern the implementation of a particular program or the resolution of adverse effects from certain complex project situations or multiple undertakings.

(1) Use of programmatic agreements. A programmatic agreement may be used:

(i) When effects on historic properties are similar and repetitive or are

multi-State or regional in scope;

(ii) When effects on historic properties cannot be fully determined prior to approval of an undertaking;

(iii) When nonfederal parties are delegated major decisionmaking responsibilities;

(iv) Where routine management activities are undertaken at Federal installations, facilities, or other land-management units; or

(v) Where other circumstances warrant a departure from the normal section 106 process.

(2) Developing programmatic agreements for agency programs.

(i) The consultation shall involve, as appropriate, SHPO/THPOs, the National Conference of State Historic Preservation Officers (NCSHPO), Indian tribes and Native Hawaiian organizations, other Federal agencies, and members of the public. If the programmatic agreement has the potential to affect historic properties on tribal lands or historic properties of religious and cultural significance to an Indian tribe or Native Hawaiian organization, the agency official shall also follow paragraph (f) of this section.

(ii) Public participation. The agency official shall arrange for public participation appropriate to the subject matter and the scope of the program and in accordance with subpart A of this part. The agency official shall consider the nature of the program and its likely effects on historic properties and take steps to involve the individuals, organizations and entities likely to be interested.

(iii) Effect. The programmatic agreement shall take effect when executed by the Council, the agency official and the appropriate SHPOs/ THPOs when the programmatic agreement concerns a specific region or the president of NCSHPO when NCSHPO has participated in the consultation. A programmatic agreement shall take effect on tribal lands only when the THPO, Indian tribe, or a designated representative of the tribe is a signatory to the agreement. Compliance with the procedures established by an approved programmatic agreement satisfies the agency's section 106 responsibilities for all individual undertakings of the program covered by the agreement until it expires or is terminated by the agency, the president of NCSHPO when a signatory, or the Council. Termination by an individual SHPO/THPO shall only terminate the application of a regional programmatic agreement within the jurisdiction of the SHPO/THPO. If a THPO assumes the responsibilities of a SHPO pursuant to section 101(d)(2) of the act and the SHPO is signatory to programmatic agreement, the THPO assumes the role of a signatory, including the right to terminate a regional programmatic agreement on lands under the jurisdiction of the tribe.

(iv) Notice. The agency official shall notify the parties with which it has consulted that a programmatic agreement has been executed under paragraph (b) of this section, provide appropriate public notice before it takes effect, and make any internal agency procedures implementing the agreement readily available to the Council, SHPO/ THPOs, and the public.

(v) If the Council determines that the terms of a programmatic agreement are not being carried out, or if such an agreement is terminated, the agency official shall comply with subpart B of this part with regard to individual undertakings of the program covered by the agreement.

(3) Developing programmatic agreements for complex or multiple undertakings. Consultation to develop a programmatic agreement for dealing with the potential adverse effects of complex projects or multiple undertakings shall follow Sec. 800.6. If consultation pertains to an activity involving multiple undertakings and

the parties fail to reach agreement, then the agency official shall comply with the provisions of subpart B of this part for each individual undertaking.

(4) Prototype programmatic agreements. The Council may designate an agreement document as a prototype programmatic agreement that may be used for the same type of program or undertaking in more than one case or area. When an agency official uses such a prototype programmatic agreement, the agency official may develop and execute the agreement with the appropriate SHPO/THPO and the agreement shall become final without need for Council participation in consultation or Council signature.

(c) Exempted categories.

(1) Criteria for establishing. An agency official may propose a program or category of agency undertakings that may be exempted from review under the provisions of subpart B of this part, if the program or category meets the following criteria:

(i) The actions within the program or category would otherwise qualify as "undertakings" as defined in Sec. 800.16;

(ii) The potential effects of the undertakings within the program or category upon historic properties are foreseeable and likely to be minimal or not adverse; and

(iii) Exemption of the program or category is consistent with the purposes of the act.

(2) Public participation. The agency official shall arrange for public participation appropriate to the subject matter and the scope of the exemption and in accordance with the standards in subpart A of this part. The agency official shall consider the nature of the exemption and its likely effects on historic properties and take steps to involve individuals, organizations and entities likely to be interested.

(3) Consultation with SHPOs/THPOs. The agency official shall notify and consider the views of the SHPOs/THPOs on the exemption.

(4) Consultation with Indian tribes and Native Hawaiian organizations. If the exempted program or category of undertakings has the potential to affect historic properties on tribal lands or historic properties of religious and cultural significance to an Indian tribe or Native Hawaiian organization, the Council shall follow the requirements for the agency official set forth in paragraph (f) of this section.

(5) Council review of proposed exemptions. The Council shall review a request for an exemption that is supported by documentation describing the program or category for which the exemption is sought, demonstrating that the criteria of paragraph (c)(1) of this section have been met, describing the methods used to seek the views of the public, and summarizing any views submitted by the SHPO/THPOs, the public, and any others consulted. Unless it requests further information, the Council shall approve or reject the proposed exemption within 30 days of receipt, and thereafter notify the agency official and SHPO/THPOs of the decision. The decision shall be based on the consistency of the exemption with the purposes of the act, taking into consideration the magnitude of the exempted undertaking or program and the likelihood of impairment of historic properties in accordance with section 214 of the act.

(6) Legal consequences. Any undertaking that falls within an approved exempted program or category shall require no further review pursuant to subpart B of this part, unless the agency official or the Council determines that there are circumstances under which the normally excluded undertaking should be reviewed under subpart B of this part.

(7) Termination. The Council may terminate an exemption at the request of the agency official or when the Council determines that the exemption no longer meets the criteria of paragraph (c)(1) of this section. The Council shall notify the agency official 30 days before termination becomes effective.

(8) Notice. The agency official shall publish notice of any approved exemption in the Federal Register.

(d) Standard treatments.

(1) Establishment. The Council, on its own initiative or at the request of another party, may establish standard methods for the treatment of a category of historic properties, a category of undertakings, or a category of effects on historic properties to assist Federal agencies in satisfying the requirements of subpart B of this part. The Council shall publish notice of standard treatments in the Federal Register.

(2) Public participation. The Council shall arrange for public participation appropriate to the subject matter and the scope of the standard treatment and consistent with subpart A of this part. The Council shall consider the nature of the standard treatment and its likely effects on historic properties and the individuals, organizations and entities likely to be interested. Where an agency official has proposed a standard treatment, the Council may request the agency official to arrange for public involvement.

(3) Consultation with SHPOs/THPOs. The Council shall notify and consider the views of SHPOs/THPOs on the proposed standard treatment.

(4) Consultation with Indian tribes and Native Hawaiian organizations. If the proposed standard treatment has the potential to affect historic properties on tribal lands or historic properties of religious and cultural significance to an Indian tribe or Native Hawaiian organization, the Council shall follow the requirements for the agency official set forth in paragraph (f) of this section.

(5) Termination. The Council may terminate a standard treatment by publication of a notice in the Federal Register 30 days before the termination takes effect.

(e) Program comments. An agency official may request the Council to comment on a category of undertakings in lieu of conducting individual reviews under Secs. 800.4 through 800.6. The Council may provide program comments at its own initiative.

(1) Agency request. The agency official shall identify the category of undertakings, specify the likely effects on historic properties, specify the steps the agency official will take to ensure that the effects are taken into account, identify the time period for which the comment is requested and summarize any views submitted by the public.

(2) Public participation. The agency official shall arrange for public participation appropriate to the subject matter and the scope of the category and in accordance with the standards in subpart A of this part. The agency official shall consider the nature of the undertakings and their likely effects on historic properties and the individuals, organizations and entities likely to be interested.

(3) Consultation with SHPOs/THPOs. The Council shall notify and consider the views of SHPOs/THPOs on the proposed program comment.

(4) Consultation with Indian tribes and Native Hawaiian organizations. If the program comment has the potential to affect historic properties on tribal lands or historic properties of religious and cultural significance to an Indian tribe or Native Hawaiian organization, the Council shall follow the requirements for the agency official set forth in paragraph (f) of this section.

(5) Council action. Unless the Council requests additional documentation, notifies the agency official that it will decline to comment, or obtains the consent of the agency official to extend the period for providing comment, the Council shall comment to the agency official within 45 days of the request.

(i) If the Council comments, the agency official shall take into account the comments of the Council in carrying out the undertakings within the category and publish notice in the Federal Register of the Council's comments and steps the agency will take to ensure that effects to historic properties are taken into account.

(ii) If the Council declines to comment, the agency official shall continue to comply with the requirements of Secs. 800.3 through 800.6 for the individual undertakings.

(6) Withdrawal of comment. If the Council determines that the consideration of historic properties is not being carried out in a manner consistent with the program comment, the Council may withdraw the comment and the agency official shall comply with the requirements of Secs. 800.3 through 800.6 for the individual undertakings.

(f) Consultation with Indian tribes and Native Hawaiian organizations when developing program alternatives. Whenever an agency official proposes a program alternative pursuant to paragraphs (a) through (e) of this section, the agency official shall ensure that development of the program alternative includes appropriate government- to-government consultation with affected Indian tribes and consultation with affected Native Hawaiian organizations.

(1) Identifying affected Indian tribes and Native Hawaiian organizations. If any undertaking covered by a proposed program alternative has the potential to affect historic properties on tribal lands, the agency official shall identify and consult with the Indian tribes having jurisdiction over such lands. If a proposed program alternative has the potential to affect historic properties of religious and cultural significance to an Indian tribe or a Native Hawaiian organization which are located off tribal lands, the agency official shall identify those Indian tribes and Native Hawaiian organizations that might attach religious and cultural significance to such properties and consult with them. When a proposed program alternative has nationwide applicability, the agency official shall identify an appropriate government to government consultation with Indian tribes and consult with Native Hawaiian organizations in accordance with existing Executive orders, Presidential memoranda, and applicable provisions of law.

(2) Results of consultation. The agency official shall provide summaries of the views, along with copies of any written comments, provided by affected Indian tribes and Native Hawaiian organizations to the Council as part of the documentation for the proposed program alternative. The agency official and the Council shall take those views into account in reaching a final decision on the proposed program alternative.

Sec. 800.15 Tribal, State, and Local Program Alternatives [Reserved]

Section 800.16 Definitions

(a) Act means the National Historic Preservation Act of 1966, as amended, 16 U.S.C. 470-470w-6.

(b) Agency means agency as defined in 5 U.S.C. 551.

(c) Approval of the expenditure of funds means any final agency decision authorizing or permitting the expenditure of Federal funds or financial assistance on an undertaking, including any agency decision that may be subject to an administrative appeal.

(d) Area of potential effects means the geographic area or areas within which an undertaking may directly or indirectly cause alterations in the character or use of historic properties, if any such properties exist. The area of potential effects is influenced by the scale and nature of an undertaking and may be different for different kinds of effects caused by the undertaking.

(e) Comment means the findings and recommendations of the Council formally provided in writing to the head of a Federal agency under section 106.

(f) Consultation means the process of seeking, discussing, and considering the views of other participants, and, where feasible, seeking agreement with them regarding matters arising in the section 106 process. The Secretary's "Standards and Guidelines for Federal Agency Preservation Programs pursuant to the National Historic Preservation Act" provide further guidance on consultation.

(g) Council means the Advisory Council on Historic Preservation or a Council member or employee designated to act for the Council.

(h) Day or days means calendar days.

(i) Effect means alteration to the characteristics of a historic property qualifying it for inclusion in or eligibility for the National Register.

(j) Foreclosure means an action taken by an agency official that effectively precludes the Council from providing comments which the agency official can meaningfully consider prior to the approval of the undertaking.

(k) Head of the agency means the chief official of the Federal agency responsible for all aspects of the agency's actions. If a State, local, or tribal government has assumed or has been delegated responsibility for section 106 compliance, the head of that unit of government shall be considered the head of the agency.

(l)(1) Historic property means any prehistoric or historic district, site, building, structure, or object included in, or eligible for inclusion in, the National Register of Historic Places maintained by the Secretary of the Interior. This term includes artifacts, records, and remains that are related to and located within such properties. The term includes properties of traditional religious and cultural importance to an Indian tribe or Native Hawaiian organization and that meet the National Register criteria.

(2) The term eligible for inclusion in the National Register includes both properties formally determined as such in accordance with regulations of the Secretary of the Interior and all other properties that meet the National Register criteria.

(m) Indian tribe means an Indian tribe, band, nation, or other organized group or community, including a native village, regional corporation, or village corporation, as those terms are defined in section 3 of the Alaska Native Claims Settlement Act (43 U.S.C. 1602), which is recognized as eligible for the special programs and services provided by the United States to Indians because of their status as Indians.

(n) Local government means a city, county, parish, township, municipality, borough, or other general purpose political subdivision of a State.

(o) Memorandum of agreement means the document that records the terms and conditions agreed upon to resolve the adverse effects of an undertaking upon historic properties.

(p) National Historic Landmark means a historic property that the Secretary of the Interior has designated a National Historic Landmark.

(q) National Register means the National Register of Historic Places maintained by the Secretary of the Interior.

(r) National Register criteria means the criteria established by the Secretary of the Interior for use in evaluating the eligibility of properties for the National Register (36 CFR part 60).

(s)(1) Native Hawaiian organization means any organization which serves and represents the interests of Native Hawaiians; has as a primary and stated purpose the provision of services to Native Hawaiians; and has demonstrated expertise in aspects of historic preservation that are significant to Native Hawaiians.

(2) Native Hawaiian means any individual who is a descendant of the aboriginal people who, prior to 1778, occupied and exercised sovereignty in the area that now constitutes the State of Hawaii.

(t) Programmatic agreement means a document that records the terms and conditions agreed upon to resolve the potential adverse effects of a Federal agency program, complex undertaking or other situations in accordance with Sec. 800.14(b).

(u) Secretary means the Secretary of the Interior acting through the Director of the National Park Service except where otherwise specified.

(v) State Historic Preservation Officer (SHPO) means the official appointed or designated pursuant to section 101(b)(1) of the act to administer the State historic preservation program or a representative designated to act for the State historic preservation officer.

(w) Tribal Historic Preservation Officer (THPO) means the tribal official appointed by the tribe's chief governing authority or designated by a tribal ordinance or preservation program who has assumed the responsibilities of the SHPO for purposes of section 106 compliance on tribal lands in accordance with section 101(d)(2) of the act.

(x) Tribal lands means all lands within the exterior boundaries of any Indian reservation and all dependent Indian communities.

(y) Undertaking means a project, activity, or program funded in whole or in part under the direct or indirect jurisdiction of a Federal agency, including those carried out by or on behalf of a Federal agency; those carried out with Federal financial assistance; those requiring a Federal permit, license or approval; and those subject to State or local regulation administered pursuant to a delegation or approval by a Federal agency.

APPENDIX A TO PART 800—CRITERIA FOR COUNCIL INVOLVEMENT IN REVIEWING INDIVIDUAL SECTION 106 CASES

(a) Introduction. This appendix sets forth the criteria that will be used by the Council to determine whether to enter an individual section 106 review that it normally would not be involved in.

(b) General policy. The Council may choose to exercise its authorities under the section 106 regulations to participate in an individual project pursuant to the following criteria. However, the Council will not always elect to participate even though one or more of the criteria may be met.

(c) Specific criteria. The Council is likely to enter the section 106 process at the steps specified in the regulations in this part when an undertaking:

(1) Has substantial impacts on important historic properties. This may include adverse effects on properties that possess a national level of significance or on properties that are of unusual or noteworthy importance or are a rare property type; or adverse effects to large numbers of historic properties, such as impacts to multiple properties within a historic district.

(2) Presents important questions of policy or interpretation. This may include questions about how the Council's regulations are being applied or interpreted, including possible foreclosure or anticipatory demolition situations; situations where the outcome will set a precedent affecting Council policies or program goals; or the development of programmatic agreements that alter the way the section 106 process is applied to a group or type of undertakings.

(3) Has the potential for presenting procedural problems. This may include cases with substantial public controversy that is related to historic preservation issues; with disputes among or about consulting parties which the Council's involvement could help resolve; that are involved or likely to be involved in litigation on the basis of section 106; or carried out by a Federal agency, in a State or locality, or on tribal lands where the Council has previously identified problems with section 106 compliance pursuant to Sec. 800.9(d)(2).

(4) Presents issues of concern to Indian tribes or Native Hawaiian organizations. This may include cases where there have been concerns raised about the identification of, evaluation of or assessment of effects on historic properties to which an Indian tribe or Native Hawaiian organization attaches religious and cultural significance; where an Indian tribe or Native Hawaiian organization has requested Council involvement to assist in the resolution of adverse effects; or where there are questions relating to policy, interpretation or precedent under section 106 or its relation to other authorities, such as the Native American Graves Protection and Repatriation Act.

APPENDIX L

WORKSHEETS

Building Materials and Elements Worksheet and Checklist　　　Part 1

Material

Location

Photo/sketch

Describe the Appearance

Photo/sketch

Describe the Condition

Photo/sketch

Describe the material as commonly seen.
Describe any evident variations in
the material

Building Materials and Elements Worksheet and Checklist   Part 2

Window Casing

Checklist items

What to ask

1.   What is the profile of the window casing?
2.   Is all the casing present?
3.   Has some of the casing been removed in the past?
4.   Is any of the casing deteriorated?
5.   Is there any water damage to the casing?

What to look for

1.   Different shapes of wood that may have been added at different times.
2.   Cracked wood
3.   Wood that is covered with mold.
4.   Water stains.

Photo

Building Materials and Elements Worksheet and Checklist   Part 2

Brick masonry

Checklist items
What to ask

1.   Is the mortar between the bricks present?
2.   What is the bond?
3.   What is the coursing?
4.   What is the color and texture of the brick?
5.   What is the color and profile of the mortar?
6.   When has the last tuckpointing taken place?
7.   Is there any discoloration on the brick?
8.   Is there flashing above the bricks?
9.   Are the bricks reinforced?
10.   Are the bricks "true" dimension or "nominal.?"

What to look for

1.   Missing mortar.
2.   Cracks that extend diagonally across the face of the building
3.   Cracks that are present in the middle of the bricks
4.   Cracks that vary in width

Photo

Building Materials and Elements Worksheet and Checklist   Part 2

Terra Cotta

Checklist items

What to ask

1.   Is the terra cotta cracked?
2.   Is the terra cotta discolored?
3.   What is the condition of the metal ties?
4.   What are the profiles?
5.   How many profiles are there?
6.   What is the original color of the terra cotta?
7.   What is the original glaze on the terra cotta?

What to look for

1.   Cracks that extend through the terra cotta.
2.   Replacement pieces made from concrete and installed previously.
3.   Rusted or delaminated steel ties within the wall.
4.   Whether or not flashing is present.

Photo

Building Materials and Elements Worksheet and Checklist   Part 2

Columns

Checklist items

What to ask

1.   Are the columns wood or stone?
2.   What Order are the columns?
3.   If the columns are wood has the wood deteriorated?
4.   If the columns are stone has the stone chipped away?
5.   How do the columns attach to the adjacent parts of the building?

What to look for.

1.   Mold on the wood.
2.   Cracks that extend through the column if the column is stone
3.   Dried and cracked wood.
4.   Spalling or flaking of stone.
5.   Structural support within the column.

Photo

Building Materials and Elements Worksheet and Checklist   Part 2

Dormers

Checklist items

What to ask

1.   Do the Dormers have columns on them?
2.   What is the condition of the flashing around the dormers?
3.   Are the dormers original to the building?
4.   What kind of window is in the dormer?

What to look for.

1.   Water damage at the intersection of the dormer and the roof.
2.   Mold on the wood at the base of the dormer
3.   Cracked wood at the base of the dormer.
4.   Whether the roof is sagging due to inadequate framing.

Photo

Building Materials and Elements Worksheet and Checklist   Part 2

Corners

Checklist items

What to ask

1.   What does the corner of the building look like?
2.   Is there any wood trim at the corner?
3.   Are there quoins on the corner of the building?
4.   Does the gutter and downspout assembly wrap the corner?

What to look for.

1.   Wood that has begun to curve outward and away from the corner.
2.   Water damage due to leaky gutters and downspouts.

Photo

Building Materials and Elements Worksheet and Checklist   Part 2

Doors and Casings

Checklist items

What to ask

1. What is the profile of the door casing?
2. Is all the casing present?
3. Has some of the casing been removed in the past?
4. Is any of the casing deteriorated?
5. Is there any water damage to the casing?
6. What is the panel configuration for the door?
7. What is the stain finish on the door?
8. What kind of door hardware is present?
9. Are the doors and hardware original?

What to look for

1.   Discoloration of the wall that would indicate removed casings.
2.   Changes in casing profile.
3.   Water damage.
4.   Moldy wood.

Photo

Building Materials and Elements Worksheet and Checklist   Part 2

Entablatures

Checklist items

What to ask

1.   What Order is the entablature
2.   Is the entablature wood, stone, or metal?
3.   Is there a gutter associated with the entablature?

What to look for

1.   Rotten wood.
2.   With metal entablatures, corroded or rusty metal
3.   Integral gutters that are not visible from grade.
4.   Cracked wood.
5.   Missing flashing.
6.   Water damage.

Photo

Building Materials and Elements Worksheet and Checklist   Part 2

Gutters and Downspouts

Checklist items

What to ask

1. Where are the gutters and downspouts?
2. Are the gutters applied or integral?
3. What are the gutters and downspouts made of
4. Do the gutters slope properly?
5. Is there water damage near the gutters and downspouts?
6. Are the gutters and downspouts original?
7. Are the gutters and downspouts ornamented?

What to look for

1. Integral gutters
2. Water stains on the exterior wall.
3. Missing mortar due to moisture damage.
4. Soil erosion at the base of the downspout.

Photo

Building Materials and Elements Worksheet and Checklist   Part 2

Fireplaces and chimneys

Checklist items

What to ask

1.   Is the fireplace operable?
2.   When is the last time the chimney was "swept"?
3.   Does the damper work?
4.   Is there a fireplace surround?
5.   Is there a chimney cap?
6.   Is there a hearth?
7.   Is the chimney flashed properly to the roof at the exterior?

What to look for

1.   Animals living in the chimney.
2.   Cracks in the exterior face of the chimney.
3.   Firebrick in the inner part of the fireplace.
4.   Non-combustible material at the base of the fireplace opening.
5.   Proper clearance from the top of the chimney.
6.   Lightning rods.

Photo

Building Materials and Elements Worksheet and Checklist   Part 2

Flashing

Checklist items

What to ask

1.   What material is the flashing?
2.   What gauge is the flashing?
3.   Is the flashing deteriorated?
4.   Is the flashing ornamented?

What to look for

1.   Missing flashing
2.   Missing gutters.
3.   Water stains on interior walls and ceilings

Photo

Building Materials and Elements Worksheet and Checklist   Part 2

Plaster

Checklist items

What to ask

1.   What is the color and texture of the plaster?
2.   Is the plaster cracked?
3.   Is the substrate in good condition?
4.   Is there any ornamental plaster?

What to look for

1.   Cracked plaster.
2.   Moldy plaster
3.   Cracks that change in width from top to bottom
4.   Sections of plaster that may have fallen

Photo

Building Materials and Elements Worksheet and Checklist   Part 2
Mechanical equipment

Checklist items

What to ask

1.   Are the mechanical systems operable?
2.   Where are the least obtrusive places for additional equipment?
3.   When were the systems installed?
4.   Have the systems been maintained routinely?
5.   Who runs the physical plant?

What to look for

1.   Leaks from pipes and machinery
3.   Duct runs
4.   Pipe runs.
5.   Air intake and exhaust
6.   Missing grilles

Photo

Building Materials and Elements Worksheet and Checklist   Part 2

Lighting

Checklist items

What to ask

1.   Are current lighting levels adequate?
2.   Are there existing fixtures that may be adapted with new lamps?
3.   What is the condition of the associated electrical systems?
4.   Where can new lighting be added ?
5.   Where can additional hidden light sources be installed?
6.   How will the new wiring be installed if additional light sources are
        required?

What to look for

1.   Frayed wiring
2.   Wiring in spiral flexible conduit
3.   Missing lamps (light bulbs)
4.   Lighting color

Photo

Building Materials and Elements Worksheet and Checklist   Part 2

ADA

Checklist items

What to ask

1.   What modifications need to be made to make the building accessible?
2.   Are ramps required
3.   Are new hardware and signage required
4.   Where is the best place for a ramp to be located?
5.   How much space would be required for a ramp?
6.   Are the rest rooms accessible?
7.   What modifications are required in the rest rooms?

What to look for

1.   Places to put a new ramp
2.   Places to put new elevator
3.   Space for accessible toilet stalls.
4.   Wall space for new signs.

Photo

Building Materials and Elements Worksheet and Checklist   Part 2

Skylights

Checklist items

What to ask

1. Are there existing skylights that have been covered with roofing material?
2. Do the existing skylights leak?
3. Are the skylights insulated?
4. Are the skylights made of stained glass?

What to look for

1. Framing that would indicate that a skylight may be present
2. Water stains where moisture has penetrated the building
3. Odd shapes on the roof that have been covered with roofing that may indicate a skylight might be underneath

Photo

Building Materials and Elements Worksheet and Checklist   Part 2

Stained glass

Checklist items

What to ask

1.   What is the condition of the wood frame?
2.   Does the stained glass bow inward?
3.   Was plastic added to the exterior of the stained glass?
4.   Are any pieces of stained glass missing?
5.   When was the last time the stained glass was repaired or cleaned?

What to look for

1.   Sagging glass
2.   Yellow polymer applied to the outside frame
3.   Rotten frames
4.   Cracked frames
5.   Missing caming
6.   Cracked glass

Photo

Building Materials and Elements Worksheet and Checklist   Part 2

Elevators

Checklist items

What to ask

1.   Is the elevator existing?
2.   Is there an ornamental frame around the elevator door?
3.   Is the elevator machinery operable?
4.   Is a new elevator required by code?
5.   Where is the least obtrusive place to locate a new elevator?
6.   Is there clearance for the elevator over-ride?
7.   Is there access to an elevator pit?

What to look for

1.   Machinery locations.
2.   Ornamental metal trim
3.   Open areas that would permit a new shaft to be built

Photo

Building Materials and Elements Worksheet and Checklist   Part 2

Foundations

Checklist items

What to ask

1.   What is the foundation wall made of?
2.   What is the footing made of?
3.   Is there a footing?
4.   Does the foundation wall leak?
5.   Is there a foundation drain along the perimeter of the foundation wall?

What to look for

1.   Cracks in the foundation
2.   Evidence of a footing
3.   Connections between the foundation wall and the framing above

Photo

Building Materials and Elements Worksheet and Checklist   Part 2

Walls

Checklist items

What to ask

1.   What are the walls made of?
2.   Are any cracks in the walls present?
3.   Are the walls plumb?
4.   Which walls are load bearing and which are not?
5.   Which walls are original and which walls may have been added later?

What to look for

1.   Water damage
2.   Cracks that would indicate movement
3.   Irregular framing that would indicate changes in configuration
4.   Framing that extends in a manner to suggest load bearing capacity

Photo

Building Materials and Elements Worksheet and Checklist   Part 2

Floors

Checklist items

What to ask

1.   What is the floor system made of?
2.   Are any cracks present in the floor?
3.   What does the underside of the floor look like?
4.   Has the floor been patched or filled in?

What to look for

1.   Warped flooring
2.   Flooring with mold on it
3.   Buckled flooring

Photo

Building Materials and Elements Worksheet and Checklist   Part 2

Roofs

Checklist items

What to ask

1.   What is the roof structure made of?
2.   What is the roofing material?
3.   Are the roof pitches original?
4.   Are all roofs original?

What to look for

1.   Sealant and flashing at valleys and perimeters
2.   Punctured roofing materials
3.   Large puddles
4.   Stains on the roofing to indicate dried puddles

Photo

Building Materials and Elements Worksheet and Checklist   Part 2

Posts

Checklist items

What to ask

1.   Are the wood posts in the basement original
2.   Is there any evidence of termite damage
3.   Is there any evidence of water damage
4.   Are the posts resting on a footing?
5.   Is the beam above the posts connected to the posts?

What to look for

1.   Rotten wood at the base of the posts
2.   Footings under the posts
3.   Connections at the base of the post to the footing
4.   Connections at the top of the post to the structure above

Photo

Building Materials and Elements Worksheet and Checklist   Part 2

Fences

Checklist items

What to ask

1.   What kind of fence exists on the property?
2.   Does a new fence meet code requirements?
3.   Where is the fence required for privacy?
4.   Where is the fence required for security?
5.   Will the fence have gates?
6.   Will the fence have intermediate posts?
7.   Will the fence change heights?

What to look for

1.   Other fences in the area that are attractive
2.   Light from automobile headlights that should be shielded
3.   Light from other sources that should be shielded
4.   Areas that require privacy

Photo

Building Materials and Elements Worksheet and Checklist   Part 2

Additions

Checklist items

What to ask

1.   What is the primary and secondary massing of the existing building?
2.   Are there other additions that preceded the planned addition?
3.   How can the addition be differentiated from the existing structure?
4.   How can the addition be an extension of the existing structure?

What to look for

1.   Existing materials
2.   Existing fenestration
3.   Existing roof pitch
4.   Adjacent landscaping
5.   Existing building systems

Photo

Building Materials and Elements Worksheet and Checklist   Part 2

Trim

Checklist items

What to ask

1. What kind of trim exists on the building?
2. Is the trim ornamental
3. How does the trim define the scale of the building/?
4. Is there evidence of trim that had been removed in the past
5. Is the trim wood or metal or another material
6. Is the trim original to the building?

What to look for

1. Stained wood indicating removed trim
2. Moldy wood
3. Rusty metal
4. Cracked wood

Photo

Building Materials and Elements Worksheet and Checklist   Part 2

Garages

Checklist items

What to ask

1.   What kind of garages exist nearby
2.   Is there a pattern of outbuilding and primary building?
3.   Are there coach houses nearby?
4.   Are the garages attached to the houses or detached from them
5.   Is there an alley access to the garage?
6.   Can the garage be used for other uses other than automobile storage?

What to look for

1.   Adequate width for garage doors, intermediate piers, and space for
       opening car doors.
2.   Vehicular access
3.   Potential shadows caused by the new construction
4.   Architectural detail in the main building that may be designed into the new
       building.

Photo

Building Materials and Elements Worksheet and Checklist   Part 2

Porches

Checklist items

What to ask

1.   Are the columns on the porch deteriorated?
2.   Is the porch original to the house?
3.   Has the porch been rebuilt to look like an original porch?

What to look for

1.   Rotten wood
2.   Cracked wood
3.   Floor slope
4.   Foundations

Photo

INDEX

A

Abacus, 96, 120
Acanthus leaf, 62
Additions, 145-152
Advisory review, 190-191
Americans with Disabilities Act
    (ADA), 95
Applied columns, (see Pilasters)
Arc de Triomphe, Paris, Fig. 1.55
Arches, 23
Architectural form, 3, Figs. 1.3, 1.4
    Greek, 9
    Roman, 9
Architectural Orders, 9
Architectural ornament (see Ornament)
Arcosanti, Paolo Soleri, Arizona,
    Fig. 1.59
Athens, Greece, 4, Fig. 1.8
ATT Building, Philip Johnson, New
    York, Fig. 1.82
Attic vents, 122
Auditorium Building, Adler and Sullivan,
    Chicago, Fig. 1.51
Axial asymmetry, 50, 52
Axial symmetry, 50

B

Balusters, Fig. 2.03
Balustrade, 77-78, Figs. 2.01, 2.02
Bartolommeo, Michelozzo di, Fig. 1.49
Base, middle, and top, 56-61
Bases, 4, 23, 56

Basilican window frame, 108
Belle Mont Plantation, 4, Fig. 1.9
Beman, Solon, 12, Fig. 1.57
Binding review, 190-191
Bird screen, 123
Black Mountain College, North Carolina,
    Fig. 1.47
Brick masonry, 83
Brick tie backs, 83
Building codes, 77
Building components and materials, 78
Building elements, 96
Building fronts, Fig. 1.8
Building materials, 78
Burnham and Root, Fig. 1.27

C

Caming, 114
Canyon de Chelly, Navajo Nation,
    Arizona, Fig. 1.60
Casings, 119
Ceiling, 3, 23
Center, 3, 23
Charleston code, 202
Charter for New Urbanism, 202
Chicago, Illinois 15, 16, Figs. 1.27,
    1.51, 1.59, 1.75
Chimney cap, 123
Chimney stacks, 124
Chippendale, 47
Church of Christian Science, Evanston,
    Illinois, 12, Fig. 1.22

Church of San Marco, Venice, Fig. 1.53
Circle-top windows, 108
Classical, 5, 9, 12, 61
Coliseum (see Flavian Amphitheatre)
Column, 34, 62, 96-97
    double, 4, Figs. 1.5, 1.6
    Latrobe's Water Works, 4
    placement, 9, Figs. 1.8, 1.32
    types, Fig. 1.29
Composite Order, 9, Fig. 1.19
Contributing structures, 192-203
Corbelling of masonry, 35
Corinthian Order, 9, Fig. 1.18
Corners, 98-99, 102-103
Court of the Urbino Palace, Fig. 1.101
Cranbrook, Bloomfield Hills, Michigan,
    20, Figs. 1.31, 1.48, 1.56, 1.83
Crawlspace vents, 122
Cricket, 125
Cubes, 3, 43, Figs. 1.2, 1.70-1.72
Curtain walls, 141
Cylinders, 3, 20, Figs. 1.1, 1.5-1.6

D

Districts, 63
Domes, 32, Fig. 1.52
Doors, 3, 51, 52, 119
Doric Order, 9, Figs. 1.16, 1.21
Dormers, 116
Double columns, 4, Fig. 1.8
Downspouts, 120
Drayton Hall, North Carolina, 41,
    Fig. 1.67

E

Early American, 4
Eiffel Tower, 20, Fig. 1.34
Elevators, 134

Entablature, 46, 119-120
Entasis, 78, 97
Erechtheum, 4, Fig. 1.8
Evanston, Illinois, 12

F

Fences, 156-163
Fenestration, 50-56
Fenestration patterns, Figs. 1.89-1.93
Fireplaces, 123
Flashings, 124-126
Flavian Amphitheatre, Rome, Italy, 12
Floors, 3, 23, 141-142
Floor plane, 26, Fig. 1.42
Florence, Italy
    Palazzo Riccardi, Michelozzo di
    Bartolommeo, Fig. 1.49
Flue, 123, 124
Fluting, 61
Formal archetypes, 3
    geometric expressed as building,
    Figs. 1.3-1.4
Foundation systems, 135, 138-139

G

Gable, 3
Gale House, Frank Lloyd Wright, Oak
Park, Illinois, 41, Figs. 146, 1.66
Garages, 153-156
Geometry in architecture, 3
Graceland, Elvis Presley's, 9, Fig. 1.13
Greece
    Athens, 4, Fig. 1.8
    Temple of Athena Nike, 4, Fig. 1.8
    Theater at Epidaurus, Fig. 1.43
Greek architecture, 9
Greek Doric Order, 12, Fig. 1.22
Groin vaults, 32

Gunston Hall, Springfield, Virginia,
    Fig. 1.76
Gutters, 120

H

Hearth, 123
Height, 98, Fig. 2.28
Hinges, 119
Historical architecture, 52
Historic preservation, 77-78
Holabird, William, Fig. 1.75
Horizontal planes, Figs. 1.37-1.38
HVAC, 128, 132

I

International Council on Monuments
    and Sites (ICOMOS), 202
Interpretation, 171-180
Ionic Order, 9, Fig. 1.17
Italian Renaissance, 4
Italy
    Rome, 9
    Vicenza, 5, Fig. 1.10

J

Johnson, Philip, 47
Joists, 23
Jones, Inigo, 9

L

Latrobe, B. Henry, 4, Fig. 1.7
Legend and ornament, 61-62
Light pollution, 133-134
Lighting, 132-133
Lightning rods, 123
Lime-based mortars, 83

Load bearing construction, 23
Locks, 119
Loggias, 62
London, England, 9

M

Marble, 61-62
Mass, 46
Mausoleum at Halicarnassuss, 16
Mechanical equipment, 126-134
Middle, 56
Mississippi, 14
Modernist, 51, 61, Figs. 1.87-1.88
Monadnock Building, William
    Holabird, Chicago, Fig. 1.75
Mortar joints, 83, Fig. 2.06
Mount Vernon, Virginia, Figs. 1.85-1.86
Mullions, 103, 107, 108
Muntins, 103, 107
Muscle Shoals, Alabama, 4, Fig. 1.9
Myths and legends, 61-62

N

Nature, 61
Navajo Hogan, Canyon de Chelly,
    Navajo Nation, Arizona, Fig. 1.54
Nelson's Column at Trafalgar Square,
    London, England, 20, Fig. 1.30

O

Orders, 9, 97-98
    Composite, Fig. 1.19
    Corinthian, Fig. 1.18
    Ionic, Fig. 1.17
    Doric, Figs. 1.16, 1.21
    Tuscan, Figs. 1.15, 1.20
Origins of the Dwelling House, 61-62
Ornament, 3, 61-62

P

Palladian window, 108
Palladroi, Andrea, 4-5, Fig. 1.10
Palazzo Riccardi, Michelozzo di
    Bartolommeo, Florence, Fig. 1.49
Pantheon, 9, Fig. 1.12
Pediments, 3, 41, Figs. 1.2, 1.65,
    1.68-1.69
People's Savings and Loan Association,
    Louis Sullivan, Ohio, Fig. 1.74
Philadelphia, Pennsylvania, 3, Fig. 1.7
Piazza Publico, Sienna, Fig. 1.45
Pilasters, 12, 78, 99, Figs. 2.04, 2.29-2.30,
    2.32
Plaster, 141
Policy, 180-189
Porches, 63-64
Pork-chop eave, 98, Figs. 2.32, 2.45b
Porte cochere, 35
Portico, 4, 5
Posts, 145
Post and beam construction, 23
Probst, Graham Anderson and White 16
Profiles, 62
Property owners, 200
Proportion, 46
Public space, 163-169
Pulley and weight system, 108
Pullman neighborhood, Solon Beman,
    Chicago, Figs. 1.58, 1.100
Pyramids, 3, 35, Figs. 1.1, 1.61
Pyramid top, Charleston, South
    Carolina, Fig. 1.64

Q

Quoins, 99, Fig. 2.31

R

Relieving angles, 83
Replacement of materials, 77
Restroom facilities (ADA), 95-96
Reverse corner detail, 102
Ridge vents, 122
Robie House, Frank Lloyd Wright,
    Fig. 1.62
Roman architecture, 9
Roman Doric Order, 12, Fig. 1.21
Roman Ionic, Figs. 1.23-1.26
Rome, 9, 12
Roof systems, 144
Rooftop, 3
Rookery Building, Chicago, 15,
    Fig. 1.27, Fig. 1.50
Room, 3
Rustication of stone, 61

S

Saddle, 125
Scale, 46
Scope of authority, 190-191
Scott Mansion, Earnest Mayo,
    Evanston, Illinois, Fig. 1.65
Size, 46, Figs. 1.77-1.80
Size, mass, proportion, and scale, 46-50
Skylights, 108-113
Slab construction, 23
Soffit vents, 122
Spaces between buildings, 62-65
Spheres, 3, 32, Fig. 1.2
Spider Rock, Navajo Nation, Arizona,
    2, Fig. 1.33
St. Paul's Covent Garden, 9, Fig. 1.11
Stained glass, 114-115
Strauss building, Chicago, Illinois, 16,
    Fig. 1.28

Structure, 3
Suburb, 68-70
Suburban land use, Fig. 1.116

T

Taliesin West, Scottsdale, Arizona, 1.44
Temple of Athena Nike, 4, Fig. 1.8
Terra cotta, 86, 91-94
  color, 91
  corrosion, 91
Terraces, 62
Theater at Epidaurus, Greece, Fig. 1.43
Thickened planes, 3, 23, Figs. 1.1, 1.36
Thomas Jefferson, 12
Tooling, 83
Top, 56
Town square, 3
Tripartite composition, 56-57,
  Figs. 1.96-1.99
True divided lites, 107
Truss construction, 35
Tuckpointing, 83
Tuscan Order, 9, Figs. 1.15, 1.20

U

Union Terminal, Cincinnati, Ohio, 9,
  Fig. 1.14
University of Virginia, Charlottesville,
  12, 47, Figs. 1.20, 1.23, 1.24, 1.81
Urban land use, 71
Urban row houses, 52

V

Vaults, 32, 35
Veining, 61
Vents, 120, 122
Verandas, 62

Vertical marker, 20
Vertical planes, 23, Figs. 1.39-1.40
Villa Capra, Vicenza, Italy, Figs. 1.10,
  1.99
Villa Rotonda, 5
Vinyl, 78, 81-82
  advantage over wood, 81-82
Vitruvius, 61-62
Void, 23
Volutes, 14

W

Walls, 3, 78, 138-141
Washington Monument, 20, Fig. 1.35
Water Works, B. Henry Latrobe, 4,
  Figs. 1.1, 1.21
Waverly Plantation, Mississippi, Figs.
  1.25-1.26
Window casing, 108
Windows, 50, 52, 103, 107, 113-115,
  Figs. 1.94-1.95
Winslow House, Frank Lloyd Wright,
  River Forest, Illinois, Figs. 1.58, 1.63
Wood, 61
Wright, Frank Lloyd, 28, 35, 41, Figs.
  1.44, 1.46